D0944354

# IN DENIAL

# IN DENIAL

### Historians,
### Communism
### &
### Espionage

JOHN EARL HAYNES
HARVEY KLEHR

ENCOUNTER BOOKS
SAN FRANCISCO

Copyright © 2003 by John Earl Haynes and Harvey Klehr

All rights reserved. No part of this publication may be reproduced, stored in a retrieval system, or transmitted, in any form or by any means, electronic, mechanical, photocopying, recording, or otherwise, without the prior written permission of Encounter Books, 665 Third Street, Suite 330, San Francisco, California 94107-1951.

Published by Encounter Books, an activity of Encounter for Culture and Education, Inc., a nonprofit tax exempt corporation.

Encounter Books website address: www.encounterbooks.com
Manufactured in the United States and printed on acid-free paper.

The paper used in this publication meets the minimum requirements of ANSI/NISO Z39.48-1992 (R 1997) (*Permanence of Paper*).

FIRST EDITION

Library of Congress Cataloging-in-Publication Data

Haynes, John Earl.
    In denial : historians, communism and espionage / John Earl Haynes and
    Harvey Klehr.
       p.   cm.
    Includes bibliographical references and index.
    ISBN 1-893554-72-4 (alk. paper)
    1. Communist Party of the United States—History—Archival
resources.   2. Espionage, Soviet—United States—History—Archival
resources.   3. Communism—United States—History—Archival
resources.   4. Spies—Soviet Union—History—Archival resources.
5. Spies—United States—History—Archival resources.   6. Institut mark-
sizma-leninizma (Moscow, Russia)—Archival resources.   I. Klehr,
Harvey.   II. Title.
JK2391.C5H38 2003
327.1247073'09'045—dc21
                                                              2003053121

10   9   8   7   6   5   4   3   2   1

*For my sons, Benjamin, Gabriel, Joshua and Aaron. HK*

*For Amanda and Bill. JEH*

# CONTENTS

# NOTE ON NOMENCLATURE

To simplify the text we follow several conventions for referring to organizations. The leading Soviet internal security and foreign intelligence agency went through numerous formal titles and acronyms, from its initial Cheka (Russian acronym for the All-Russian Extraordinary Commission to Combat Counterrevolution and Sabotage), GPU (State Political Directorate), OGPU (United State Political Directorate), NKVD (People's Commissariat of Internal Affairs), GUGB (Main Administration of State Security), NKGB (People's Commissariat of State Security), MGB (Ministry of State Security), KI (Committee of Information), MVD (Ministry of Internal Affairs) and finally, from 1954 until the collapse of the USSR, the KGB (Komitet Gosudarstvennoy Bezopasnosti or Committee for State Security).

To avoid using multiple titles and acronyms for a single agency depending on when the event occurred, the single acronym of KGB will be used for all periods. Similarly, despite several name changes and reorganizations of their institutional histories, the chief Soviet military intelligence agency will be referred to as the GRU; the American Communist Party will be the Communist Party USA (CPUSA); and America's chief cryptologic agency will be the National Security Agency (NSA).

# INTRODUCTION

More than fifty years ago, American, British and Soviet armies crushed Nazi Germany and destroyed one of the most murderous regimes in human history. Its collapse did not mean a loss of interest in or concern with fascism; as the years have passed, Nazism has remained seared in the memory, not only of the Jews who were its major victims, but of millions of others around the globe determined never to allow its resurgence. Efforts to "normalize" the Holocaust and minimize its horror continue to elicit anger and repugnance.

It has only been a little more than a decade since the collapse of the Soviet Union and the meltdown of the Communist world it once led. Communist regimes survived for much longer than Nazi Germany, and their combined victims vastly outnumber those murdered by European fascism. Yet the enormous human cost of communism barely registers in American intellectual life. Worse, a sizeable cadre of American intellectuals now openly applaud and apologize for one of the bloodiest ideologies of human history, and instead of being treated as pariahs, they hold distinguished positions in American higher education and cultural life. How is it possible that the memory of Communist crimes could have vanished so swiftly while the memory of Nazi crimes remains so fresh?

The Cold War was not only a struggle between nations but also an ideological struggle within nations. While there was no significant fascist tendency among American intellectuals, the

United States, like all other democracies, harbored a significant Communist movement that drew support disproportionately from intellectuals. Thus the nostalgic afterlife of communism in the United States has outlived most of the real Communist regimes around the world. Although the Cold War on the ground has ended, the Cold War in history rages on, and it is more than just a squabble among scholars. By their determined effort to rehabilitate communism, a number of writers and professors are seeking to transform Americans' memories of their own national experience, what will be remembered and what will be forgotten, and the lessons of that history that will shape our understanding of the challenges of the twenty-first century.

Both of us have been deeply involved in these ongoing scholarly debates. Separately and together we have written eleven books and nearly one hundred articles dealing with some aspect of the contentious topic of American communism.[1] Our focus has not been on Cold War diplomacy but rather on the domestic controversy about American communism, a dispute going back to the late 1940s and the creation of postwar American culture. These disagreements—often involving different evaluations of how to weigh certain kinds of evidence, different views about the significance of certain statements, and different accounts of motives and outcomes—generated much heat and little closure because, at heart, they were based on very different moral assessments of communism and of America. One viewpoint, which we shared, was critical of American communism, seeing the Communist Party of the United States of America (CPUSA) as profoundly antidemocratic in both theory and practice. This "traditionalist" interpretation also saw America's constitutional order as deserving the loyalty and support of its citizens, and attacked American Communists for their subordination to a hostile foreign power. The opposing "revisionist" stance took a benign view of communism, arguing that Marxism-Leninism embodied the most idealistic dreams of mankind and that American Communists were among the most heroic fighters for social justice in the nation's history. Revisionists saw American democracy as a fraud camouflaging capitalist oppression and aggressive imperialism. By the early 1990s, the two contending perspectives in the scholarly world had been thoroughly aired out and neither had managed to persuade the other of the error of its ways.

The contention between these two positions was at high tide in August 1991 when a small group of Soviet officials, in alliance with the old guard of the Communist Party of the Soviet Union (CPSU), launched a coup against the government of Mikhail Gorbachev in an attempt to halt his program of reforming Soviet communism. They succeeded in placing Gorbachev under house arrest, but Boris Yeltsin, president of the USSR's Russian Republic, rallied the people of Moscow against the coup. When the Soviet army refused to fire on the crowds gathered at Yeltsin's headquarters, the coup leaders lost their nerve. Not only did the coup collapse, but Yeltsin seized the initiative to overthrow the entire Communist system. By January 1992 he had pushed Gorbachev aside, formally dissolved the Union of Soviet Socialist Republics and established the authority of a non-Communist Russian Republic under his own leadership. The Russian government dissolved the Communist Party of the Soviet Union and declared its assets to be public property, among them the Institute of Marxism-Leninism, the chief archive of CPSU records.

Anxious to expose Communist misdeeds, Yeltsin's government opened the archive to both Russian and foreign scholars.[2] For the first time, researchers were able to search through previously closed records of Communist activities going back to the origins of the Bolshevik movement and the creation of the Soviet state. In the summer of 1992 Harvey Klehr visited this newly opened archive, becoming the first American to examine the enormous documentary collections of the Communist International (Comintern), the Soviet agency that had guided foreign Communist parties from 1919 until its dissolution in 1943 and absorption into the CPSU's bureaucracy.

In addition to a rich collection of reports and minutes from the American Communist Party and similar reports and minutes from Comintern offices overseeing American communism, Klehr found extensive correspondence between the Comintern and American Communists, copies of Comintern orders, reports from Comintern representatives in America who supervised the CPUSA, reports from the American party, and thousands of pages of transcribed testimony from American Communist officials who journeyed to Moscow each year to appear for days before Comintern commissions that questioned them regarding the movement in America. The history of American communism, previously pieced together from snippets of such material and extensive reliance on newspaper accounts, personal interviews and American government files—and subjected to the ideological views of their creators—could now be examined more objectively in light of records generated by Communists themselves.

As Klehr was going through the files, he began to come upon a number of messages between someone named Pavel Fitin and Comintern chief Georgi Dimitrov. Although he did not recognize the former name, two things stood out. First and most obviously, the messages were stamped "TOP SECRET." Second, Fitin was asking in 1944 and 1945 for information in Comintern files about individual American Communists, many of whom Klehr immediately recognized as having been accused by Elizabeth Bentley in 1945 of being participants in her espionage apparatus. (Several generations of hostile historians had subsequently dismissed Bentley's charges as the "imaginings of a neurotic spinster.")[3] After the documents were translated in the United States and we had identified Fitin as the wartime head of the foreign intelligence directorate of the NKVD (later the KGB)—the chief of the Kremlin's foreign espionage operations—the significance of this material became clear. These Fitin-Dimitrov messages provided direct archival corroboration of Bentley's testimony about the espionage activities of a number of important American government employees during World War II.

Other material from the Comintern archive demonstrated that the American Communist Party had created a clandestine "secret apparatus" that not only provided security for party political activities and infiltrated rival political groups but also cooperated with Soviet intelligence agencies. (The idea of an organized CPUSA underground had also been an object of widespread ridicule and disbelief among historians.) The Comintern records held by the Russian State Archive of Socio-Political History (RGASPI) are immense, more than twenty million pages, and the archive had not been aware of the potential significance of this material. Our book *The Secret World of American Communism* appeared in 1995 as one of the first volumes of Yale University Press's "Annals of Communism" series, using documentation from the newly opened Russian archives. The book highlighted material, such as the Fitin-Dimitrov messages, that provided abundant evidence of the cooperation between the Communist International, the CPUSA and Soviet foreign espionage agencies.[4] In response, the SVR, Russian successor to the Soviet KGB, "resecretized" those Comintern files containing KGB material to prevent other researchers from having further access to them.

In January of 1993 John Earl Haynes made his first trip to Moscow to examine a collection that had not been available during Klehr's earlier visit: the central headquarters records of the CPUSA itself. In 1926 the Communist International in a secret resolution urged its "sections," as it termed the various national Communist parties, to centralize their records with those of the Comintern itself. The American party responded, and from then until the Comintern dissolved in 1943, it shipped more than 435,000 pages of material to Moscow. After the Comintern's dissolution, the Communist Party of the Soviet Union took over the records; and after the dissolution of the CPSU in 1991, the Russian government took ownership of the archive. Here in Moscow at the Russian State Archive of Socio-Political History were the minutes and protocols of the American Communist Party's executive agencies, correspondence with district party officials and local organizers from New York to San Francisco, and thousands of pages of internal memoranda of the party's powerful trade union secretariat, the vital organizational bureau, the agitation and propaganda secretariat, its women's bureau, and its vast array of ethnic and foreign language affiliates. Combining the Comintern material and the CPUSA records, we produced another book for the Annals of Communism series, *The Soviet World of American Communism*.[5] This volume stressed documents showing the Communist International's secret financial subsidies of the American party as well as Comintern control over the CPUSA's policies and leadership.

Immediately after publication of *The Secret World* in 1995, Senator Daniel Patrick Moynihan invited us to testify before a joint congressional–executive branch commission he chaired studying the issue of government secrecy. Some of the material we had located in Moscow appeared to relate to the Venona project, a highly secret American effort to break Soviet codes in the 1940s that, rumor held, had led to the arrest of several Soviet spies. In our appearance, we commented on the anomaly of finding important information on Soviet espionage and Venona in Moscow even while the American government continued to deny access to American documents about the project in American archives. Senator Moynihan pressed newly appointed CIA director John Deutsch, a member of his commission, to consider declassifying Venona. Several months later the National Security Agency (the chief U.S. code-breaking agency) opened the Venona documents and by the end of 1997 released almost three thousand fully or partially decrypted Soviet cables, enabling us to write another book for Yale University Press. *Venona: Decoding Soviet Espionage in America* showed that during World War II, Soviet intelligence agencies exploited the USSR's wartime alliance with the United States as an opportunity to launch a wide-ranging espionage offensive against the U.S. The deciphered Venona messages alone identified more than three hundred Americans, the vast majority of them Communists and a disturbing number highly placed in the government, who cooperated with Soviet intelligence. The messages also showed that their assistance to Soviet espionage was carried out with the knowledge and organizational aid of the Communist Party of the United States of America.

These books received a great deal of notice in the media, much of it favorable. *The Secret World of American Communism* drew much more press attention than most scholarly books because it provided the first archival glimpse into the netherworld of Communist espionage in the 1940s and was the first book to contain extensive revelations from previously closed Russian archives. Not surprisingly, conservative commentators saw vindication for the anticommunism that had been a central element of conservative and much of liberal politics since World War II. (George Will's admiring column about the book concluded that many leftists "cannot face the fact that the left was on the losing side of history, and deserved to be.") Veteran anti-Stalinist liberal intellectuals such as Arthur Schlesinger Jr. (in the *New Republic*) and Murray Kempton (in the *New York Review of Books*) also applauded the book.[6] But despite these volumes' documentary nature, academic reviewers—who, in the redefinitions of the 1960s, now saw themselves as "progressives" rather than "liberals"—were largely hostile to our conclusion that the CPUSA had significant financial, organizational and espionage links to the Soviet Union and that several hundred American Communists had spied for Moscow.

When you write a series of books that challenge deeply held beliefs, you expect to receive some strong responses, and even more so when those deeply held beliefs are the prevailing views of the historical discipline. While most Americans regard communism as a lost cause, and deservedly so, a significant number of American academics still have soft spots in their hearts for the CPUSA, either because they applaud the causes it championed, deplore what they see as the persecution of those who fought for "social justice," romanticize the party's accomplishments, disdain American capitalism, culture and constitutional democracy, or honor parents or other relatives who were party members.

Still, we were most taken aback by the vehemence of the reaction among a large segment of academics who resisted considering new evidence, and by the intellectual contortions they practiced to keep from smelling the cordite of the smoking gun

we had uncovered. It became apparent that the response to our
books raised larger issues about historians and the writing of history. We came to see our experience as an illustration of how an
alienated and politicized academic culture misunderstands and
distorts America's past, and of the crucial role played by historical gatekeepers such as professional journals in misshaping cultural memories to fit the ideological biases of the academic
establishment.

Our earlier books were chiefly research volumes dealing
with primary documents or narratives about some part of the
history of American communism. This book takes a step back
to see how contemporary scholars and intellectuals have failed
to confront new evidence about the history of American communism and Soviet espionage. We believe that some academics,
including several prominent and influential ones, have written
bad history in the service of bad politics. Their political enthusiasms have distorted their professional vision to the detriment
of the historical profession and the search for truth about the
past.

The Cold War is over and communism as an organized political force is dead. True, Communists still rule in the world's most
populous nation as well as in Cuba and North Korea. But Chinese communism is an empty shell; its nominal ideology has less
and less to do with the realities of China's economic and social
life. Cuban communism awaits only the death of Fidel Castro
for its implosion. And North Korea is a bizarre nightmare state,
a living hell that has starved millions of its own citizens to death
and crippled an entire generation of children through malnu-
trition. Communism as social fact is dead. But communism as a
pleasant figment of the "progressive" worldview lives on, giving
a phantom life to the illusions and historical distortions that sustained that murderous and oppressive ideology. The intellectual
Cold War, alas, is not over. Academic revisionists who color the
history of American communism in benign hues see their teaching and writing as the preparation of a new crop of radicals for
the task of overthrowing American capitalism and its democratic

constitutional order in the name of social justice and peace. Continuing to fight the Cold War in history, they intend to reverse the victory of the West and convince the next generation that the wrong side won, and to prepare the way for a new struggle.

# CHAPTER 1

# *Revising History*

Studying historians and their methods is, for the most part, the stuff of boring graduate seminars. It means taking one step back from the actual events and people that make history interesting and dramatic. Generally it requires tedious discussion of sources and methods, among other technical issues, and carping about interpretations of documents or recondite epistemological questions. But historiographic debates can also be illuminating, and it is important that they be allowed to run their course.

In 2000, to take one prominent example, a historiographic argument moved out of the seminar and into a British court and the international public square when David Irving, a British writer, sued American historian Deborah Lipstadt. Irving charged that Lipstadt had libeled him by labeling him a Holocaust denier in a book devoted to that topic. A prodigious researcher and prolific writer, Irving did not deny that he had maintained in books, in speeches and on his website that there were no gas chambers at Auschwitz and that most of Hitler's Jewish victims succumbed to disease instead of being murdered. Nor did he deny that he had claimed that the number of Jewish dead during World War II had been grossly inflated for political reasons and that the eyewitness testimony of most Holocaust survivors was worthless. Irving also maintained that Hitler had no plan to exterminate Jews; indeed, he claimed that Hitler actually tried to curb Nazi excesses. The trial, and Lipstadt's subsequent victory, drew worldwide attention to the bizarre intellectual netherworld where a cadre of so-called historians labored to "prove" that the Holocaust never happened in scholarly-looking books, complete with footnotes, scientific-sounding analyses and extensive interviews.

As a practical matter, Irving could not have sued in an American court. Under American law, with its tradition of maximizing free speech and debate, the burden of proof is on the plaintiff bringing the action. To get into an American court, Irving would have been required to demonstrate that Lipstadt's statements were false and were made with premeditated malice. Under British libel law, however, the burden of proof is on the defendant to show the complete accuracy of any statement resented by the plaintiff. If Lipstadt had failed to substantiate her description of Irving with ample evidence and expert analysis, her statements would have been held libelous, she would have faced crippling monetary damages, and her publisher would have had to withdraw her book from sale. It has long been common for historians facing a British libel action to withdraw controversial statements, even though they were confident of their factual accuracy, rather than risk financial ruin from an unsympathetic judge or jury. But Irving had misgauged his foe as well as ignoring the evidence she could bring into court.

With the military defeat of the Nazi regime in 1945, millions of documents became available to scholars. While many records were destroyed, notably those from many of the extermination camps, there were enough traces and trails in what had survived to make the story of Nazi crimes clear. There was, for example, the chilling "Wannsee Protocol" of a 1942 planning conference of Nazi regime officials, which began with the statement, "SS-Obergruppenfuehrer Heydrich gave information that the Reich Marshal had appointed him delegate for the preparations for the final solution of the Jewish problem in Europe and pointed out that this discussion had been called for the purpose of clarifying fundamental questions."[1] More directly, the liberated concentration camps provided irrefutable proof of dreadful Nazi crimes: not only piles of corpses and mass graves, but surviving victims as well, pitiful half-starved creatures whose pictures shocked the civilized world.

Expert witnesses called by Lipstadt's defense team demolished the scholarly pretensions and claims to objectivity of the Holocaust revisionists and demonstrated, as the judge in the case noted, that Irving misquoted sources, mistranslated documents, wrenched material out of context, twisted the meaning of documents and used dubious sources. When eyewitnesses supported his thesis, Irving accepted their testimony; when they cast doubt on it, he belittled the value of eyewitness testimony. But unlike a merely incompetent historian, who might be expected to make errors in a random way, the judge found, Irving consistently misconstrued his material all in one direction: to exonerate Hitler and minimize the horrors of the Holocaust.[2]

Holocaust revisionism has never established a beachhead within the historical profession—at least not yet. The challenge to the facts of the Holocaust came from cranks and amateurs who lacked training in historical methods and arguments. Some, like Irving himself, fancied themselves professional historians but had no graduate degrees in history or appointments in academic institutions. Those few professors who engaged in Holocaust revision were usually in disciplines far removed from history, like Arthur Butz, an engineering professor at Northwestern University, or Robert Faurisson, a prominent literary scholar in France whose Holocaust "investigations" were praised by MIT linguist Noam Chomsky.[3]

Defense of Nazi mass murder is not acceptable in the scholarly world and shouldn't be. But another species of historical revisionism, one that is equally repugnant, is practiced with impunity in the academy. The number of apologists for the former Soviet Union and its mass murders dwarfs the handful of aberrant pro-Nazi academics in America. Sympathy for the Communist project and distaste for attacking it are today fully accepted in American higher education.

It was not always this way. From the 1930s onward the temper of the academic world had been liberal but not sympathetic to communism. The "Popular Front" variety of liberalism, in covert alliance with the Communist Party, gained some popularity among liberals in the late 1930s, but the Nazi-Soviet Pact of 1939 soured many on that relationship. The 1942–45 wartime alliance of the United States and the USSR briefly resurrected Popular Front liberalism, but that died quickly when the Cold War flamed up from the ashes of the Nazi defeat. By the late 1940s, 1950s and into the 1960s the political tone of academic life was set by an anticommunist liberalism that defined itself as equally hostile to fascism and communism, both seen as varieties of totalitarianism.

But in the 1970s, the American academic world began to change. The anticommunist consensus that had dominated American culture since the late 1940s broke down in the scholarly world, although not among most Americans. The unpopularity of the Vietnam War, and the conviction that anticommunism had led America into it, was likely the largest factor in discrediting opposition to communism. Contributing as well, however, was a belated backlash against the excesses of McCarthyism, a moment when some conservatives had used anticommunism to bludgeon not just Communists and their sympathizers, but liberals, leftists, the Democratic Party and the New Deal heritage as well. More to the point, many younger scholars entering the academic world had been activists in the militant "New Left" of the late 1960s and early 1970s or sympathetic with its radical goals. This new generation of radical scholars regarded the United States, not the USSR, as the chief menace in the world.

These radical academics thoroughly changed the ideological atmosphere of the scholarly world. In particular, their hostility toward anticommunism affected two fields: the history of Soviet communism and the history of domestic American communism.

### Revising the History of Stalinism

The Soviet regime was a tyranny from its origins. It took power in 1917 in an armed coup and dispersed at gunpoint the freely elected Constituent Assembly in 1918 when a majority refused to support Bolshevik rule. The Soviet state not only suppressed democratic liberties; it engaged in mass murder from its very beginnings. But Lenin's "Red Terror" was only a prelude to Stalin's reign, with its use of violence and deliberate starvation to collectivize agriculture and break the peasantry, followed by ideological show trials and the "Great Terror" of the 1930s. In 1956, Soviet leader Nikita Khrushchev acknowledged some of the mass murder in a famous speech to a Soviet Communist Party congress, putting the blame on one man, Joseph Stalin, and his "cult of personality." Khrushchev allowed a highly restricted opening of the record, releasing only material that indicted Stalin (while Lenin went unmentioned), but even this partial opening, which proceeded with fits and starts, came to an end when Khrushchev was displaced as Soviet supreme leader in 1964. Decades of stonewalling, closed archives, dishonest official history and repression followed the brief period of de-Stalinization. In contrast to the ready availability of seized Nazi records, most of the sensitive material that might embarrass the Soviet regime or expose the crimes of the Lenin and Stalin eras remained hidden in archives that tightly controlled not only who was given access but which files they were allowed to see. Particularly sensitive material—including documentation on covert funding of foreign Communist parties, subsidies to foreign terrorist organizations and crimes against humanity such as the Katyn Forest massacre of prisoners of war—was pulled out of ordinary archives and secreted in special repositories.

Despite the unavailability of documentation, however, there was a public record that could be sifted by scholars and there were witnesses: people who had escaped from the USSR in the 1930s and 1940s, Gulag prisoners rehabilitated after Stalin's death, and Soviet defectors.[4] The Soviet regime also permitted large numbers of Jews and ethnic Germans to emigrate to the West in the 1970s. Soviet dissidents gathered bits and pieces of evidence and interviewed survivors. Using this evidence on the broad issue of the Soviet regime's character, Adam Ulam, Richard

Pipes, Martin Malia and other scholars emphasized the totalitarian nature of Stalinism and the centrality of Stalin in shaping the lethal brutality of the Soviet state.[5] But no book did more to publicize the crimes of communism than Aleksandr Solzhenitsyn's monumental *Gulag Archipelago,* smuggled out of the Soviet Union in the early 1970s, which constructed a history of the Gulag prison labor system based on underground literature and survivors' memoirs. Within the scholarly world, Robert Conquest's *The Great Terror: Stalin's Purge of the Thirties* (1968), *Kolyma: The Arctic Death Camps* (1978) and *The Harvest of Sorrow: Soviet Collectivization and the Terror-Famine* (1986) provided a similar portrait of the Stalinist nightmare, in which millions starved to death in the collectivization drive of the late 1920s and early 1930s, were executed in the Great Terror or died in the Gulag, or survived but were imprisoned or forcefully exiled to remote parts of the USSR. Allowing that the lack of access to Soviet archives required extrapolation from incomplete data, Conquest estimated the total of those killed from the collectivization campaign, the state-induced Ukrainian famine of 1932–33 and the "Great Terror" of 1937–38 at more than twenty million.

From the late 1970s onward, however, a determined group of younger American scholars began an effort to "normalize" the Stalinist regime by minimizing the number of victims of the Terror and the Gulag. Attacking the reigning view of Soviet history, they argued that responsibility for the Terror lay not so much with Joseph Stalin and the Communist system as with a bureaucratic process that got out of control. These Soviet history revisionists had fewer obstacles to overcome in their effort to rehabilitate Stalin or Lenin than the Holocaust revisionists had faced. Until 1991 the Soviet regime remained in power and zealous in presenting a totally favorable view of its history. There were no photos of the KGB's mass burial sites and no liberating armies freeing Gulag labor camp prisoners. Soviet archives were largely closed to Western research, and Soviet authorities vetted what was open to insure that nothing damaging to the regime was accessible.

Under these circumstances, revisionists reinterpreted the limited and sometimes ambiguous documentary record to present a benign view of Stalinism. They belittled testimony by survivors of the Gulag as the biased complaints of anticommunists or embittered exiles. Solzhenitsyn, for example, was widely derided as a "reactionary, chauvinistic, messianic Russian nationalist" and smeared as anti-Semitic to boot. Whereas Conquest had estimated the number of deaths from Stalin's Great Terror in the late 1930s as being in the millions, pioneering revisionist Jerry F. Hough (Duke University) in 1979 wrote that "a figure in the low hundreds of thousands seems much more probable than one in the high hundreds" and that a lower figure of only "tens of thousands" was "even probable." Another leading revisionist, Professor Sheila Fitzpatrick of the University of Chicago, also placed the maximum number executed in the "low hundreds of thousands." Robert Thurston (Miami University of Ohio) devoted an entire essay in *Slavic Review* to assailing Conquest's work, and J. Arch Getty (University of California, Riverside) included an attack on Conquest's research in his influential *Origins of the Great Purges*. Getty avoided providing a numerical estimate of Stalin's victims but insisted that the totals were very low, not in the millions or even hundreds of thousands. All he would concede was that "many thousands of innocent people were arrested, imprisoned and sent to labor camps. Thousands were executed." Getty absolved Stalin of responsibility for planning mass murder, depicting him as a moderate unable to control an intrabureaucratic struggle that regrettably got out of hand. A widely used textbook written by the University of Pennsylvania and Central European University's Alfred Rieber, *A Study of the USSR and Communism*, was equally dismissive of the claims about millions of victims, saying that "estimates place the total arrests in the hundreds of thousands and the total executions in the tens of thousands."[6]

Minimizing the numbers murdered in Stalin's terror was not merely a perverse pastime, it was a cornerstone in the larger revisionist project to discredit the view that Soviet communism was a species of totalitarianism or even especially oppressive. The

chief goal was to depict the Soviet Union as not so very different from societies in the West and, consequently, nothing to fear
and even something to admire.

The collapse of the USSR in 1991 and the opening of Soviet-
era archives damaged the revisionist program of normalizing
and rehabilitating the Soviet regime. To the body of previously
existing evidence of nightmarish conditions under communism,
the archives added millions of additional documents of unim-
peachable authenticity. A new body of literature based on these
materials began to appear almost immediately. Richard Pipes
and Dmitri Volkogonov examined the Leninist origins of Stalinist crimes, while Vladimir Brovkin looked at the evidence of
popular alienation from Bolshevik rule in the 1920s. Anne Applebaum published the first comprehensive history of the Gulag
system since Solzhenitsyn's Soviet-era underground volumes,
while Jonathan Brent, Vladimir Naumov, Joshua Rubinstein and
Gennadi Kostyrchenko documented Stalin's frame-up and execution of Soviet Jewish leaders. Alexander Dallin, William Chase
and Fridrikh Firsov demonstrated the often-lethal cynicism of
Stalin's dealings with foreign Communists and the execution or
imprisonment of thousands of foreign Communists within the
Comintern apparatus. Ronald Radosh, Mary Habeck and Gerald Howson revealed the dark underside of Communist involvement in the "good fight" in the Spanish Civil War.[7]

The human toll of the Soviet regime has also become much
clearer. Survivors of the Gulag and their children and grandchil-
dren have raised their voices. A new Russian civic organization,
Memorial, dedicated itself to exposing the extent of Stalin's
crimes and remembering his victims. It searched for and located
mass graves and publicized archival records of the Terror.
Although major elements of the Russian government continue
to drag their feet, a "Presidential Commission for the Rehabilitation of Victims of Political Repression" chaired by Alexander
Yakovlev, a former adviser to Mikhail Gorbachev, has sought to
open up records of Soviet-era crimes.[8] And the archival record
itself, although incomplete with large collections still closed, was

devastating nonetheless. Interestingly enough, while no direct order signed by Hitler ordering mass murder of the Jews has ever been located, historians have unearthed orders from Stalin approving the execution of old Bolshevik comrades and setting arrest and execution quotas for the political police.

### The Katyn Forest Massacre: A Case Study

The treatment of the Katyn Forest massacre illustrates the determined myopia of revisionists in the decades prior to the collapse of the USSR and the opening of its archives. When the Nazis conquered the western USSR in 1941 they discovered several mass graves, most prominently one in the Katyn Forest near Smolensk. The graves contained the bodies of more than twenty thousand Polish prisoners of war captured by the Soviets in 1939, when they annexed eastern Poland as their share of the Nazi-Soviet Pact, and then executed in 1940. They were not ordinary Polish soldiers but commissioned and noncommissioned officers, chiefly reservists mobilized when Nazi Germany attacked; they were the backbone of Polish civil society—businessmen, midlevel government officials, lawyers, engineers, doctors, teachers and professionals of all sorts. Stalin had these POWs murdered to remove the potential leaders of the newly conquered Polish territory.

In 1943 the Nazis released news of the mass graves in hopes of driving a wedge between the Soviet Union and the Polish government-in-exile. In this they succeeded. The USSR denied the murders, blaming Germany. But Polish authorities demanded an independent investigation. In response, the Soviets accused them of cooperating with the Nazis and broke off diplomatic relations. Soviet stonewalling, however, only delayed the discovery of evidence. Urged on by millions of Polish American voters, the United States Congress in 1951–52 conducted an investigation of the Katyn massacre that produced direct forensic confirmation from captured German records, along with voluminous corroborative testimony from Soviet defectors and lower-ranking Polish POWs who were released after the Nazi attack on the USSR. Cumulatively, the investigation produced damning evidence of Soviet guilt for an abominable act of mass murder.[9]

And how did revisionists handle the issue of Katyn? Most chose to pass over it in silence. Silence, indeed, is a widespread practice among revisionist scholars in the face of evidence or events that reflect poorly on the Communist enterprise. They treat historical evidence as a cafeteria where one can pick out the items one likes and ignore distasteful ones, constructing just the savory historical meal one desires. When what happened at Katyn could not be avoided, other revisionists insisted that the evidence was unclear and took a studied neutral stance. For example, Peter M. Irons, a senior professor at the University of California, San Diego, in "The Test Is Poland: Polish Americans and the Origins of the Cold War," gave Katyn only casual mention, four paragraphs in a fifty-seven-page essay, despite its major impact on the attitudes of Polish Americans at the beginning of the Cold War. In his cursory treatment Irons reported the German claims and the Soviet denial, but offered no opinion about what the truth might be, although at a point or two he slyly insinuated that the evidence of Soviet guilt was weak. He referred to "anxious Polish inquiries about the fate of several thousand missing Polish army officers, *supposedly interned by the Soviets* but nowhere to be found." (Emphasis added.)[10]

*Supposedly interned?* There was never any doubt that the officers were interned by the Soviets. Even the USSR had agreed to that; its position was that the internment camps had been overrun by the Nazis who had subsequently shot the Poles and then blamed Moscow.

Gabriel Kolko, an influential revisionist whose books were widely assigned as college texts, also portrayed the evidence about the Katyn massacre as inconclusive, arguing that "the criminological evidence ... has been used convincingly to prove the culpability of both sides" and adding that possible motives for either side's guilt were "equally persuasive." Perhaps realizing that the weight of the evidence against the Soviets was too heavy for this agnosticism to be convincing, Kolko then downplayed Soviet guilt, saying that even if one believed that the evidence pointed to Moscow, "Katyn was the exception" in Soviet behavior and "its relative importance ... must be downgraded very considerably." Why anyone should downgrade the moral significance of the cold-blooded slaughter of twenty thousand helpless prisoners is not clarified, except that Kolko went on to comment that the Poles murdered at Katyn were the elite of the Polish nation and, consequently, "whoever destroyed the officers at Katyn had taken a step toward implementing a social revolution in Poland." Since Kolko left no doubt that he approved of social (read: Communist) revolution in Poland and elsewhere, his fallback position artfully endorsed Stalin's strategy of revolution through mass killings without actually admitting that Stalin had instigated the killings.[11]

The partial opening of Russian archives in the last years of the Gorbachev era and the larger opening after the collapse of the Communist regime undercut the ability of revisionists to avert their eyes from Soviet crimes. Even contrived agnosticism about the Katyn Forest issue ended in 1990 when Soviet reform leader Mikhail Gorbachev ordered an investigation of the massacre. Soviet prosecutors videotaped interrogations of surviving KGB officials who had supervised the murders. In one of the tapes Vladimir Tokaryev, KGB commander at Kalinin, one of the murder sites, explained that a KGB execution team killed 250 Poles a night during April 1940. Tokaryev said that the lead executioner dressed in a leather hat, long leather apron and leather gloves (butcher's dress) that went past the elbows to keep blood off his uniform as he shot the handcuffed Poles one by one in the back of the head. Pyotr Soprunenko, KGB commander of all Polish POW camps, said during his interrogation that the order to execute the Polish officers came from the Politburo of the Soviet Communist Party and was personally signed by Stalin. Later historians located the order itself, dated March 5, 1940. Signed by Stalin and his chief aides, it said:

(1) To instruct the USSR NKVD [KGB] that it should try before special tribunals:

(a) the cases of the 14,700 former Polish officers, government officials, land owners, police officers, intelligence officers, gendarmes, settlers in the border regions and prison guards being held in prisoner-of-war camps;

(b) together with the cases of 11,000 members of various counter-revolutionary organizations of spies and saboteurs, former land owners, factory owners, former Polish officers, government officials, and escapees who have been arrested and are being held in the western provinces of the Ukraine and Belarus and apply to them the supreme penalty: shooting.

The Russian historian Dmitri Volkogonov also located a KGB memorandum of February 1959 stating that a review of records showed that from April through May 1940, Soviet political police had executed 21,857 Poles in obedience to the above order.[12]

In the face of the new evidence on Katyn, the Gulag and the Terror, revisionists have had to adjust their stance. Even J. Arch Getty grudgingly upped the number of those executed in the late 1930s Terror and those who died in the Gulag from mere "thousands" to more than a million, and recast Stalin from moderator of a bureaucratic turf war that got out of control to one of the instigators of slaughter. "We can now see his fingerprints all over the archives," Getty admits.[13] Still determined to retain a layer of whitewashing over Stalinism, however, he depicts the whole matter as Bolshevik "self-destruction" brought on by panic, paranoia and bureaucratic blundering. Getty contends that Stalin's regime was not the "coldly efficient machine of Orwell's 1984," but one characterized by "clumsy implementation of vague plans"—as if KGB administrative sloppiness were a moral defense.

But the setting of arrest quotas, authorizing of mass executions and dispatching of emissaries to oversee the purge of remote party committees were not the result of some bureaucratic misunderstanding or carelessness. Those shot in the back of the head by Stalin's executioners were not suicides; nor did those who died in the Gulag deliberately work themselves to death. What was done was murder, planned and deliberate.

Getty has refused to withdraw his condemnation of historians such as Robert Conquest whose earlier estimates of the human toll of communism, while probably high in light of post-1991 evidence, were easily more accurate than Getty's own prior attempts to minimize this catastrophe. One can understand why Conquest, responding to a request from his publisher for a new title for the revised edition of *The Great Terror* after the opening of the archives, tartly replied, "How about *I Told You So, You Fucking Fools.*"[14]

As the case of J. Arch Getty makes clear, not even the archival documentation of Soviet mass murder could prevent academic revisionists from whitewashing Stalinism. And anyone thinking that apologetics for Stalinism are a relic of the past need only read Robert W. Thurston's *Life and Terror in Stalin's Russia, 1934–1941*, written in 1996—long after the Soviet archives had been opened—for an adventure into the land of excuse making. Thurston, a professor at Miami University of Ohio, does make some concessions to the new evidence. He abandons the absurdly low estimates of those killed under communism suggested earlier by Getty and other revisionists, but still strives to minimize the numbers, allowing only that in 1937 and 1938, the peak of the Great Terror, Soviet authorities executed 681,692 persons. He agrees that this number does not include those who died in the Gulag from deprivation or take into account the victims of farm collectivization in the early 1930s or the politically induced Ukrainian famine or those executed for political reasons before and after the Great Terror of the late 1930s.

A precise figure for the deaths caused by Soviet communism is still not available and may never be; but based on the new archival material, reasonable estimates of those killed in the various episodes of state-initiated mass violence would certainly raise the death toll past five million and probably past ten million. Yet even Thurston's minimalist reckoning equals more than *nine hundred political executions per day* for the two-year period under question. Such a number ought to awaken the moral sensibilities of any reasonable person. Thurston also admits that at least two and a half million people were arrested during the Terror of the late 1930s, nearly one in twenty of the adult male population. Still, he implausibly insists that despite millions of political arrests and more than six hundred thousand political executions, "extensive fear did not exist" and there was no "mass terror." He is dismayed by how negatively Joseph Stalin has been characterized, for in his view Stalin was "more human than others have portrayed him." Stalin, claims Thurston, "was not guilty of mass first-degree murder from 1934 to 1941 and did not plan or carry out a systematic campaign to crush the nation."[15]

Thurston's tactic of admitting to horrifying facts and then blandly denying that they are horrifying is morally cognate to the word games and creation of straw men engaged in by Holocaust deniers. "First-degree murder" is a concept in American criminal law that has no real relevance to politically inspired mass murder carried out by government agents, whether Nazi or Communist. And whether or not Stalin had a "plan" for a "systematic campaign" of terror is just as irrelevant to his five or ten million victims as was the question of Hitler's plans to the six million Jews who were exterminated. Thurston's claim that Stalin, "this fear-ridden man," just "reacted, and over-reacted, to events" parallels Holocaust revisionists' apologias for Hitler.[16]

Another extreme example of the continued strength of academic Stalinophilia can be seen in a 1999 essay by Theodore Von Laue, the Frances and Jacob Hiatt Professor of European History emeritus at Clark University and one of the authors of a much-used history textbook. The essay, published in the respected journal *The Historian*, actually approves of mass murder as a means of social modernization:

> How then are we to judge Stalin? Viewed in the full historical context Stalin appears as one of the most impressive figures of the twentieth century. Born in obscurity, he rose to historic significance, a fallible human being of extraordinary qualities. He supervised the near-chaotic transformation of peasant Eurasia into an

urban, industrialized superpower under unprecedented adversities. Though his achievements were at the cost of exorbitant sacrifice of human beings and natural resources, they were on a scale commensurate with the cruelty of two world wars. With the heroic help of his uncomprehending people Stalin provided his country, still highly vulnerable, with a territorial security absent in all its history.

And, Von Laue adds admiringly, "though he knew how to act his public role, Stalin himself retained a sense of fallibility and imperfection, remaining remarkably humble." There is no discussion of the grotesque cult of personality surrounding Stalin that was foisted on the entire Soviet nation by every available means of state propaganda, nor of the Soviet dictator's sociopathic personality that manifested itself in things great and small.[17]

Most of Von Laue's essay is devoted to rationalizing Soviet tyranny, the use of terror, and the killing of anyone who might potentially stand in the path of Soviet modernization and power. His text speaks for itself:

> [Russia's] vast Eurasian territories, populated mainly by uneducated peasants, did not contain the cultural resources necessary for building a modern state.... Regard for individual life was a necessary sacrifice in Lenin's ambition to enhance life in the future. In Russia, necessary changes could be accomplished only by a highly centralized dictatorship mobilizing the Russian masses with the help of the semi-religious Marxist vision of human perfection.... Can we then condemn a Russian patriot, determined to surpass the influence and success of Western nations, for wanting in 1920 to spread the Soviet model and reveal "to all countries something of their near-inevitable future"?[18]

Von Laue then defends the Great Terror as a necessary stage and expresses admiration for the "remarkable human achievement" and "sophisticated design" of the Soviet dictatorship:

> Stalin's style of leadership, although crude by Western standards, was persuasive among his disoriented peoples. The sophisticated design of Soviet totalitarianism has perhaps not been sufficiently

appreciated. However brutal, it was a remarkable human achievement despite its flaws. The Marxist ideology helped suppress the ethnic and national diversity within the Soviet Union in a common membership in the proletariat that promised a glorious communist future to follow.... Stalin has been greatly criticized for the extent to which he used terror as an instrument to transform traditional attitudes and to force submission to the discipline imposed by the Communist Party—far greater than under Lenin. There is no need here to go into detail on this subject as it has been highly dramatized.

He closes his defense of mass murder with a revisionist cliché: "by 1938 the terror was scaled down, and Stalin himself admitted that *'mistakes' had been made.*" (Emphasis added.)[19] It is hard to imagine any academic historian foolish enough to make similar assertions about Hitlerism or any academic journal so morally obtuse as to publish them. There would be—and deservedly so—an uproar should a scholarly journal publish an essay with the passage, "The sophisticated design of Nazi totalitarianism has perhaps not been sufficiently appreciated. However brutal, it was a remarkable human achievement despite its flaws." But when it comes to the grand vision of communism, far too many American academics are willing to excuse the murder of "uneducated peasants" and exculpate, even admire, a ruthless dictator and the elegant design of his coercive mechanisms.*

While historians led the way, politically committed academics from other fields eagerly jumped onto the revisionist bandwagon. In the course of reviewing a book by two fellow leftist scholars, Barbara Foley, an English professor at Rutgers University, objected to their critical stance toward "Stalinism," writing that "the term 'Stalinism' perhaps needs deconstruction more than any other term in the contemporary political lexicon." She

---

*Logically, Von Laue's praise of the sophisticated design of Stalinism conflicts directly with Getty's portrait of endemic bureaucratic bungling and vague central control, but it is rare to find revisionists of these two approaches criticizing each other's views. While conflicting on the surface, the two interpretations are but different paths to the common goal of justifying Stalinism.

went on to endorse Arch Getty's revisionist account of the Soviet Union and labeled Robert Conquest an "offender against what I consider responsible scholarship." In her own book, after some perfunctory acknowledgement that there was a dark side to Stalinism, Foley enthusiastically praised its "tremendous achievements ... the involvement of millions of workers in socialist construction, the emancipation of women from feudalistic practices, the struggle against racism and anti-Semitism, the fostering of previously suppressed minority cultures ... the creation of a revolutionary proletarian culture, in both the USSR and other countries." Grover Furr, an English professor at Montclair State University, lauded the creation of Communist regimes in an essay-review entitled "Using History to Fight Anti-Communism: Anti-Stalinism Hurts Workers, Builds Fascism." In Furr's view, "billions of workers all over the world are exploited, murdered, tortured, oppressed by capitalism. The greatest historical events in the twentieth century—in fact, in all of human history—have been the overthrow of capitalism and establishment of societies run by and for the working class in the two great communist revolutions in Russia and China." Fredric Jameson (Duke University), one of the most influential and frequently cited figures in literary studies over the past several decades, has also been an enthusiastic defender of Stalinism. In 1990 he brushed aside the millions who died under Soviet rule and insisted that "Stalinism is disappearing not because it failed, but because it succeeded, and fulfilled its historical mission to force the rapid industrialization of an underdeveloped country (whence its adaptation as a model for many of the countries of the Third World)."[20]

## Revising the History of American Communism

Revisionism of the kind represented by Robert Thurston and Theodore Von Laue, although influential and highly vocal, never achieved domination of Soviet history studies; but revisionism has been much stronger among historians of American communism.

Although the Communist Party of the United States of America never became a major player in American political life, it had always been a controversial group whose activities evoked tremendous passions among both supporters and opponents. During the 1930s, the CPUSA played an important role in a number of organizations and crusades that helped to shape American life: the rise of industrial unions, the resistance to fascism and the struggle over the proper scope of governmental activism in social and political life that gave rise to the dominant New Deal political coalition of Franklin Roosevelt. Communists led or were part of the leadership group of unions that held a quarter to a third of the membership of the Congress of Industrial Organizations (CIO), an impressive achievement although some histories brush aside the fact that the vast majority of American unionists were in noncommunist CIO unions or the resolutely anticommunist American Federation of Labor. During the Popular Front of the late 1930s Communists also achieved a limited entry into mainstream politics in such states as New York, California, Washington, Michigan, Minnesota, Wisconsin, Oregon and Illinois, although remaining on the far margins in most of the country.

In 1948, Communists and their allies attempted to seize the leadership of American liberalism by creating the Progressive Party and backing former vice president Henry Wallace for the presidency. But Wallace's defense of the 1948 Communist coup in Czechoslovakia and his repeated excuse making for Stalin's actions, as well as exposure of the Communist Party's secret role in the Progressive Party, doomed this effort. As the Cold War intensified, and particularly during the Korean War, when American troops were directly engaged with Communist forces, the CPUSA became the pariah of American society. As evidence accumulated of extensive Soviet espionage against the United States, the party's standing fell further. Congressional committees probed Communist influence in every nook and cranny of American life, ranging from the pineapple plantations of Hawaii to the steel mills of Buffalo, with frequent stops in Hollywood. Anticommunism swept the country and Communists were ejected from the trade union movement, the Democratic Party and most liberal political institutions. No Supreme Court term was complete without at least one case challenging a statute or regulation bearing on communism as a violation of some provision of the Bill of Rights. Increasingly isolated and damaged by sustained government harassment, the CPUSA imploded when Khrushchev's confirmation of Stalin's crimes and the Soviet suppression of the Hungarian Revolution shattered the dream world of many members. By 1958 it was down to three thousand members and as an organization it never again played a significant role in American political and social life.

In America's intellectual life, however, communism and anticommunism have continued to loom large. In 1987 an annotated guide listed more than two thousand books, articles and dissertations on the topic.[21] If a new edition were prepared today, it would contain three times as many citations. Sometimes it seems as if never have so many written so much about so few.

The first substantial group of scholarly works on the CPUSA, the "Communism in American Life" series, the result of a grant from the Fund for the Republic, appeared in the late 1950s.[22] One of the most difficult tasks faced by the authors—Theodore Draper, Nathan Glazer, Daniel Aaron, David Shannon and others—was simply to gather documentary source material. Little was available, apart from newspaper stories and the transcripts of congressional investigations. Draper, in particular, was indefatigable, interviewing scores of ex-Communists, gathering internal party documents from expelled party leaders like Earl Browder and rummaging in long-forgotten Communist publications.

Not everyone was happy with the results. Some conservatives objected to the liberal and left-wing backgrounds of many of the authors and thought some volumes understated the extent to which some liberals had cooperated with Communists in the Popular Front era of the late 1930s. And several projects suffered from the limited availability of archival documentation. But many of these pioneering books uncovered fascinating material and remain useful guides to the American Communist experience.

In particular, Theodore Draper's *The Roots of American Communism* and *American Communism and Soviet Russia* told the political and organizational history of the CPUSA to 1929 with an insight and rigor that have still not been surpassed. Although most of the authors were left-of-center, all shared an anticommunist perspective. Many were veterans of bruising battles with Communists and their allies in trade unions, intellectual organizations and political groups, and they had observed the work of secret Communist caucuses, their manipulation of issues and abrupt shifts of policy in response to Moscow's needs. Some had gone through the CPUSA itself and learned to distrust it from the inside. Although not part of the same series, the only comprehensive (from origins to the 1950s) one-volume history of the CPUSA written in this era, Irving Howe and Lewis Coser's *The American Communist Party: A Critical History,* shared its perspective, reflecting the authors' anti-Stalinist Trotskyist experience.[23]

Most of the authors, implicitly or explicitly, accepted the "Red fascism = Brown Bolshevism" view that saw Nazism and Communism as left and right varieties of a similar totalitarian impulse. This interpretation began to gain widespread acceptance on the democratic left in the 1930s and won broad public acceptance after the Nazi-Soviet Pact of 1939. Two influential political scientists, Evron Kirkpatrick and Herbert McClosky, summarized the similarities of the Nazi and Stalinist regimes: no freedom of the press, speech or association, including no independent labor union movement; a monopoly political party that dominated social and civil institutions as well as the state; an absence of free, competitive elections; a court system that was a political-administrative extension of the party-state rather than an independent judiciary; the existence of a state-sponsored propaganda system aimed at the constant mobilization of the masses for state goals; the existence of a special political police that enforced the rule of the party-state; the acceptance of the "great leader" principle in the persons of Hitler and Stalin; the subordination of the individual to the state; and a state policy of external expansion. Even during the fervor of the wartime alliance with the Soviet Union, two prominent liberal educators, John Childs and George Counts, urged liberals to prepare for a break when the war ended, warning that association with the Communist Party "adds not one ounce of strength to any liberal, democratic or humane cause; on the contrary, it weakens, degrades or destroys every cause that it touches." The volumes of the Communism in American Life series took the view that the CPUSA, subordinated to the Soviet Union and infected by a rigid commitment to Leninist principles, could not by its nature be a "normal" participant in a democratic polity and had no legitimate place on the democratic left, tenets that later came to labeled "traditionalist."[24]

Draper, Howe and the books of the Communism in American Life series with their liberal anti-Stalinist perspective set the tone of academic discussion of domestic communism until the 1970s. Then, in reaction to the Vietnam War and the rise of the New Left on college campuses, a new generation of radicalized scholars launched a ferocious attack. Revisionists took it as an unchallengeable premise that McCarthyism and the popular anticommunism of the prior decades had inflicted grave damage on American culture, subverted democratic liberties, supported American imperialism and led to the Vietnam disaster. A 1974 volume, *The Specter: Original Essays on the Cold War and the Origins of McCarthyism,* brought together the newly emboldened revisionist scholars in a collection of essays that battered anticommunism in general, but anticommunist liberalism in particular, from every quarter. To these revisionists, anticommunist liberals had legitimated an inherently evil impulse of anticommunism and thereby set the stage for its logical products, America's Cold War aggression, McCarthyism and the Vietnam War quagmire.[25]

If one were to read these early revisionists' writings and nothing else, one would gain the impression that the CPUSA was largely a figment of the anticommunist imagination and that anticommunists were simply paranoids embarked on a hunt for imaginary witches. The American Communist Party, to the extent it shows up in these early revisionist histories, is treated as an organization of little importance whose activities were far too insignificant to have justified counteraction. David Caute's *The Great Fear: The Anti-Communist Purge under Truman and Eisenhower* (1977) articulated this view with casual dismissal of the American Communist movement, declaring it "clearly the case" that "American capitalism, business, free enterprise, prosperity and liberty had little to fear from domestic Communism." Instead of a real concern about the CPUSA, Caute attributed "'anti-Communist' hysteria" and "collective delusion" to fear of "the unassimilated alien, the hyphenated American still carrying the contagion of Old-World Socialism, that creeping, gradualist, Fabian New Dealism, which posed so insidious a threat to unbridled Business, big or small."[26]

While anticommunist liberal scholars of the Communism in American Life school sometimes marginalized Communist participation in the New Deal, these early revisionists made it nearly invisible. Often, the only Communists in their histories were those skeptically referred to as "alleged" Communists, while the myriad special purpose advocacy groups, such as the American League Against War and Fascism, that the CPUSA secretly sponsored and controlled were only "alleged" Communist fronts. In *The Politics of Fear,* for example, Robert Griffith discounted the relevancy of the specific characteristics of the CPUSA or Soviet communism and defined McCarthyism and other varieties of anticommunism as hostility to radicalism in any form:

> It was a natural expression of America's political culture and a logical though extreme product of its political machinery. What came to be called "McCarthyism" was grounded in a set of attitudes, assumptions, and judgments with deep roots in American history. There has long been a popular fear of radicalism in this country. . . . The mobilization and political articulation of these is the anti-Communist "persuasion."[27]

In Griffith's eyes, radicalism constituted a very good thing and opposition to it, by definition, was foul.

Where the anticommunist liberal historians of the 1950s and early 1960s had seen Nazism and Stalinism as variants of a common totalitarian impulse, revisionists treated such alleged similarities in the two regimes as little more than "emotion and simplism," in the words of leftist historians Leslie Adler and Thomas Paterson. They explained that while Nazism was a destructive movement, Soviet communism was a "system proclaiming a humanistic ideology" which had only "fail[ed] to live up to its ideal."[28] Revisionist writings were also filled with righteous indignation and emotional abhorrence toward Joseph McCarthy and McCarthyism, alongside cool aloofness toward Joseph Stalin and Stalinism.

These early revisionists had great success in discrediting left anticommunism in the university. But once this task was accomplished by the mid to late 1970s, and liberal anticommunists were an increasingly endangered species in history departments, revisionists took a different tack entirely. Where early revisionists had dismissed American Communists as so unimportant that public fears about them were irrational, the second wave of revisionists believed Communists to have been important shapers of American politics and culture.

One contributing factor was the demise of the New Left. After several years of euphoric confidence that an American revolution was imminent, the New Leftists, many of them children of Communist parents, confronted the reality of an emphatically nonrevolutionary America governed by Richard Nixon. Returning to graduate school after several years of political organizing and agitation that had left in its wake only failed radical and sometimes violent splinter groups disconnected from American life, some of them began trying to find solace in the American radical past. Although the New Left had imploded, the cultural climate encouraged the work of the revisionists: the unpopularity of the Vietnam War had fractured the public anticommunist consensus; Richard Nixon, long closely identified with domestic anticommunism, had been disgraced and forced from the presidency in 1974; and American security agencies were reeling from revelations of official misconduct and found themselves the targets of hostile congressional committees.

New documentary sources also became available. The Freedom of Information Act (FOIA), passed in 1966, partially opened
government files to scholars. Although the FBI was notoriously
slow in responding to requests, a steady stream of FBI files dealing with communism began to emerge from the J. Edgar Hoover
Building. Numerous privately held collections of Communist
Party material became available as the specter of McCarthyism
receded. New questions and fashions in historiography broad-
ened the scope of inquiry. Oral history aficionados located dozens
and hundreds of old activists and encouraged them to tell their
stories. Memoirs and autobiographies abounded. Biographers
found old veterans, some with source material, others with memories of the wrongs they felt had been done to them, eager to
justify their lives and struggles. Although several books and articles about black Communists had been written in the 1950s, the
new focus on race and ethnicity stimulated fresh research on a
variety of minority and immigrant groups in which Communists
had been active.

Some of the most assiduous revisionists decried the previous emphasis on politics and concentrated on the impact of communism on literature, the theater, music and art. The apogee of
this tendency is Michael Denning's *The Cultural Front: The Laboring of American Culture in the Twentieth Century* (1997). There isn't
much recognizable communism in the amiable Popular Fron-
tism of *The Cultural Front*. Stalin, the Gulag and the Great Terror fade into the background along with most conventional
politics and even the CPUSA as an institution. With the disagree-
able matter of real politics removed, what's left is an idealized
Popular Front of softly politicized art, literature, music, cinema
and theater, which is treated as more authentic. The impact of
communism and Popular Front styles on the arts cannot be gain-
said, and *The Cultural Front* presents an impressive analysis of
Popular Front cultural modes. But at the center of the Popular
Front phenomenon was the hard core of the CPUSA, its politics
and its drive for power. To leave out that core renders the history hollow. In the eyes of traditionalists, *The Cultural Front*

exemplified what Theodore Draper called a "genre of books about Communists-without-communism," banishing the CPUSA's Marxist-Leninist goals to a back room.[29]

Professor Maurice Isserman of Hamilton College, author of *Which Side Were You On? The American Communist Party during the Second World War,* explained the leitmotif of this new generation of historians:

> The new history of Communism has examined particular communities, particular unions, particular working class and ethnic cultures, particular generations, and other sub-groupings within the Party. Though critical of the C.P.'s authoritarian internal structure, and its overall subservience to the Soviet Union, the new historians have been alert to the ways in which the American C.P. was shaped by the environment in which it operated and by the people who enlisted under its banners.... The new Communist history begins with the assumption that nobody was born a Communist, and that everyone brought to the movement expectations, traditions, patterns of behavior and thought that had little to do with the decisions made in the Kremlin or on the 9th floor of Communist Party headquarters in New York.... [T]he new historians of Communism are willing to see American Communists ... as a group of people involved in, shaping, and shaped by an historical process.[30]

Many of these "new historians of American communism," as Isserman styled them, tied their research to their own radical sympathies, openly acknowledging that it was driven in part by a desire to validate their political needs. If the earlier generation of historians of American communism had written about a god that failed, these new revisionists, with some prominent exceptions, were searching for a past that would justify their radical commitments and offer lessons for continuing the struggle. They excoriated the traditionalists, most notably Theodore Draper, for emphasizing the CPUSA's subservience to the USSR, arguing that he gave short shrift to the independent, local sources of Communist activities and the "lived life" of individual members of the party. In hundreds of articles and scores of books, these revisionists emphasized the heroic battles that Communists had fought in places like Spain or the auto plants of Detroit, the severe repression they had endured and the progressive causes like the civil rights and union movements they had enriched. Some, like Isserman, conceded the Soviet ties, but minimized their impact or seriousness; others brushed them off as largely symbolic professions of faith that had little relevance for the workaday activities of most American Communists; still others argued for seeing the CPUSA as having achieved a happy blend of an indigenous radical movement and a Soviet-inspired party.

Logically, these later revisionists, whose writings began to appear in the late 1970s, were in factual disagreement with the earlier ones who had depicted domestic Communists (the "alleged" Communists) as too weak and insignificant to justify concern. On the contrary, American Communists had been important and influential participants in the labor movement and the New Deal coalition whose great contributions to American life had been slighted by history. Ideologically, however, both groups of revisionists were on the same side and the latter regarded the former as having cleared their path by discrediting anticommunist liberalism's influence in the scholarly world.

Despite the revisionist tide, some scholars carried on the traditionalist approach. But by the early 1990s, assisted by the post-1960s consensus in historical circles that the McCarthy era represented the most disgraceful episode in twentieth-century American life and by fading memories of a post–World War II Communist menace, the revisionists had taken control of the history of American communism.[31] When the controversial federally funded "National History Standards" for elementary schools were released in 1994, traditionalists charged that the revisionist view of American communism was being foisted onto schoolteachers. The conservative scholar David Gelernter observed in exasperation that this guide for teachers "mentioned McCarthy twenty-some odd times—amazing but typical of the weight this man swings. (Edison got zero mentions. The Wright brothers, also zero.) Don't honesty and pure curiosity impel you to acknowledge this strange situation and explain it?"[32] Most of the graduate students working in the field treated opposition to communism as an unpalatable byproduct of an unenlightened and paranoid era. They attributed the collapse and failure of the CPUSA not to its undemocratic and unpopular ideology or to its blind support for Soviet totalitarianism, but to a repressive, even fascistic American security regime that had spied upon, disrupted and destroyed a radical movement that in their minds had embodied many of the best impulses and values of American democracy.

### Genovese's Question

The collapse of all the Communist regimes in Eastern Europe and of the Soviet Union itself in 1991 and the concomitant discrediting of the Communist dream shook the revisionist consensus in the academic world (although not the drafters of the National History Standards). It also prompted one prominent historian to excoriate his colleagues for their refusal to confront the ideology and movement to which many had looked for sustenance.

Eugene Genovese, a prominent Marxist historian and one of the most distinguished interpreters of American slavery, had also been a political activist, dating back to his days as a young Communist and continuing in the 1990s during his transition to Catholic conservatism. In 1994 he asked, in the democratic socialist magazine *Dissent,* "What did we know and when did we know it?" about the crimes of communism. After delivering a *mea culpa* about his own sinister credulity, Genovese challenged historians whose claims to ignorance about the human toll inflicted by Communist regimes amounted to intellectual complicity, a "willful refusal to examine the evidence that had been piled high from the beginning," and accused them of "professional incompetence." Acknowledging his own complicity, he noted, "In a noble effort to liberate the human race from violence and oppression we broke all records for mass slaughter ... we have a disquieting number of corpses to account for." But many of those on the left, Genovese charged, had adopted the tactic of admitting nothing, explaining nothing and apologizing for nothing.[33]

Because of his authority as a former leftist and a celebrated scholar, Genovese's *J'accuse* had an impact—but a surprisingly minimal one. Several critics responded by dancing around his main point and complaining that he had unfairly conflated distinctions within the left, ignoring or gliding over the fervent anti-Stalinism of democratic socialists. None of these critics, however, regretted or even noted that in the academic world in the 1970s and 1980s revisionists had, with considerable success, demonized the anti-Stalinist left as accessories to McCarthyism. Two prominent revisionist historians, Eric Foner and Robin D. G. Kelley, tried to deal with Genovese's challenge more directly.

The DeWitt Clinton Professor at Columbia University, past president of both the Organization of American Historians and the American Historical Association, Eric Foner has received numerous academic awards and honors. He is also a member of a well-known family of Communists; his father and two uncles lost teaching jobs because of their party membership. His uncle Philip Foner wrote more than a dozen books extolling the CPUSA and was treated as a pioneer by the much younger generation of revisionists.

Responding to Genovese, Eric Foner insisted that "the question" of Communist crimes had been discussed in his "Old Left family" ever since 1956.* Since several Foners in this family were historians, it was striking that it took Nikita Khrushchev's 1956 admission for them to begin to credit the voluminous information about Stalin's crimes that was publicly available before then. Since the 1930s, journalists, scholars, diplomats, exiles and defectors had written hundreds of accounts of Stalin's Terror. But to

---

*"Old Left" is a euphemism often used by revisionists for "Communists." The historian Sean Wilentz "remembered an argument I had a few years back with a young, leftist editor, who angrily took me to task for referring, in draft, to a well-known scholar and member of the Communist party as a Communist. 'Old Leftist,' I learned, was the approved term; to call a communist a Communist, even matter-of-factly, was to indulge in red-baiting." Sean Wilentz, "The Question: The Responses," *Dissent* 41, no. 3 (Summer 1994): 384–85.

be a Communist was to be part of a rigid mental world tightly sealed from outside influences and this seal partitioned the Foners from reality. In fact the entire American Communist movement reacted as the Foners did in 1956. The CPUSA's theoretical journal *Political Affairs* editorialized on "the impact of the Khrushchev *revelation*," "these *revelations*" and "the *shocking disclosures*." William Z. Foster, the party's chairman, referred to "the *sweeping revelations* of the Stalin cult of the individual." Max Weiss, a longtime leading party figure, said, "the disclosure of the mistakes made under Stalin's leadership came as a *stunning surprise* to our Party leadership and membership," and party chief Eugene Dennis wrote, "*the facts disclosed* about the errors of Stalin ... *are, of course, new to us.*" (Emphases added.) The historian Aileen Kraditor observed that Dennis's comment was "a literal lie but a deeper truth: the facts were not new; their meaning was. Truth was not what fitted reality; it was what [authoritative ideological leaders] ... uttered. The source of a doctrine, news item, or any other statement carried more weight than the content of it; the feeling about the source preceded and determined the true believer's reaction." In other words, Dennis, Foster and the Foners did not credit the overwhelming evidence of Stalin's crimes until an authoritative *Soviet* leader, Nikita Khrushchev, ruled that they were crimes.[34]

While calling for "a balanced reassessment of the history of American communism," most of Foner's reply to Genovese was not a discussion of the substance of his essay but a barbed personal attack ending with the ultimate ostracism: a declaration that Genovese was no longer part of the left. Foner's call for balance was entirely rhetorical, since his steadfast cheerleading for communism in the face of its worldwide collapse has been remarkable. In 1990 he returned from a trip to the Soviet Union, then in economic disarray and on the verge of disintegration, to grouse that Soviet historians no longer accepted his negative views of America and that to younger Russian academics "America has become the land of liberty and prosperity." To his irritation, these young Russians even praised Thomas Jefferson and the values of the American Declaration of Independence. Historians have often written of their duty to fill in the "blank pages of history," but Foner bitterly reported on a Moscow public exhibition on the Soviet Gulag system and denounced "the obsessive need to fill in the blank pages in the history of the Soviet era." In 1991 he railed against the growing movements in Latvia, Lithuania, Estonia and Georgia to leave the USSR and regain their national independence; they should be treated in the same way as the southern states that had attempted to leave the American union in 1861, he raged, calling on Gorbachev to deal with the secessionists as Lincoln had. The subsequent decomposition of communism taught him nothing, and in *The Story of American Freedom,* published in 1998 and lavishly praised in academia, Foner made the American Communist Party into a heroic organization that profoundly changed American history for the better, "the center of gravity for a broad democratic upsurge" and one of the "focal points of a broad social and intellectual impulse, a 'cultural front' that helped to redraw the boundaries of American freedom." His account of the American Communist Party was so unbalanced that Theodore Draper judged it "bizarre," noting that in his book Foner had shown "no such enthusiasm for any other organization in all of American history." Reviewing his writings, the senior scholar John Patrick Diggins called Foner, regarded in the academic world as one of the nation's foremost historians, "both an unabashed apologist for the Soviet system and an unforgiving historian of America."[35]

New York University professor Robin D. G. Kelley, author of a romantic account of black Communists in Alabama, also defended left-wing historians against Genovese's charge, arguing that they had begun a serious reassessment of the USSR and the Comintern, but without offering any concrete examples. How little this avowal meant was vividly revealed by an interview that Kelley conducted with longtime Communist and historian Herbert Aptheker and published in the prestigious *Journal of American History* in 2000. Going well beyond the issues of American slavery and the writings of W. E. B. Du Bois, where

Aptheker had made significant contributions to historical scholarship, Kelley treated Aptheker's membership in the American
Communist Party as evidence of virtue. He never asked Aptheker
about his books and articles filled with praise for North Korea's
grotesque Stalinist regime, his defense of the Soviet invasion of
Hungary, his whitewashing of Soviet anti-Semitism, or his justifications of the Soviet suppression of the Czechoslovak attempt
at creating "socialism with a human face."[36]

When Aptheker smeared the prominent historian Oscar
Handlin as a onetime member of the CPUSA who had "completely sold out and became some big shot at the Library of Congress," Kelley lacked the wit to tell him that he had confused
Handlin—who was never a Communist—with another prominent historian, Daniel Boorstin, who had been a party member
and left in disgust after the Nazi-Soviet Pact.[37] Neither the editors of the *Journal of American History* nor any outside academic
reviewers of this interview bothered to check the accuracy of this
defamation of two senior historians before publishing Kelley's
article.

At the end of the interview Kelley asked Aptheker what
advice he would give to younger radical historians like himself,
who were "anticapitalists." Part of Aptheker's answer was that
leftist historians must make "intense partisanship" an integral
part of their scholarship. He stated that he could not "understand the idea of objectivity" in history because objectivity meant
"being part of the Right," and he could not "understand how a
human being who has some comprehension of history, of the
past and its struggles, can align himself with the Right." In an
afterword Kelley offered words of praise for Aptheker's partisanship and determination to overturn "racism, capitalism and
imperialism."[38]

Gerda Lerner, professor of history emerita at the University of Wisconsin, shares several traits with Foner. Like him, she
is a much-honored star of the contemporary academy. Her election as president of the Organization of American Historians in
1981 was an early sign of the leading role achieved by radical

historians in professional associations. While Foner came from a family of Communists, Lerner was a Communist Party activist for a decade, not leaving the CPUSA until after Khrushchev's confirmation of Stalin's crimes. After dropping out of the CPUSA she became a "post-Marxist" radical as well as a pioneering feminist historian. In an autobiography published in 2002, Lerner acknowledges that since the collapse of Soviet communism "everything has become far more complex and disturbing" and that she no longer defends the Nazi-Soviet Pact or Stalin's purges as she once did. She explains, "I wanted the Soviet Union to be a successful experiment in socialist democracy and so I checked my critical facilities when it came to that subject, and instead accepted what I wanted to hear on faith. It is easy to see now, in hindsight, that that was a serious mistake, but it was not so easy to see it then." Lerner admits that she "fell uncritically for lies I should have been able to penetrate and perceive as such. Like all true believers, I believed as I did because I needed to believe: in a utopian vision of the future, in the possibility of human perfectibility, in idealism and heroism, and I still need that belief, even if the particular vision I embraced has turned to ashes."[39]

But Lerner's recognition of the lies she accepted about the Soviet Union has done little to mitigate her loathing for the United States. A refugee from Nazism, she once compared life in America to living under Adolf Hitler. ("It was not dissimilar to the state of existence I had experienced in Vienna after the Anschluss.") Looking back, Lerner does concede that her judgment that fascism "could and it did" come to America "was objectively wrong," but she assures her readers that such an assessment "was appropriate for me and my own experience."[40] While she now recognizes that communism had its faults, in Lerner's view opposition to communism is always inappropriate. She attributes the collapse of Soviet communism to internal factors, giving no credit to Western resistance and making clear her continued hatred of America's decision to fight the Cold War.

## A Matter of Terminology

Even the terminology used to describe the combatants in this intellectual war has remained contested ground. We refer to those historians who took a benign view of American communism as "revisionists" in the usual historiographic sense that they were "revising" an earlier established interpretation, that of the Communism in American Life series. In the same fashion, we refer to the approach that we and others pursue as "traditionalist" in the sense that it has its roots in the interpretations first advanced by authors of the Communism in American Life series. There are alternative formulations. Maurice Isserman preferred the "new historians of American communism" to "revisionists," but it proved too cumbersome and never caught on. Alternative labels for the traditionalist view include "orthodox" and "Draperite."

In this contest, terminology is ideology in disguise. Some revisionists like to refer to traditionalist historians as "conservative," "right-wing" or "anti-Communist." In the space of one statement, Rutgers professor Norman Markowitz denounced traditionalist historians as "triumphalist," "counter-revisionist," "romantics," "rightwing romantics" and "reactionaries" who belong to the "HUAC school of CPUSA scholarship."[41] "Conservative" and "right-wing" are misleading, however, because many traditionalist scholars, indeed most of the original Communism in American Life authors, were liberals or radicals, and the pre-eminent traditionalist, Theodore Draper, has always remained a man of the left. Revisionists are well aware of this, but those depicting all traditionalists as conservatives do so in order to make it more difficult for liberal historians to take a traditionalist stance.

What some revisionists want is terminology that contrasts "anti-Communist historians" (biased and unscholarly) with themselves as just plain "historians" (unbiased and scholarly). For example, in a bizarre attempt at guilt by association, Brown University historian Paul Buhle has charged that traditionalists are identical to the most partisan Communists in their bias. In a featured essay in the newsletter of one of the major historical organizations, Buhle wrote, "Every scholar has a perfect right to political and personal views: rigidly anti-Communist, Communist or (for the great majority of us) 'other.'"[42] Leave aside the less-than-perfect balance (anti-Communists are *rigid* while Communists are simply Communists) and focus instead on the sly claim that historians like Buhle—committed left-wing revisionists—work in some wide scholarly consensus that lies between the rigid certainties of the anti-Communists on the hand and the Communists on the other.

In reality, the span of acceptable politics in Buhle's world-view is far from the center. He is willing to put Stalin on the left, but only if you agree that Harry Truman is a corresponding extremist of the right. Writing in *Radical History Review,* Buhle judged Harry Truman to be "America's Stalin" and went on to declare, "when the judgment of the twentieth century's second half is made, every American president will be seen as a jerk. After Truman, Nixon yields only to Reagan—still another Truman heir—as the jerkiest of all." *Radical History Review,* where Buhle publishes frequently, is not a journal *about* radical movements but a journal *by* radical historians published by "MARHO: The Radical Historians' Organization." Paralleling Herbert Aptheker's scorn for objectivity and support for politicized history, *Radical History Review* proudly states that it "rejects conventional notions of scholarly neutrality and 'objectivity,' and approaches history from an *engaged, critical, political stance.*" (Emphasis in the original.) Buhle, a former New Left activist, is a radical historian by any reasonable definition, and indeed it is a title he claims for himself in his essay "Reflections of an Old New Leftist" published recently in *Radical History Review.* His suggestion in the Organization of American Historians newsletter that he is just part of some middle-of-the-road "other" is a deception belied by his extremist views. If Buhle's radicalism really is in the academic mainstream, it illustrates the profession's unbalanced tilt to the left.[43]

The history profession is in fact politically skewed, with many academics writing on communism unable to recognize where political partisanship ends and scholarship begins. Consider *The State of American History* (2002), a book of essays by senior historians contemplating the status of historical scholarship. In the course of assessing the history of communism and anticommunism, Michael J. Heale complains that in the last decade, "conservative politics ... received a boost with the ending of the Cold War and the 'victory' of the United States." He laments that this "victory" has led some scholars to offer positive judgments of conservative American presidents. In particular, he deplores the "rehabilitation of Reagan, the sometime FBI fink" (this last snide comment referring to Reagan's cooperation with the FBI regarding Communist infiltration of the Screen Actors Guild when he served as its president). Not that Heale is particularly fond of liberal American presidents either; after all, they too fought the Cold War. He reminds readers, "As has often enough been pointed out, Kennedyite liberalism can sometimes be difficult to distinguish from conservatism." And he threatens scholars that any "who took an unsympathetic view of American communism risked being labeled neoconservative," clearly a deadly charge in his eyes.[44]

In 1993, twelve revisionists published essays in *New Studies in the Politics and Culture of U.S. Communism*. In the opening essay Michael Brown (Northeastern University) dismissed the writings of traditionalists Draper, Starobin and Klehr as not scholarship at all, but "outside of social science" and only "an extraordinary overtly tendentious type of satire." He linked the reappearance of "orthodox" historical writings about communism in the 1980s to "the introduction of a durable fascist element at the center of the United States polity," presumably meaning that Ronald Reagan's election was somehow equivalent to the rise of Adolf Hitler. In contrast he praised the work of leftists Maurice Isserman, Paul Lyons, Mark Naison and Ellen Schrecker, commenting that "what appears to be sympathy" for American communism in their writing "is in fact simply a willingness to accept responsibility for the only perspective from which a critical historiography can proceed."[45] By "critical historiography" Brown meant critical of American society.

While it is not difficult to differentiate "traditionalists" from "revisionists," one must note that the latter includes scholars with perspectives that sometimes clash. Those revisionists who take the view that the CPUSA was never or almost never wrong have denounced those revisionists who, while judging the party's history positively, have been critical of key aspects of CPUSA history. For example, Isserman's *Which Side Were You On?* offered a positive portrayal of an attempt by Earl Browder to Americanize the party toward the end of World War II. Moscow denounced Browder's reforms, he was ousted in mid-1945, and "Browderism" became a Communist heresy. His positive views on Browderism earned Isserman a rebuke from Norman Markowitz, who censured him as one of a "new group of anti-Communist caretakers." Similarly, although Mark Naison of Fordham University presented a flattering picture of the Communist Party in his 1983 *Communists in Harlem during the Depression,* he also noted the CPUSA's subordinate relationship to Moscow. That observation prompted another revisionist historian, Gerald Horne of the University of North Carolina, to denounce Naison for "rot" and "bad scholarship." Professors Markowitz and Horne published these attacks in *Political Affairs,* the theoretical/ideological journal of the CPUSA itself.[46]

AMERICAN COMMUNISTS SOUGHT nothing less than the revolutionary transformation of society into a perfect egalitarian socialism that delivered material and cultural abundance without oppression of any sort. This was no gentle utopianism, however, but a messianic romanticism that hated the existing world with its myriad imperfections and looked forward to apocalyptic change. In 1935 Lincoln Steffens, a prominent journalist and Communist sympathizer, assured Communists that they had the task "to make and cross a bridge from one age to another ...

from our old Christian-Greek culture to the communist culture which will probably prevail for the next two thousand years."[47] The generation of radicals who entered the academic world in the 1970s, although not willing to operate within the rigid confines of the CPUSA, shared the Communist movement's devotion to a revolutionary transformation of society and its eagerness to cross Steffens' bridge.

Many revisionist historians explicitly stated their radical loyalties, their admiration for Marxism-Leninism and their hatred of capitalism. Paul Lyons (Stockton College), whose 1982 book, *Philadelphia Communists, 1936–1956,* has often been cited as a model of "new historians" grassroots study, said that he regarded Communists as "people committed to a vision of social justice and a strategy of social change that make them my political forebears. And like my biological parents, they merit a love that includes—in fact, requires—recognition of their faults and errors. Needless to say, such a love also rests on an honoring." He wrote that he considered his book a "contribution" toward the achievement of "socialist cultural hegemony."[48]

In *Many Are the Crimes: McCarthyism in America* (1998), Yeshiva University historian Ellen Schrecker declared, "I do not think that I conceal my sympathy for many of the men and women who suffered during the McCarthy era nor my agreement with much (though not all) of their political agenda." Schrecker clearly acknowledged that those who suffered were chiefly Communists instead of hiding behind the smokescreen that they were innocent liberals falsely accused of being Communists. Norman Markowitz enthusiastically endorsed the Communist "dictatorship of the working class," calling it "a higher form of democracy." A senior historian at Rutgers University, Markowitz is also an admirer of Joseph Stalin, lauding his "consistent strategy ... to construct socialism across the huge territory of the Soviet Union, and to outmaneuver the British Empire, France, Imperial Japan, Nazi Germany, the United States and lesser capitalist states." When Gorbachev's reforms allowed Russians to discuss the horrors of the Stalin era openly, Markowitz was enraged, and denounced "those in the Soviet Union ... who have adopted a version of the traditional anti-Communist view of the Stalin era."[49]

Usually, but not always, the benign view of communism was coupled with hostility to the United States. University of Michigan professor Alan Wald, who has published numerous revisionist essays and books on cultural history, wrote:

> United States capitalism and imperialism remain absolute horrors for the poor and people of color of the world, and ultimately hazardous to the health of the rest of us. Therefore, the construction of an effective oppositional movement in the United States remains the most rewarding, and the most stimulating, task for radical cultural workers. That is why I choose to assess the experience of Communist writers during the Cold War era from the perspective of learning lessons, finding ancestors, and resurrecting models of cultural practice that can contribute to the development of a seriously organized, pluralistic, democratic, and culturally rich left-wing movement.

Scott Lucas lectured historians at the 2001 conference of the Society for Historians of American Foreign Relations on his adherence to "rational anti-Americanism" and noted that while he officially taught "American Studies" at the University of Birmingham (Great Britain), his real pursuit was "anti-American studies." After the Cold War ended with American victory, Bard College professor Joel Kovel wrote of his "bitterness that those I had considered, as the Sandinista anthem put it, the 'enemy of humanity,' [Americans] were strutting about and boasting that history had ended on their terms."[50]

Another prominent revisionist professor, Gerald Horne, published a defense of Communist libels that the United States had engaged in bacteriological warfare in Korea in the *Journal of American History*. After the September 11, 2001, terrorist attack on the United States, Horne said that the fault lay with the United States and gloated, "the bill has come due, the times of easy credit are drying up, it is time to pay." When asked his reaction to the September 11 attack, Professor Robin Kelley thundered a call for war not against the terrorists but against the American state: "In 1932, a group of French and Caribbean Surrealists got together and wrote a brief called 'Murderous Humanitarianism,' vowing to change 'the imperialist war, in its chronic and colonial form, into a civil war.' I say the same thing: We need a civil war, class war, whatever, to put an end to U.S. policies that endanger all of us." In an essay featured in the *OAH Newsletter,* revisionist historian Alan Singer (Hofstra University) allowed that the 9/11 attack had been "horrific" but insisted that America was guilty of much, much worse: "The events of September 11 do not compare in magnitude with a number of actions taken by the United States since the end of World War II including the bombing of Hiroshima and Nagasaki and the systematic destruction of Vietnam, Iraq, and now Afghanistan." And Eric Foner, one of the historical profession's leading figures, demonstrated his sense of historical proportion by noting soon after September 11, "I'm not sure which is more frightening: the horror that engulfed New York City or the apocalyptic rhetoric emanating daily from the White House."[51]

Not all revisionists, of course, shared such knee-jerk hostility to the United States. Mark Naison responded, "if anyone said anything about America's imperialist activities making it the moral equivalent of the Taliban and Al Qaeda I would beat them up."[52] But for most of them, the deeply ingrained anti-Americanism of their intellectual world could not help but make these revisionists view the attack on this country as the secular equivalent of divine retribution.

### Demonizing Anticommunism

Given such views, it is not surprising that revisionists have castigated traditionalists for having brought anticommunist values to their studies. A critical stance toward communism constitutes an unforgivable sin in the eyes of revisionists. As Ellen Schrecker put it, opposition to communism "tap[ped] into something dark and nasty in the human soul." Historian Blanche Wiesen Cook of the City University of New York asserted that because of its fight against communism, America "stand[s] morally isolated before the world, allied with ... killer countries ... always bellowing, when we are not shrieking, and thumping and bumping and burping our bombs and tanks and missiles," adding that "everything fine and creative in American thought has been splattered and smeared" by hostility to communism. Rutgers professor Norman Markowitz added, "primal anti-Communism is generally associated with Vichy collaborators and Nazi occupiers in World War II, and later with U.S. Cold Warriors. The purpose of 'primal anti-Communism' was to suppress all forms of critical thought and dissent."[53]

In Schrecker's *Many Are the Crimes,* anticommunism is presented as an insidious evil responsible for most of the ills of American society since 1945. Lest that description seem a rhetorical exaggeration, it is worth considering the crimes Schrecker attributes to hostility toward communism. In this book, anticommunism is guilty of having destroyed the civil rights movement's ties to the "anti-imperialist left" (euphemism for the Communist-aligned left) and, Schrecker claims, thereby "deprived the African nationalists of their main American ally, thus indirectly strengthening that continent's colonial regimes." Schrecker also holds anticommunism responsible for the restrictions on labor union power in the Taft-Hartley Act and adds, "debilitating as Taft-Hartley was, it was not solely responsible for labor's disastrous failure to replenish its ranks. Here, again, the anticommunist crusade bears much of the responsibility, for it diverted the mainstream unions from organizing the unorganized." Anticommunism is also culpable for the failure of national health insurance, for governmental inefficiency and for incompetent American foreign intelligence and diplomacy.[54]

Nor is this all. In Schrecker's eyes, anticommunism's malevolent influence included slowing the development of feminism, driving talented musicians from major orchestras, and even producing bad movies and dull television programming. (In reaction to McCarthy, Hollywood studios promoted "the good

guy/bad guy polarization of the Westerns, the unthinking patriotism of the war movies, the global triumphalism of the bible
epics, and the constricted sexuality of the romantic comedies.")
Having ruined television and the movies, anticommunism also
compelled serious painters to abandon realism for modernism
by having "destroyed the artistic vision of the Popular Front, mar-
ginalizing entire schools of representation and severing the connection between art and social responsibility." Schrecker also
blames anticommunism for retarding the natural sciences, for
crippling American higher education and, of course, for leading to Richard Nixon's abuse of presidential powers.[55] Many are
the crimes, indeed!

The *ne plus ultra* of demonizing opposition to communism,
however, is *Red Hunting in the Promised Land: Anticommunism and
the Making of America* by Joel Kovel of Bard College. Professor
Kovel begins with a "few terminological points," distinguishing
Communism with a capital 'C' from communism with a lowercase 'c.' Capital 'C' Communism involved "actually existing movements, governments, and so on which took life from the Bolshevik
Revolution and its many offshoots" including the CPUSA and
the Soviet Union. Lowercase 'c' communism designated "whatever inherently belongs to the ideal form of the vision of a classless society." Kovel explains that the "Soviet system while nominally
Communist was, given its hierarchy, exploitation and lack of
democracy, neither communist nor even authentically socialist."
And because his book is "about anticommunism and not anti-
Communism" therefore "little effort will be made to sort out the
vast complexities of the [Soviet] Communist experience except
as they cast light on our own ideological system." Thus, because
his book is not about those hostile to Soviet Communism, Kovel
claims he didn't have to spend much time on real Communists,
the real USSR or the embarrassing reality of Stalinism. Instead,
his book is about those who oppose "the ideal form of the vision
of a classless society."[56]

Kovel's argument, however, is a bait-and-switch game, and
it turns out that anyone who opposed the CPUSA or was critical

of the USSR was in Kovel's view just camouflaging depraved low-ercase 'c' anticommunism. For Kovel, anticommunists (who turn out to be identical with uppercase 'C' anti-Communists) are men-tally sick. In his telling, Senator Hubert Humphrey, longtime lib-eral leader, U.S. senator, vice president, and the Democratic Party's presidential candidate in 1968, was afflicted by an anti-communism that, Professor Kovel intuits, was "a ritual of male bonding within which the signifier 'father' links Hubert Humphrey, Jr., Hubert Humphrey, Sr., Lyndon Johnson, and the whole ethos of America as a land where 'real men stand tall' and stand together." And as for the FBI's J. Edgar Hoover, Dr. Kovel presents him as a sexually perverted archdemon for whom anti-communism "might be interchangeably a womb or anus."[57]

Kovel presents the America nation as a nightmarish mon-strosity since its origins. He explains that the colonial Puritans were lowercase 'c' anticommunists who feared native Indians because the latter lived in communal societies and were "the first communists in America." Consequently, Indians became the "object of the first 'red scare'" waged by Americans. Again sub-stituting wordplay for analysis, he writes that Americans like "red-hunting" because "the hunt retains a near-sacred character for Americans, as the politics of the National Rifle Association attest." And of course, Cold War anticommunism was not really about Soviet Communism but about American hatred of the ideal of the classless society. American Cold War anticommunism, Kovel claims, plunged the world into a nightmare: "millions of inno-cents lie dead, whole societies have been laid to waste, a vigor-ous domestic labor movement has been castrated, and the political culture of the United States has been frozen in a retro-grade position." Kovel further explains that American "anticom-munism is an exploitation of the deep structures of racism for the purpose of managing threats to capitalist rule," and also a "black hole" and "a pathology which had become the civil reli-gion of the U.S." Indeed, in Kovel's eyes, so satanic is opposition to communism that "anticommunism destroys time itself."[58]

WHILE MANY REVISIONISTS INTEREST themselves with varied and far-flung manifestations of anticommunism, few in contrast have been particularly interested in the Soviet Union or Joseph Stalin as factors precipitating domestic anticommunism. Only a few of the revisionists compare or contrast American communism with Soviet communism or bother to discuss the USSR at all; most treat Soviet communism as a massive irrelevancy. Yet it is clear that Moscow was the overwhelming presence in the minds of American Communists whom these revisionists defend and romanticize.

The American Communist poet Tillie Olsen wrote in 1934 that Stalin's Soviet Union was "a heaven ... brought to earth in Russia." In 1935 a CPUSA spokesman wrote that Stalin "has directed the building of Socialism in a manner to create a rich, colorful, many-sided cultural life among one hundred nationalities differing in economic development, language, history, customs, tradition, but united in common work for a beautiful future.... [A] world leader whose every advice to every Party of the Comintern on every problem is correct, clear, balanced, and points the way to new, more decisive class battles." In 1940, one of the CPUSA's leading teachers lectured at a secret school for young cadre marked for party leadership:

> The single country where the dictatorship of the proletariat has triumphed represents a wedge driven into world capitalism by the world proletariat. The USSR is the stronghold of the world proletariat; it cannot be looked on as merely a nation or a country; it is the most advanced position of the world proletariat in the struggle for a socialist world. When the Red Army marches, it is the international proletariat marching to extend its sphere of operations in the struggle against world imperialism. In the period of capitalist superiority in strength, the Party splits world imperialism by taking advantage of its inherent contradictions; it also builds up the strength of the USSR to provide the world working class with greater might. Stalin, the great genius of socialism, stands like a colossus of steel as the leader of the world proletariat.

Junius Scales, a student at the 1940 cadre school and afterwards head of the CPUSA in North Carolina, later wrote, "We students felt that the Bolsheviks truly created and practiced 'scientific' socialism.... [W]e felt we must learn from those real pros who had already built a heaven on earth. Consequently we regarded Soviet ideology as tested truth and believed that the Bolshevik experience offered guidance in every area of political work." In 1941 the party's theoretical journal declared that Stalin was the "greatest man of our era.... With every passing hour the titanic figure of this magnificent leader becomes more inextricably bound up with the very destiny of world humanity." Elizabeth Gurley Flynn, another party leader, called Stalin "the best loved man on earth of our time." And Alexander Bittelman, one of the party's chief ideologists, declared, "Stalin's greatness and genius stand out so clearly and beautifully that progressive humanity has no difficulty in recognizing them.... To live with Stalin in one age, to fight with him in one cause, to work under the inspiring guidance of his teachings is something to be deeply proud of and thankful for, to cherish."[59]

Did this Stalin worship have some practical effect? Devoted as many are to reconstructing the daily world of the average Communist activist, it would seem that the revisionists should be curious about the question of whether their commitments mentally prepared American Communists to assist Soviet intelligence agencies in espionage against the United States. The USSR in 1944 gave Gregory Silvermaster, a midlevel U.S. government economist, a Soviet decoration for his espionage on behalf of the Soviet Union. The KGB officer who secretly delivered the news to him reported that Silvermaster was "sincerely overjoyed and profoundly satisfied with the reward given him in accordance with your instructions. As he says his work for us is the one good thing he has done in his life." Harry Gold, who spent more than a decade as a key Soviet industrial spy, later said, "The chance to help strengthen the Soviet Union appeared as such a wonderful opportunity." And shortly before he began his work as a Soviet spy inside the atomic bomb project, Ethel Rosenberg's brother David Greenglass wrote his wife, "I have been reading a lot of books on the Soviet Union. Dear, I can see how farsighted and intelligent those leaders are. They are really geniuses, everyone of them.... More power to the Soviet Union and a fruitful and abundant life for their peoples."[60]

Given the primacy of the USSR in the mind of American Communists, the lack of concern about Soviet communism among many revisionist historians of American communism borders on the absurd. Such parochialism is equally apparent in revisionist judgments on anticommunism in American life. Neither a philosophical rejection of Marxism-Leninism nor fear of the popular support commanded by the CPUSA inspired the militancy of American anticommunism. Rather, most anticommunists feared what they saw in the Soviet Union and loathed the CPUSA not because it advocated peace or civil rights or labor unions, but because they believed that American Communists wished to bring the barbarities of the Soviet system to America. Yet many of the revisionists seek to explain domestic anticommunism as if the history and character of communism in the Soviet Union, Eastern Europe and China were irrelevant.

University of South Florida professor Fraser Ottanelli maintains that "the course of the CPUSA was shaped by a homespun search for policies which would make it an integral part of the country's society as well as by directives from the Communist International." The party's process of Americanization during the Popular Front years "was initiated and defined, in its various phases, by United States Communists," while the Communist International's activities merely "provided new opportunities and more room to maneuver."[61] In the course of his book on the party in the 1930s, however, Ottanelli presents the important decisions of the party as mostly "homespun," and Moscow almost disappears from view.

The difficulty with this variety of revisionism is illustrated by Ottanelli's tortured treatment of the Nazi-Soviet Pact. In the late 1930s the party had centered its successful Popular Front policy around antifascism, an international alliance against Nazi aggression, and support for President Roosevelt. The Nazi-Soviet Pact of August 22, 1939, required a drastic shift, given the party's subordination to Moscow's foreign policy. The CPUSA did not hesitate for even one day, but immediately endorsed the pact without reservation. However, the Communist International in Moscow had not given the American Communists any forewarning or policy direction, so party leaders had to guess at the full implications of the pact. Initially CPUSA spokesmen presented the pact as a stroke against Nazi aggression. The day after it was announced, Earl Browder told the *New York Times* that the pact made "a wonderful contribution to peace," while the *Daily Worker* proclaimed, "German fascism has suffered a serious blow."[62] The notion that the Nazi-Soviet Pact contributed to peace ended with the German attack on Poland on September 1. Still thinking anti-Nazism was the Soviet line, American Communists initially cheered Polish resistance to the Nazis. Browder announced on September 3 that the party gave "full moral, diplomatic and economic help for the Polish people and those who help Poland defend its national independence."[63] Not quite two weeks later the Communist International informed the CPUSA that this was a wrong guess about the Nazi-Soviet Pact's meaning and provided some guidance on its proper interpretation, a central part of which was opposition to Polish resistance and Polish national independence. Obediently, the party immediately denounced the Polish government as fascist and dropped all concern for Polish national independence. A few days after that, the USSR invaded and annexed half of Poland as provided by secret agreements between Hitler and Stalin, and independent Poland ceased to exist.

The Comintern's directive, however, did not deal with domestic policy, and Browder sought to salvage what he could of the Popular Front alliance by not directly attacking Roosevelt, although the party had become hostile to Roosevelt's foreign policy. In mid-October the Comintern informed Browder that this was an incorrect interpretation and ordered a complete break with Roosevelt. He complied, abandoning the policies under which American Communists had thrived since 1935. After being among the earliest to cheer on a possible third-term candidacy for FDR, American Communists turned savagely against him and attempted to sabotage his third-term election through their positions in liberal and labor organizations all across the United States.

The only reasonable lesson of this episode is the primacy of Moscow's wishes over domestic American considerations. Yet Ottanelli insists that it proved the reverse: "the unwillingness of American Communists to accept the implications of the new course of Soviet policy is in itself an unequivocal refutation of any notion that the United States Communists automatically aligned themselves to the 'twists and turns' of Moscow's policies."[64] Ottanelli's claim illustrates the perception gap between traditionalists and revisionists. The latter are able to transmute a scant few weeks of wrong guesses about what Moscow wanted, promptly corrected when concrete instructions arrived, into maverick independence. It was no such thing.

# CHAPTER 2

# The Archives Open

The documentary material newly accessible in Soviet-era Russian archives after 1991 added a wealth of detail and color to previous work. It also resolved a number of issues that had previously been hotly contested between traditionalist and revisionist historians. There was now a mountain of evidence, for instance, to confirm the close, at times suffocating, oversight exercised by the Communist International over the CPUSA. There was clear evidence that for most of its history the CPUSA had been financially subsidized by Moscow and that the subsidies were much larger than had been suspected. There was further confirmation of the role played by the Comintern and the Soviet Communist Party in choosing American Communist Party leaders, showing that this practice extended into the 1930s and 1940s, a period when many revisionist scholars had claimed that the CPUSA was autonomous from the USSR. Finally, there was abundant proof that on matters of policy both significant and trivial the American Communist Party leadership hesitated to act before consulting Moscow and that in all matters Moscow's wishes prevailed.

That revisionists would not find much good news in the Moscow archives was only to be expected. The CPUSA had never hidden its positive accomplishments, and no one seriously thought that Moscow had a trove of documents about unknown incidents that would burnish its image. Despite the claims of revisionists that American Communists were really just idealistic progressives seeking social justice, no one was so naive as to expect to find in Comintern files, for example, a report that the American party's Political Bureau had secretly sent a stern letter to Joseph Stalin expressing doubts about the Moscow Trials and demanding that Nikolai Bukharin and Grigorii Zinoviev be given an opportunity to defend themselves before an unbiased commission. Nor did anyone expect to find documents showing that the CPUSA's leaders discussed the possibility, say, of breaking with Moscow over the Nazi-Soviet Pact or even expressed serious reservations about the pact. Revisionists could only hope that revelations from the archives would not be too damaging and that they could still practice effective damage control.

There were a few revisionist historians who dealt forthrightly with the new archival resources. In 1981, James Ryan had written a doctoral dissertation on Earl Browder, the longtime chief of the CPUSA, arguing that at his core Browder was less a Stalinist than a Kansas Populist-in-a-hurry and a thoroughgoing American. As a historian at Texas A&M University, Ryan traveled to Moscow in 1993 to examine the Comintern and American Communist Party records. After his return he remarked that his earlier views of Browder could not withstand the documentary evidence he had seen in Moscow. "It is difficult to overstate the significance of these materials," he wrote in his 1997 book, *Earl Browder: The Failure of American Communism.* "They offer a perspective on American radicalism available nowhere else." Ryan concluded that Browder "lacked the vision and courage to separate himself and the organization totally from a foreign monster."[1]

Another historian, Vernon Pedersen, went through a similar experience. His 1987 master's thesis, a study of the Communist Party of Indiana, had been firmly in the revisionist camp. But after a 1993 research stint at the newly opened Moscow archives, Pedersen concluded: "The opening of the Russian archives confirmed the traditionalists' long-held claims."[2] Pedersen's Ph.D. dissertation on the Maryland Communist Party, revised and published in 2001 as *The Communist Party in Maryland, 1919–57,* combined an intense focus on the local activities of rank-and-file Communists with a clear-eyed understanding of the CPUSA's centralized nature, antidemocratic ideology and subordination to Moscow.

Other revisionists who have ventured to Moscow continue to uphold the revisionist stance while quietly conceding some points. In his 1972 doctoral dissertation on the CPUSA and Black Americans, Professor Mark Solomon of Simmons College had minimized the role of the Comintern, arguing, for example, that African Americans "virtually originated the idea of Black Belt self-determination," referring to the CPUSA's controversial stand in the late 1920s and 1930s which held that the black population of the American South had the right to national independence. After extensive use of the archives, Solomon remained highly sympathetic to the CPUSA but was a little more realistic and even a bit defensive. In *The Cry Was Unity: Communists and African Americans* (1998), he no longer dismissed the Comintern's supervisory role but tried put a benign spin on Moscow's supremacy by saying that Comintern orders to the CPUSA "were reminiscent of a parent's tough love for an errant child" and others "provided a needed sense of distance and perspective to straighten out muddles in national parties." He admitted, however, that American Communists often confused "Soviet state interests with a loftier internationalism" and this habit "more often than not led to willing acquiescence to foreign-made decisions that were often applied reflexively in the United States." He also acknowledged that the idea of Black Belt self-determination originated in Moscow.[3]

Sometimes the use of insights from the archives is so grudging as to be virtually invisible. University of Delaware historian Edward Johanningsmeier's *Forging American Communism: The Life of William Z. Foster* (1994), a biography of a leading figure in the party from the 1920s to the 1950s, tried to gain wiggle room, saying that the CPUSA's "rank-and-file membership *did not act completely autonomously,* even though it is now clear that the relationships between shop-floor and community-level organizers and the party hierarchy were characterized by a significant degree of independence," and that Foster was, "in the end,

profoundly American." (Emphasis added.) "Did not act completely autonomously" was Johanningsmeier's ever-so-slight modification of the earlier revisionist insistence on American
communism's autonomy—the CPUSA from Moscow and local
Communists from the party's leadership. As to whether Foster
was "profoundly American," later in his book Johanningsmeier
admitted that after being chastised in 1929 by Stalin and the
Profintern (the Comintern's trade union arm), Foster never
again deviated from Moscow's leadership and "recomposed his
utopian vision in the 1930s to conform with the totalitarian ethos
of Stalinism." He also said that Foster's "radicalism was based on
a powerful and genuine alienation from the central assumptions
of American politics" and quoted a statement by Gerhard Eisler,
onetime Comintern representative to America, that Foster and
Eugene Dennis, who jointly led the CPUSA from 1945 to 1959,
"interpret American problems as foreigners." Whatever Foster
was, he was not profoundly American.[4]

Professor James Barrett (University of Illinois) made more
extensive use of Moscow archives than Johanningsmeier for his
*William Z. Foster and the Tragedy of American Radicalism* (1999).
Although taking a revisionist perspective, he gently criticized
Johanningsmeier for minimizing the importance of the Comintern in shaping Foster's views: "His own instincts and ideas
were constrained and often distorted by the exigencies of international communist politics.... [By the late 1930s] he seemed
to become more fixed on the Soviet line and more rigid in his
understanding and application of Marxism-Leninism." Barrett
interpreted Foster's life as a lamentable conflict between indigenous radicalism and a foreign commitment, eventually won by
the latter.[5]

### Triumphalism

While historians have typically been excited by the emergence
of important new primary source material, many revisionists
were not pleased either by the new material available in Moscow

after 1991 or by the uses to which it was put. The news, for instance, that the Soviet Union had massively subsidized the CPUSA, that U.S. businessman Armand Hammer, among others, had laundered Soviet money, that the American party had created a secret apparatus that cooperated with Soviet intelligence agencies, that evidence substantiated the claims of defectors from Soviet espionage such as Elizabeth Bentley and Whittaker Chambers, that, in short, the CPUSA had been a subsidiary of the USSR—all supported by documents from Russian archives—sent them into paroxysms of outrage.

One common revisionist response was to denounce both the information and the traditionalists who used it for a "triumphalism" that applauded the Cold War victory of the West. Ellen Schrecker, editor of the American Association of University Professors journal *Academe*, devoted an entire paper delivered at the American Historical Association annual meeting to criticizing the "triumphalism" of "people like Klehr, Haynes and Radosh." She then presented a grotesque conspiracy theory according to which work based on the former Soviet archives was part of "the broader campaign to delegitimize professional scholarship" financed by conservative foundations. Scott Lucas, a diplomatic historian, angrily complained in the *Journal of American History* that newly published traditionalist books were "part of the continued effort to win the history of the Cold War, at home as well as abroad." Professor Hugh Wilford (University of Sheffield, U.K.) denounced the "triumphalist declarations" of "neo-orthodoxy." Robert Shaffer (Shippensburg University) lamented the "political agenda of using 'proof' from within the former Soviet Union as a way to claim not only victory but righteousness for the U.S. in the Cold War."[6]

A number of traditionalists were convicted of exactly this sin at the April 2002 "Cold War Triumphalism" conference sponsored by New York University's International Center for Advanced Studies. More than a dozen academics poured out their scorn for books based on new findings from Moscow archives while also denouncing the post–September 11 war against international

terrorism as a new act of American imperial aggression following the similarly unjustified American launching of the Cold
War. In accord with contemporary academic fashion—and Soviet
trials under Stalin—those put on trial were not invited to mount
a defense or dispute their conviction.[7]

Someone accused of "triumphalism" apparently was guilty
of finding satisfaction in the West's Cold War victory or, as Robert
Shaffer put it, concluding there was any "righteousness" to the
American cause. No such charge would have been made, however, against those writing books about the outcome of the Allied
war against the Nazis. In the vast literature dealing with fascist
Germany and World War II, the assumption implicit or explicit
in most scholarly work is that the Allied victory was a positive
event and, decidedly, a righteous cause. We do not know of an
example of reviewers in any major historical journal denouncing a book on World War II because it was written from a "triumphalist" anti-Nazi or pro-Allied perspective. Scholarly studies
of fascism or Hitlerism obviously sought to locate and evaluate
as many primary documents as possible and objectively weigh
the evidence as to what happened, but there was—and is—no
expectation that historians should be blind to the moral and
political implications of what a Nazi victory would have meant.

The Cold War should be no different. The western democracies stood firm for more than forty years and triumphed over
an oppressive tyranny. To millions of Latvians, Lithuanians, Esto-
nians, Georgians, Armenians, Ukrainians and other nationalities, the end of the Cold War and the collapse of the Soviet
Union meant liberation from Soviet imperialism. Modern-day
Russia and the successor republics of the USSR are no bastions
of democratic politics, but the most repressive is only a pale
reflection of Soviet tyranny and several are seriously attempting
to create democratic states. For Poland, Hungary, Bulgaria,
Czechoslovakia, East Germany and Romania, the victory of the
West meant liberation from Soviet suzerainty, the collapse of
hated Communist one-party dictatorships, and the creation of
democratic polities. In calling the documentation of this event

"triumphalism," revisionist scholars are saying that they regret the USSR's defeat in the Cold War and are enraged that anyone should take satisfaction from it.

### Following the Money

Revisionists also professed themselves scandalized that Yale University Press received funding for its Annals of Communism series from "conservative" foundations. In the *Journal of American History,* Ellen Schrecker indignantly charged that our books "were, it turns out, funded in this project by several well-known right-wing foundations."[8]

"It turns out" is a nice touch, implying that Schrecker had ferreted out some secret that Yale University Press was trying to keep hidden. Actually, in accordance with standard scholarly practice, the press had listed the donors to the Annals of Communism project in the front matter of all its books in the series. In an essay in *The Nation,* however, Schrecker and Maurice Isserman disparaged traditionalist historians as hired guns of a vast right-wing conspiracy. They asserted: "of course the foundations that are funding research by Radosh, Haynes, Klehr and the others— the John M. Olin Foundation and the Lynde and Harry Bradley Foundation, to name two—are the same people who brought us the assaults on affirmative action, the welfare state and all the other legacies, real and imagined, of the sixties" and "a broader campaign to delegitimize the academy, long targeted by contemporary conservatives as the last stronghold of the sixties radicals."[9]

They added, "one need not be a conspiracy theorist" to believe these charges. Actually, one does. Using Schrecker's own logic, one would be justified in denigrating her study of McCarthyism, *No Ivory Tower: McCarthyism and the Universities,* because the Louis Rabinowitz Foundation supported her research. Victor Rabinowitz, who ran the foundation after his father's death, admitted in his autobiography to being a secret member of the CPUSA for many years. He used the foundation's assets to support radical authors and proudly noted that two of the board

members who helped select worthy recipients were Harry Magdoff and Carl Marzani, both of whom covertly cooperated with
Soviet intelligence agencies in carrying out espionage against
the United States. If our work is somehow tainted by association
with a foundation that opposed affirmative action and the welfare state, what does it say about Schrecker's work that it was
funded by a foundation run by secret Communists and Soviet
spies? But this whole approach is a diversion: the openly acknowledged Rabinowitz Foundation funding of Schrecker's book is as
irrelevant to evaluating the contents of *No Ivory Tower* as are the
openly acknowledged sources of funding for Yale's Annals of
Communism series.[10]

The intellectual double standard that revisionists use to
decide when a source of funding taints a project is also illustrated by their very different reactions to covert CIA and Soviet
subsidies. For instance, Frances Stonor Saunders' *The Cultural
Cold War* (originally published in Britain in 1999 as *Who Paid the
Piper?*) took on the story of the Congress for Cultural Freedom.
In the early 1970s it was revealed that in the early years of the
Cold War, the U.S. Central Intelligence Agency had funded anti-
communist intellectual writings and activities through secret subsidies to this European-based organization. The CCF concentrated
on encouraging liberal and left-wing intellectuals in Western
Europe to support a pro-democratic and anticommunist per-
spective in the intellectual debates in Europe over the Cold War.
On a much smaller scale, covert CIA funding also went to the
CCF's American affiliate, the American Committee for Cultural
Freedom (ACCF), for similar activities. Saunders provided new
and abundant detail regarding the CIA's program of covertly
subsidizing cultural activities that assisted the West in the Cold
War. The secret funding, she argued, irretrievably tainted and
compromised those involved. A feature essay in the *Chronicle of
Higher Education* cheered Saunders on, praising her portrait of
the "dark years of American anti-Communist paranoia" when
cooperating intellectuals were "dupes" or "passengers on the
C.I.A. gravy train" who did "the dirty work of propaganda" for

the CIA. Similarly, Brown University historian Paul Buhle declared that because of the secret subsidies, those intellectuals associated with the Congress of Cultural Freedom should be considered "instruments of the CIA."[11]

Research into secret CIA subventions in the cultural front of the Cold War is a legitimate historical project. Knowing that the CCF operated with CIA funds and consulted with the CIA over use of those funds puts a different perspective on how one judges its activities. The CCF's public image as an independent, private entity was false. While possessing some autonomy, it operated with secret government oversight and its history must be understood in that light.[12]

It is not legitimate, however, for revisionists to have smeared the reputations of pioneering traditionalist scholars by falsely linking them to this secret CIA funding. In "Secret Subventions: Troubling Legacies," featured in the Organization of American Historians newsletter, Paul Buhle charged that "the highly prestigious scholarly series, 'Communism in American Life,' was secretly planned by the board of the American Committee for Cultural Freedom, with generous funding arranged for a handful of scholars." Yet the source Buhle cited, Sigmund Diamond's *Compromised Campus,* made no such charge. Diamond, a vociferous critic of the ACCF, discussed the *attempt* of the ACCF to play a role in the Communism in American Life project and its recommendations for authors. But Diamond also wrote that the Fund for the Republic, creator of the Communism in American Life project, *rejected* the proposals from the ACCF and he said nothing about CIA funding of the project. Contrary to Buhle's assertion, there is no evidence that the series was planned by the ACCF or that the CIA arranged the funding.[13]

So revisionist historians eagerly follow Yale University Press's openly acknowledged funding if it will lead to "right-wing foundations" that they can use to taint traditionalist scholars, eagerly follow secret CIA funding of the Congress for Cultural Freedom if it will discredit Cold War anticommunist liberal intellectuals, and are so eager to discredit the Communism in American Life book series that they invent nonexistent CIA funding. But when the money trail leads to Moscow, they lose their taste for the hunt.

Indeed, money—"Moscow Gold," as it was once called—is one area of historical controversy about which the Russian archives have provided abundant documentation. By the 1930s there was already widespread suspicion that the USSR secretly funded the American Communist movement. A number of former Communists, including ex-CPUSA chief Benjamin Gitlow, claimed that the Comintern provided generous subsidies, often smuggled to the United States in the form of gold and jewelry. American Communists, however, angrily denounced such charges as anticommunist paranoia. And while some documentation of such subsidies existed, it was far from definitive. Consequently, traditionalist historians could say no more than that there was evidence of subsidies, but their extent and how long they continued after the CPUSA's founding was unclear. Revisionist historians, meanwhile, passed over the matter in silence or treated it as trivial and a bit of a joke. Victor Navasky, a prominent revisionist writer, professor of journalism at Columbia University, and publisher of *The Nation* recounted that in 1983 he interviewed Gus Hall, head of the CPUSA, to ask him about reports, supported "only by anonymous FBI sources," that "Moscow Gold" had been financing American communism. According to Navasky, Hall "scoffed at the idea." He explained that the party's files were in Moscow and invited Navasky to write him a letter requesting permission to use them. Navasky did so, but a few weeks later "permission was denied."[14] Instead of stimulating his suspicions, this experience led Navasky to defer to Hall's stonewalling. Neither he nor his journal followed up on the matter and Navasky remains in denial about it today.

The question was answered once and for all with the opening of Russian archives. The Soviet subsidies turned out to have been quite large and to have lasted until the eve of the USSR's collapse. In *The Secret World of American Communism* and *The Soviet World of American Communism* we reproduced, for example, an accounting sheet of the first Soviet subsidies handed over to the American party in 1919, as well as a handwritten and signed receipt from Gus Hall, dated 1988, when he accepted a bag containing $3,000,000 in cash from a Soviet KGB officer and a copy of the KGB memo to the International Department of the Soviet Communist Party confirming that the $3,000,000 had been delivered to the CPUSA in accordance with the orders of the Soviet leadership.

We were not the only ones to establish the abundant money trail from Moscow to New York. The *Washington Post* published documentary evidence, as did the Russian historian Dmitri Volkogonov and the former Soviet dissident and writer Vladimir Bukovsky. Overseas, journalists and historians published similar documents showing astoundingly high levels of Soviet subsidies for every foreign Communist Party and other radical groups that had accepted Soviet direction. For example, a 1973 accounting sheet of the secret "International Assistance Fund" of the Communist Party of the Soviet Union showed for that year the Italian Communists got $5,200,000, the French Communist Party got $2,250,000, the American Communist Party got $1,500,000 and so on for a total of $16,680,200 distributed to sixty-nine foreign Communist parties and allied organizations.[15]

Details of an astounding project carried out by the Federal Bureau of Investigation also surfaced. The civil rights historian David Garrow in 1981 identified two senior figures in the CPUSA, brothers Morris and Jack Childs, as longtime informants for the FBI who had conveyed secret Soviet subsidies to the CPUSA. More information came to light in 1995 after journalist John Barron published *Operation Solo: The FBI's Man in the Kremlin* using FBI material to show that the Childs brothers had been central figures in smuggling Soviet subsidies from Moscow to the United States from the late 1950s to the 1970s, accounting for more than $28,000,000, all the while reporting on every transaction to the FBI.[16]

Revisionist historians reacted to the avalanche of discomforting facts in a variety of ways. Edward Johanningsmeier took the view that the question asked about CIA funding of anticommunists

in Frances Stonor Saunders' *Who Paid the Piper?* shouldn't be asked
about Soviet funding of Communists. He argued, "funding is
not *prima facie* evidence of motivation" and unless one can "link
funds delivered to specific policy initiatives," then secret payments were irrelevant to the question of CPUSA subordination
to Moscow. This suggestion that Moscow gave the CPUSA block
grants to use as it pleased was silly and directly contradicted by
the evidence. Many of the documents from the 1920s and 1930s
contained specific, line-item appropriations as well as general
operating subsidies. Further, in view of the Comintern's domination of the CPUSA, tying every dollar to specific policy initiatives would have been unnecessary. Johanningsmeier also called
documentation of Soviet subsidies "unsurprising," as if what had
been denied or ignored for so long was a long-accepted fact
hardly worth noting. Ellen Schrecker joined him in that evaluation by dismissing the documentation on Soviet subsidies as "old
news." But, in fact, anyone whose knowledge of American Communist history came from reading the voluminous revisionist literature, where the idea of "Moscow Gold" was laughed at or
ignored, would have been very surprised indeed.[17]

Some revisionist historians, however, continued to ignore
or minimize the existence of Soviet subsidies, no matter how
compelling the new evidence. As was typical of revisionist works,
the original 1990 edition of the *Encyclopedia of the American Left*
gave little attention to the issue of Soviet funding of American
communism. The second edition came out in 1998, after the
appearance of ample documentation that the subsidies were no
myth. In the second edition Paul Buhle, who later falsely linked
traditionalist historians to CIA funding, offered a convoluted
way of dealing with Soviet funding of the American Communist
Party. He argued that secret ties between immigrant radicals and
their homelands were not unusual. In the nineteenth and twentieth centuries Germans, Irish and other ethnic Americans were
constantly sending money back to comrades in their homelands
and "inevitably, legal niceties were avoided." Of course, this was
money *from* America to foreign countries, not the other way

around. Buhle did allow that the Bolshevik revolution had changed this pattern in some ways. But while conceding that there were Soviet subsidies to American Communists, he insisted that most of the money still flowed the other way, from Americans to the USSR: "the overwhelming flow of money went from American shores to the Soviet Union, mainly for specific campaigns, such as food support in the early 1920s and war relief in the 1940s."[18] The huge amount of funds openly raised and openly sent to the USSR for famine relief in the early 1920s and for war relief in World War II cannot be compared to Moscow's clandestine subsidies to a revolutionary political movement within the United States. Further, the bulk of the famine and war relief sent to Russia was not even from immigrant radicals as Buhle implied but from a broad spectrum of Americans motivated by humanitarian concerns. For example, Herbert Hoover, no friend of Bolshevism, spearheaded the Russian famine relief campaign in the early 1920s.

As for the Cold War era, Buhle does not acknowledge the existence of Soviet subsidies despite the abundant new evidence. Instead, in an *Encyclopedia of the American Left* essay written with Dan Georgakas (New York University), Buhle attributed the CPUSA's ability to support a daily newspaper despite a lack of advertising and a paucity of members largely to "the strength of library subscriptions in the Soviet Union and its bloc." The claim of the importance of "the subsidy provided by East European library subscriptions" is repeated in another Buhle-authored entry as well. In contrast to these relatively benign-sounding library subscriptions, Buhle once more diverted attention by pointing to the CIA: "Heavily funded by CIA sources . . . Jay Lovestone, now fervently anti-Soviet, used his personal network of associates to shape labor's own counterintelligence agency. Millions of dollars were passed to friendly labor officials in Europe, particularly in France and Italy." East bloc libraries and institutions did purchase several thousand subscriptions to CPUSA publications. But these subscriptions were a minor, indirect subsidy of American Communist activities and were not in the same league with Soviet delivery to the CPUSA of millions of dollars in cash subsidies—subsidies that go unexamined in *The Encyclopedia of the American Left.*[19]

The very first document reproduced in *The Secret World of American Communism* detailed Comintern payments to a variety of foreign Communists, including John Reed, one of the founders of the American Communist movement, as subsidies to jump-start the newly formed foreign Communist parties. According to the document, Reed had been given valuables worth just over one million rubles. We translated a word for describing the form in which the subsidy was transmitted to Reed as "value" and explained that in the context of the Comintern accounting sheet it meant jewels, gold or items of value rather than currency. Reed attempted to return secretly to the United States via Finland in 1920. Finnish security police captured him and confiscated a large quantity of diamonds in his possession.

In that era when the new Bolshevik regime had only limited access to world financial markets, it often used confiscated Tsarist and Russian church gold and jewels as a way to subsidize foreign Communists. For example, *Revelations from the Russian Archives,* a volume of translated documents published by the U.S. Library of Congress in cooperation with the Federal Archival Service of Russia, transcribed a Soviet memorandum noting the 1919 delivery to a courier for the Communist Party of Great Britain of 35 diamonds along with 206 pearls. The same memo noted receipt by the Comintern, for later distribution to foreign Communists, of two shipments of valuables consisting of 173 individual diamonds along with a sapphire broach, two platinum bracelets with diamonds, four strands of pearls, a ring with a pearl and a diamond, one pearl pin, a broach with three large diamonds, a brooch with both a diamond and a sapphire, a diamond pendant, a pearl stud, a diamond stud with a sapphire, a ring with a ruby and a diamond, a horseshoe charm with diamonds and sapphires, two pearl earrings, a charm with pearls and diamonds, a circular diamond brooch set in platinum and one diamond ring.[20] The term "Moscow Gold" as shorthand for such subsidies probably derived from this use of looted jewelry to subsidize revolution. The particular Communist International accounting sheet reproduced in *The Secret World of American Communism* recapitulated scores of Soviet payments during 1919 and 1920 to nearly a dozen foreign Communist parties. Some payments were made in hard currencies (Swedish krona, English pounds) and some in the form of valuables. We noted that the 1,008,000 ruble figure given for the valuables provided to Reed was the rough equivalent of more than one million U.S. dollars, an enormous sum at the time.

Before the book appeared, several Russian translators had checked the document translations. *The Secret World,* of course, was in English and for the benefit of our readers a complete translation of the Comintern accounting sheet was part of the text. One revisionist reviewer, University of Akron professor Michael Carley, claimed we had mistranslated the accounting sheet, saying, "there is no proof for this supposition" that Reed had been given valuables. He asserted that the word on the document that we translated as "value" was probably *valiuta* or *stoimost,* Russian terms that would have indicated paper currency rather than valuables. "But whatever the Russian word, 'value' does not mean or suggest valuable in the sense meant by the editors," Carley said. He then went on to explain that the Russian paper ruble was worthless as foreign exchange in 1919, so the rubles given Reed were of trivial use—although he never explained why the Soviets would give foreign Communists valueless paper rubles, nor did he address the other evidence of Soviet use of gold and jewels for subsidizing foreign parties.[21]

Carley literally didn't know what he was talking about. The word was not *valiuta* or *stoimost* as he had guessed, but *tsennosti,* and its meaning was exactly what we had indicated. Carley's review was on an internet discussion group, H-Russia, part of the H-Net family of internet history discussion groups. Authors can quickly respond to a review, and we did, pointing out the mistake in his speculation about the original Russian word and the irresponsibility of his assertion that we had mistranslated a document he had never seen. We also noted that our coauthor, Fridrikh Firsov, was both a native Russian and a senior historian of the Comintern and could not have made the error that Carley claimed to have uncovered. Finally, we noted that the same document had been cited and characterized the same way by Dmitri Volkogonov in his newly published biography of Lenin and by the head of the Federal Archival Service of Russia, Rudolf Pikhoia. Carley responded by admitting that he had not seen the original document. But he refused to withdraw his claims and went on to defame the Russian scholars who were native Russian speakers, had actually seen the document and had all agreed on the meaning of the word. Carley declared, "no critical reader should be prepared to take their word on Comintern subsidies to the CPUSA," but didn't explain why a "critical reader" should not credit Firsov and Pikhoia. Nor did he explain why a critical reader should ignore other documents demonstrating frequent Moscow subsidies to American Communists. He did discuss why a critical reader should not trust Volkogonov; after all, he "is a special assistant to Russian president Boris Yeltsin; I would not be the first commentator to note that his views, however interesting, should not be accepted uncritically, since Yeltsin wishes to discredit Soviet history in order to defeat his present political enemies."[22] (Most revisionists hated Yeltsin for his role in defeating the hard-line Communist coup against Gorbachev and ending Soviet rule.)

The most creative attempt to distort information about Soviet subsidies by misunderstanding words came from Professor Michael E. Parrish (University of California, San Diego) in commenting on a document in *The Soviet World of American Communism,* where the Comintern specified that two-thirds of a particular subsidy was to be spent on "legal work." Parrish wrote in the journal *Diplomatic History* that this allocation was only what "one might expect in a country known for its litigiousness." As *The Soviet World* explained, however, "legal work" in Comintern terminology referred to open, above-ground political activity. It was distinguished from "illegal work," which referred to clandestine or underground political activity. The Comintern was directing that the subsidy be divided, with one-third for the American party underground arm and the rest for its above-ground work. "Legal work" has nothing to do with American litigiousness or attorney's fees. Parrish either missed or ignored the explanation, but his gaffe enabled him to pretend that the Soviet Union was just helping an organization constantly being harassed by the American legal system.[23]

Several revisionists, faced with the evidence of Soviet espionage and the CPUSA's role in it, did some quick rewriting of historiography and, just as with the case of "Moscow Gold," insisted they knew it all along. Edward Johanningsmeier pondered "documents showing the cooperation of C.P. leaders and cadre with Soviet intelligence gathering operations" and concluded that it was "unsurprising."[24] Professor Athan Theoharis of Marquette University declared:

> The Venona and KGB records confirm that leaders of the American Communist party had served either as couriers or had recruited individuals to steal U.S. secrets for the Soviet Union.... The fact that the Soviets spied on the United States ... is in itself not a startling revelation. The recently opened records confirm only what presidents, most people in the intelligence community, and sophisticated political commentators already suspected. These records do not demand a reassessment of the conventional wisdom, adding at best helpful detail.

Unsurprising? Not startling? Conventional wisdom? Perhaps out of self-protection, Theoharis omitted *historians* from his list of those who knew about or already suspected that the American Communist Party participated directly in Soviet spying. If what one knew about the CPUSA and espionage were limited to the pre-1991 books and articles by revisionist historians like Theoharis and Johanningsmeier, the new evidence would have come as a profound shock. And certainly in the academic world, the "conventional wisdom" was that Soviet espionage had been, at most, minor and the CPUSA emphatically was not involved. One of the most-cited revisionist books, David Caute's *The Great Fear:*

*The Anti-Communist Purge under Truman and Eisenhower,* drove the point home by putting in emphasized type the unqualified statement, *"There is no documentation in the public record of a direct connection between the American Communist Party and espionage during the entire postwar period."*[25]

Caute's categorical denial that American Communists were mixed up in Soviet espionage was another article of revisionist faith that crumbled once Russian archives opened. But there had always been considerable evidence that there were Communist spies among us. In addition to falsely crying fraud, smearing opponents as Nazi collaborators and muttering about conspiracies funded by conservative foundations, the revisionist consensus also pretends that certain phenomena or people do not exist or are not worthy of scholarly examination. The way leftist academics have treated Elizabeth Bentley is a prime example.

Bentley turned herself in to the government in late 1945, and her information prompted a massive FBI internal security investigation. In 1948 Bentley testified publicly to the House Committee on Un-American Activities that she was a defector from the CPUSA and Soviet intelligence, and that during World War II she had been the liaison between the KGB and two large networks of Soviet sources in Washington, one headed by Victor Perlo and another by Gregory Silvermaster. She later testified at other congressional hearings and court cases in the late 1940s and early 1950s and wrote a popular autobiography, *Out of Bondage.* She played a major role in shaping public attitudes toward Soviet espionage and American Communists.[26] For this, she was subjected to a fierce attack, depicted as a fraud, and her testimony was denounced as lies from start to finish. *The Nation* called her testimony "smears" and "such wanton charges as hardly seem worth the dignity of denial." Eventually the historical consensus ratified that harsh judgment. Herbert Packer in his influential *Ex-Communist Witnesses,* although allowing that possibly something in her story might be true, wrote, "No witness's story is better calculated to inspire mistrust or disbelief than Elizabeth

Bentley's. The extravagance of her claims about her espionage contacts, the vagueness of her testimony about the content of the secret material that she allegedly received, the absence of corroboration for most of her story, and above all, her evasiveness as a witness, all combine to raise serious doubts about her reliability." David Caute was even less nuanced, painting Bentley as an unbelievable liar. Professor Athan Theoharis summarily dismissed Bentley's testimony, claiming her story "lacked credibility" and constituted "unsubstantiated allegations." Despite her centrality to the growth of popular anticommunism in the early Cold War era, there was no academic dissertation or book-length study of Bentley.[27]

When *The Secret World of American Communism* appeared in 1995, the top-secret Fitin-Dimitrov messages reprinted in the book provided strong new evidence that Bentley's story about espionage was credible by linking a number of the people she had named as Soviet spies to the KGB. Considering that Bentley's testimony had a major impact on public attitudes and government actions toward domestic communism, it seemed reasonable that historians would be interested in the implications for Cold War history. Most academic reviewers, however, simply averted their eyes. The *Journal of American History*'s review of *The Secret World of American Communism* did not even mention the material on Bentley. The *American Historical Review* solved the problem by not reviewing the book at all. Despite the historical establishment's effort to pretend that nothing has changed, a positive sign of the power of the new evidence was that, at long last, a scholarly biography of Elizabeth Bentley, by Kathryn Olmsted (University of California, Davis), appeared in 2002. Olmsted concluded that Bentley's 1945 statement to the FBI regarding Soviet espionage and those Americans who assisted it was accurate. A second Bentley biography, by Lauren Kessler of the University of Washington, is due out in 2003.[28]

Even when startling new information about Soviet espionage came to light, professional historical journals were reluctant to acknowledge it. In 1997, journalists Joseph Albright and Marcia

Kunstel published *Bombshell: The Secret Story of America's Unknown Atomic Spy Conspiracy,* which provided a detailed examination of American physicist Theodore Hall, an unknown but important Soviet spy within the atomic bomb project.[29] Solidly based on newly opened archival sources such as the Venona messages, FBI investigative records and documents in Russian archives, the book also benefited from interviews with Hall himself. A brilliant young physics prodigy, Hall graduated from Harvard in 1944 and was immediately recruited to work at Los Alamos. He was, however, a secret Communist, and as soon as he discovered that he was working on an atomic bomb, he contacted the KGB through the CPUSA and became a Soviet spy. While not a senior scientist, he worked on several of the key components of the bomb project. Among the many reports he delivered to the Soviets were descriptions of the implosion detonation system for the plutonium bomb and methods developed to separate the needed uranium U-235 from the unneeded U-238. Hall was also drafted into the Army as a private while at Los Alamos, but because of his scientific talent he was immediately offered an officer's commission. He accepted and swore the oath of true faith and allegiance to the United States required of all officers. He then returned to Los Alamos and proceeded to break his oath.

By any reasonable measure, Theodore Hall's atomic espionage was of significant historical interest. It raised questions about the advent of the Cold War, America's loyalty-security program, the relative importance of the Rosenbergs as atomic spies, the role of the Communist Party in Soviet espionage and, of course, the history of American's atomic weapons program. And this story had "the shock of the new," describing the activities of a man whose espionage career had remained secret from the American public and American scholars until 1995. While finding room to review books on bebop and urban planning in St. Petersburg, Florida, the *American Historical Review* declined to review *Bombshell.* The *Journal of American History* examined it only in a joint review with two other intelligence-related works. Professor Nicholas Cullather of Indiana University began this review with two paragraphs belittling histories of espionage as little better than the spy fiction of John le Carré. Having told historians not to pay any attention to these books, he then very briefly (in three paragraphs) summarized *Bombshell,* entirely ignoring the importance of atomic espionage in shaping the early Cold War and how Hall's story dramatically illuminated the role of American Communists in Soviet espionage.[30]

On contested issues such as the nature of American communism, the assumption is that scholarly controversies will be aired out in major historical journals where the opposing cases can be argued vigorously and fairly. In fact, the gatekeepers of the historical profession have effectively silenced this debate in the *Journal of American History* and the *American Historical Review.* Scholars who write traditionalist histories of American communism have produced dozens of books, worked in previously untapped archives and generated considerable historical controversy and debate. But since the triumph of revisionism in the academy in the 1970s, they have not been able to publish articles in the profession's two most prestigious journals.[31]

In 1972 the *Journal of American History* published "The Red Peasant International in America" by Lowell Dyson, describing the efforts of American Communists to organize farmers. Dyson's essay was traditionalist in orientation, placing the farm work of the CPUSA in the context of the Communist International's overall policy toward agriculture and the American party's subordination to Moscow. That was the last time any traditionalist article appeared. In the more than thirty years since then, the *Journal of American History* has not published a single article that had a critical view of the CPUSA as a substantial theme. On the other hand, it has published no less than twenty-two articles portraying American communism and the CPUSA in a positive light or demonizing domestic anticommunism.[32]

The *American Historical Review,* the other major professional journal, publishes far fewer articles dealing with twentieth-century U.S. history. Still, its record is similar. The last essay taking a critical view of American communism and a positive view of domestic anticommunism was Alonzo Hamby's "The Vital Center, the Fair Deal, and the Quest for a Liberal Political Economy," also published in 1972. In the thirty years since then, the *American Historical Review* has printed at least five revisionist articles about domestic American communism and anticommunism but no articles that take a critical view of American communism.[33]*

### McCarthyism: "A loaded word, but such a useful one."

Revisionists have done more than strain to discredit or ignore the new information; when all else fails they fall back on reviling the messengers. The first gambit in this attack has been to distort what traditionalists actually said about the role of espionage in the life of American communism. The second is to accuse them of McCarthyism.

Ellen Schrecker has commented that "McCarthyism is a loaded word" and "is invariably pejorative." But she also regards it as a "useful" epithet that "should become part of our regular historical discourse," and called on historians to use "McCarthyism" as the term of choice for "the movement to eliminate communism from American life during the late 1940s and 1950s," thereby taking in all varieties of opposition to communism with this one "pejorative" label. In her own *Many Are the Crimes* she applied that "loaded" term to any opponents of communism. She accurately termed Joseph McCarthy, his allies and imitators "McCarthyists," then went on to insist that there were "many McCarthyisms" including "a liberal version ... and there was even a left-wing version composed of anti-Stalinist radicals," charging that "Socialists and other left-wing anti-Communists functioned as a kind of intelligence service for the rest of the [anti-Communist] network." Consequently, weighed in the balance and found to be avatars of "McCarthyism" were Harry Truman, the liberal Americans for Democratic Action, the AFL, the CIO (its

---

*On issues of the Cold War, diplomacy and foreign policy, the record of these two journals is better but still unbalanced.

non-Communist majority under Philip Murray), Trotskyists, Love-stoneists, Socialists, Roman Catholics, the left-literary journal *Partisan Review* and the anti-Stalinist "New York intellectuals," Sidney Hook, Hubert Humphrey, Morris Ernst, Norman Thomas and Walter Reuther.[34]

Radical historians are not the only ones to conflate anti-communism and McCarthyism. No less an arbiter of politically correct ideas than the *New York Times* has done this as well. In 1998 *Times* reporter Ethan Bronner wrote an account of the debates among American scholars occasioned by the opening of new archival material, highlighting the conflict between those who saw extensive Soviet espionage and those, like Ellen Schrecker, who argued that "whatever harm may have come to the country from Soviet-sponsored spies is dwarfed by McCarthy's wave of terror." The editorial board of the *Times* soon signaled its agreement with Schrecker. Remarkably, on October 23, 1998, the lead editorial in America's newspaper of record denounced "Revisionist McCarthyism." The editorial charged, "Armed with audacity and new archival information, a number of American scholars would like to rewrite the historical verdict on Senator McCarthy and McCarthyism." The *Times* complained that new information from Russian and American archives was "opaque and ambiguous," although it admitted that in a few prominent cases the evidence was clear, mentioning Julius Rosenberg and "most likely" Alger Hiss. None of this, the editors declared, should be allowed to stand in the way of the consensus that it was McCarthyism — much more than any Soviet espionage or Communist infiltration of government — that "was a lethal threat to American democracy."[35]

To say that there was a significant issue of Soviet espionage in post–World War II America is not to vindicate McCarthy. The deciphered Venona messages, for example, document the CPUSA's integral role in the Soviet Union's massive espionage against the United States but offer no support for McCarthy's wild and irresponsible charges against the Truman and Roosevelt administrations. Most Americans who spied for the Soviet Union were members of the CPUSA. That organization had an underground apparatus that cooperated with both the KGB and GRU—checking out prospective spies, providing safe houses, recruiting couriers and supplying false passports. The head of this apparatus, Rudy Baker, met regularly with Earl Browder, the general secretary of the CPUSA. Browder himself functioned as a talent scout for potential spies and recruited a number of his party members for espionage against the United States. This did not mean that every American Communist was a Soviet agent. But the CPUSA was not just another American political party, operating according to the legal rules or the established practices of ordinary political organizations. Its Soviet ties defined its very *raison d'être,* and those ties made it, as the philosopher Sidney Hook argued at the time, in part a conspiracy and not a body of independent-minded heretics. The idea that anyone who linked American Communists to Soviet espionage was a McCarthyite and that those accused of Soviet espionage were innocent victims of McCarthyism is worse than nonsense.[36]

The charge of McCarthyism is a diversion from the broader issue of anticommunism. What revisionists are unable to surrender is the belief that opposition to communism is inherently wrong. Some of the more thoughtful or honest revisionist writers have either shed or, more rarely, never subscribed to the myths about American communism. But even these writers persist in clinging to the mantra that the fight against communism was morally and politically unjustified.

Operating as they do in an overwhelmingly liberal and leftist academy, what revisionists seem to fear most is that liberal and leftist anticommunism will once more become respectable as it was from the late 1930s into the 1960s. Speaking to the American Historical Association, Ellen Schrecker warned her fellow academics, "The rehabilitation of Cold War liberalism is a central tenet of the triumphalist discourse about communism and anticommunism." Writing together, Maurice Isserman and Schrecker assail the idea that Cold War liberalism is owed any credit for its struggle against communism. On the contrary, they insist, "cold war liberalism did not, in fact, 'get it right.'" At first, they seem to imply that nobody got it all right or all wrong, writing that it "would be a simpler world to understand if the devils and the angels would all line up neatly on one side or the other of contested terrain ... [with] crystal-clear vistas, in which all the actors knew then what we know now—about Stalin, about the Soviet Union." Once more we see the revisionist myth that politically conscious persons could not have known of Stalin's Great Terror, the Gulag or the totalitarian character of Soviet communism until the Soviet Union admitted it in 1956, or even until the Berlin Wall came down thirty-three years later. But in fact, in the 1930s and 1940s a great deal was known about Stalin and Soviet communism, and many people, particularly the anti-Stalinist liberals and democratic socialists disdained by Schrecker and Isserman, knew very well the nature of communism's threat to democracy.[37]

Schrecker and Isserman quite rightly call for judging American Communists "in context" and with "nuance."[38] But they should judge anticommunists with the same nuance, not write them off as devils all, without an angel in sight. Schrecker and Isserman condemn anticommunist liberals, anticommunist conservatives, anticommunist Democrats, anticommunist Republicans and anticommunist leftists. There is not a hint of either commendable intentions or laudable accomplishments on the part of any of them. While they now belatedly admit that Communists didn't get it all right, they still argue that those who opposed communism got it all wrong.

Such an assault on anticommunist liberalism is an indication that the debate is shifting from the history of communism to the history of anticommunism. In the introduction to *Many Are the Crimes,* Schrecker notes, too sweepingly but with considerable accuracy in regard to the academic world, "there is a near-universal consensus that much of what happened during the late 1940s and 1950s [referring to American anticommunism] was misguided or worse."[39] This consensus, however, takes as a premise the revisionist view that the CPUSA was a normal, albeit radical, political movement, more rooted in American traditions than subordinate to Moscow, and with no significant involvement in Soviet espionage. But as Schrecker and Isserman allow in their essay, this view cannot stand in the face of the new evidence. And with that premise crumbling, the "near-universal consensus" on anticommunism is giving way and, to the alarm of Isserman and Schrecker, there is "new life to liberal anticommunism." Their essay is in part an attempt to shore up the consensus and initiate a new line, a willingness to rethink American communism *but not* anticommunism.

It is a hopeless task. There was no party around which the anticommunist movement was built nor a core anticommunist ideology. Anticommunists were defined by what they were against rather than what they were for. Instead of a single anticommunism, there was a multitude, each with different objections to communism but all agreeing about the danger it posed to the West and to American freedom and security. The various anticommunisms did not follow a common agenda aside from their shared opposition to communism or even approve of each other. Consequently, any historical analysis of anticommunism depends upon a historical analysis of communism. The new evidence about the CPUSA bears directly on how historians judge the perspicacity and tactics of its anticommunist opponents.

But one point is beyond debate or cavil: it is the anticommunist liberals whom Schrecker, Isserman and other revisionists criticize who deserve a large part of the credit for meeting and turning back the threat of communism. One of their major themes is that anticommunists typically flogged dead horses: obsessed by a nonexistent Communist threat, anticommunists persecuted a tiny minority with little or no ability to implement its goals. For example, they write, "Hubert Humphrey ... along with [Arthur] Schlesinger and [Reinhold] Niebuhr set up the Americans for Democratic Action to protect the Democrats from the *waning* forces of the far left." (Emphasis added.)[40]

But what they fail to acknowledge is that when the ADA was established in 1947, it was only a fraction of the size of the Communist-infiltrated Progressive Citizens of America, the voice of a then influential Popular Front liberalism. Far from "waning," the forces of the pro-communist left were mounting their most ambitious assault on mainstream politics. The prospect for a political realignment appeared to exist. The Progressive Party candidate, Henry Wallace, had been a popular secretary of agriculture and then vice president under FDR. Harry Truman's presidency was in deep political trouble and he looked like a loser in 1948. The Democrats, having lost both houses of Congress in 1946, feared that a Truman defeat in 1948 would solidify the Republican congressional majority. Communists and their Popular Front allies hoped that the Progressive Party would displace the Democrats as the political vehicle for liberal and labor forces. This bold gamble failed disastrously in the 1948 election when Truman and his anticommunist liberals decisively defeated the Communists and their Progressive Party allies in a struggle for political control of the New Deal coalition and the labor movement. Only *then* did the pro-communist left wane. The crucial defeat of domestic American communism came in the struggle *within* liberalism between Popular Front and anticommunist liberals. But why did liberals reject Henry Wallace and his Popular Front policies? In large part because the ADA, led by figures such as Hubert Humphrey, Reinhold Niebuhr and Arthur M. Schlesinger Jr., persuaded liberals that Communists were not appropriate political partners for anyone holding democratic values and should be treated as pariahs.[41]

**The Cold War Is Over**

One sign that the revisionists' position has been weakened by new information from the Russian archives is a loud cry of indifference from those worried that the revisionist consensus will crumble under the weight of further research. The *New York Times Sunday Magazine* rarely carries articles of any length about scholarly debates, but in November 1999 it devoted a lengthy cover story (embellished with eight color photographs, two of them full pages) to this historical argument. The essay, entitled "Cold War without End," had a number of themes, but pervading the article was a world-weary complaint that the subject of domestic communism was played out and that the issue chiefly interested only Jews concerned about their "acceptance and assimilation" in American life and certain others with "unresolved feelings of personal betrayal" as well as "the Oedipal conflicts of red-diaper babies," all of whom had failed to "process the news that the war is over."[42] If the issue were of so little interest, of course, the question must be asked why the *Sunday Magazine* devoted such attention to it?

It is one thing for a newspaper to proclaim boredom with the Cold War because it is "over." It is quite another matter for *historians* to proclaim boredom with the past. In response to a statement that historical writing about American communism and anticommunism will continue "for many years to come," Ellen Schrecker averred that these matters are "redolent of political antiquarianism" and have "run out of steam," and she plaintively asked, "will the domestic Cold War never end?" Speaking to historians at the American Historical Association she urged scholarly neglect, saying, "We should recognize the issue of communism and Soviet espionage has become an antiquarian backwater. After all, the Cold War is over." She is not alone. In the *Chronicle of Higher Education*, American University professor Anna Kasten Nelson brushed aside two recent books on Soviet espionage and one on the Cold War with the dismissive comment, "it is time to move on."[43]

It is foolish to call upon historians to "move on" because virtually all of what historians do is study events that are "over." Rome fell a long time ago, but historical study of the Roman Empire is still lively. The English Civil War, the American Civil War, World War II and the Holocaust are over, but calls for historians to "move on" from these subjects are ludicrous. The revisionist call for an end to research is actually an attempt to call the game early with the score still in their favor. Their pleas, in other words, are for a selective end to research that threatens the revisionist consensus on American communism and anti-communism. Schrecker, indeed, lets the cat out of the bag with her insistence—a wishful fantasy, actually—that the Moscow archives have not yielded evidence requiring "that the past 30 years of scholarship [the revisionist consensus] will need to be rewritten."[44] What she is actually saying is not that historians will not find more evidence about the subversive nature of the American Communist Party, but that they should not look.

Schrecker and those whose views she represents are trying to stuff the genie back into the bottle. Revisionists dominate the academy, easily outnumber traditionalists, and control the most prominent historical journals. But traditionalist interpretations have been invigorated by the newly available archival evidence, more than a dozen scholarly books have appeared in the last decade that take a traditionalist approach, and by any measure traditionalists are on the offensive. A new academic journal, *American Communist History,* was launched in 2002 with an editorial board balanced between traditionalists and revisionists. The U.S. Library of Congress's purchase in 2000 of a microfilm copy of the CPUSA records held by the Russian State Archive of Socio-Political History (RGASPI) has made more than 435,000 pages of party headquarters records more easily available to American researchers, particularly graduate students with limited travel budgets. Other American libraries are also purchasing copies of this film. In addition, the Library of Congress is a partner in the International Committee for the Computerization of the Comintern Archive that will make available, in 2003, computer images of one million pages of the Comintern archive, including sections particularly rich in American-related material.

No wonder revisionists insist on distorting what is in the archives, attempt to minimize explosive documents, and engage in crude and inaccurate name calling. They have a losing hand and are bluffing in the vain hope that other players will just lay down their winning cards.

# CHAPTER 3

# *See No Evil*

In few areas of research have historians been so blind to new material or so eager to collaborate in maintaining myths than that of communism and espionage. The energy put into finding reasons to avert one's eyes from the new evidence or to explain it away by various rhetorical strategies has been nothing short of astounding. Poor scholarship is, of course, present in any field alongside good scholarship: some scholars are always stubbornly resistant to new evidence. But on matters of domestic communism and anticommunism, the last thirty years have seen a breakdown of the usual defenses that keep shoddy scholarship from overwhelming solid historical research. Too many revisionists have practiced a strategy of shrill and desperate denial on the core issues of the essential character of the American Communist movement and its role in American political life.

## Explaining Away the Documents

One method to avoid confronting evidence is smugly to assert, in an Orwellian way, that it does not mean what it says. Consider the Venona decryptions. Made public in 1995, these messages have been a body blow to the revisionist project.

Venona was the code name for an American code-breaking project to read ciphered telegrams between Soviet diplomatic offices in the United States and Moscow. Started in 1943 to investigate whether Stalin was considering a second Nazi-Soviet Pact that would leave the U.S. and Great Britain to face the full force of Nazi Germany, the project did not succeed in decrypting any Soviet cables until 1946. It then discovered Soviet espionage directed against the United States, not diplomatic maneuvering.

While a significant achievement, the Venona project did not provide American counterespionage agencies with a complete picture of Soviet activities. The messages were telegrams, often short and cryptic. The actual espionage "take"—stolen documents, microfilm and written reports from sources—went to Moscow via secure diplomatic pouch. And only a limited number of messages were deciphered. The Soviet Union used a labor-intensive cipher procedure, known as a "one-time pad" system, in which each message was coded in a unique, never-repeated cipher based on random numbers. The system was unbreakable if strictly followed due to the lack of repetition. But in 1942 the Soviet code-making agency, under tremendous strain to keep up with wartime demand for enciphering material, duplicated thousands of its one-time pads, making them into two-time pads, and created a vulnerability that American cryptanalysts were able to exploit. The duplication ceased after a few months, but meanwhile Soviet diplomatic offices and intelligence agencies had received thousands of duplicated and potentially vulnerable one-time pads.

American cryptanalysts were eventually able to read more than 2,900 Soviet telegrams, most sent between 1943 and 1945, still only a small fraction of the hundreds of thousands that had been sent. By 1946 most of the duplicated and vulnerable pads had been used up (each pad was used only once again). Nevertheless, the messages were an intelligence treasure trove. They identified hundreds of Americans (as well as scores of Britons, Canadians, Australians, Frenchmen and others) who assisted Soviet intelligence agencies. They demonstrated that the American Communist Party closely cooperated with Soviet spies and intelligence officers. They verified the reliability of the testimony of onetime spies such as Elizabeth Bentley and helped counterespionage officers gauge the accuracy of other information. Combined with other historical sources, the Venona cables greatly increase the ability of scholars to understand both the extent of Soviet espionage and the role that American Communists played in it.

Some revisionist scholars have attempted to minimize the significance of the decrypted KGB messages of the Venona project by suggesting that they are largely boasting and exaggeration or attempts by KGB agents to deceive their Moscow superiors. Scott Lucas says, for instance, that credulous traditionalists should take "into account the tendency of any intelligence officer to exaggerate, for political superiors, the number and importance of agents they are controlling." Professor Anna Kasten Nelson agrees, "Agents tend to tell their superiors what they want to hear." And Ellen Schrecker makes the same point:

> A careful reading of the Venona decrypts leaves the impression ... that the KGB officers stationed in the United States may have been trying to make themselves look good to their Moscow superiors by portraying some of their casual contacts as having been more deeply involved with the Soviet cause than they actually were. These documents do not tell us, for example, whether some of the New Deal officials Bentley worked with were consciously spying for the Russians or just sharing confidences with political allies and friends. A case in point is a cryptic Venona message reporting that Harry Dexter White believed the Soviets could get better terms on a loan than the American government had offered them. Was he betraying his country or merely making small talk?[1]

What is the basis for this view that Soviet field agents in America habitually deceived their superiors with fictitious recruits? Had Schrecker, Lucas and Nelson located evidence of chronic deceit by Soviet intelligence officers, particularly during World War II, the era of the Venona messages? No. They appear to have based their analysis of KGB operations in the United States on the 1959 comic film *Our Man in Havana,* where a British expatriate in Cuba cons an incompetent British intelligence service into thinking he is a master spy by submitting fictitious reports from nonexistent sources, a motif that reappears in John le Carré's more recent *The Tailor of Panama.*

The Soviet KGB, however, lived in a state of institutional-
ized anxiety, constantly on the watch for hostile intelligence services foisting double agents and disinformation on it. The
implication that a succession of KGB station chiefs in New York,
Washington and San Francisco, over a period of years, successfully conspired to conduct a massive con game, and that either
they had been bamboozled by their own field officers or they
were deceiving Moscow by claiming to have scores of fictitious
agents, is simply risible. Any officer practicing such deceit would
risk not merely recall and discipline but, during the Stalin era,
execution. KGB headquarters was not a credulous patsy but a
suspicious taskmaster. In fact, it was so suspicious about being
misled by questionable sources that in 1942 it ordered a special
investigation into the reliability of three of Moscow's most valuable spies inside the British government—Kim Philby, Anthony
Blunt and Guy Burgess—after all three reported that the British
had drastically reduced their intelligence operations directed at
the USSR as a result of the British-Soviet alliance in 1941. (The
KGB had responded to the alliance by *increasing* its espionage
assault on Great Britain.) Incredulous at reports that the British
were behaving so nobly (or naively), the KGB headquarters suspected the three of being double agents who were feeding their
KGB contacts false information. The investigation eventually
concluded that the three agents had reported accurately. But
the episode shows that Moscow was ever alert to being misled,
even to the point of paranoia.[2]

By the 1940s the KGB had developed an elaborate system
for vetting and authorizing recruitment of sources. A KGB field
officer could not recruit at will. Aleksandr Feklisov, a KGB officer in the United States during World War II, noted in his memoir: "In reality, even though the officer in charge does most of
the work, a recruitment implies a whole series of procedures
undertaken by five or six other officers. This is what is called
'studying the target.'"[3] The KGB station chief supervised the
recruitment while another field officer, section commander (sub-
chief of technical intelligence, political intelligence or other

specialty) and his assistant performed research in agency archives and reviewed the field officer's reports to avoid the bias of the field agent who was personally close to the candidate recruit.

There is ample documentary support for Feklisov's description of the background checking that the KGB undertook on candidates for recruitment. In the Comintern archive, for example, there are numerous inquiries from the KGB for background information from the Comintern on American Communists later known to have assisted Soviet intelligence. The KGB even asked the Comintern for any records it had on two American Communists whose apartments were used as safe houses. The CPUSA's liaisons with the KGB, Jacob Golos and Bernard Schuster on the East Coast and Isaac Folkoff on the West Coast, were often asked to provide background material on prospective recruits. In 1943, for example, the KGB even called upon the CPUSA to verify claims of a contact in Kabul, Afghanistan, that he had worked closely with a leader of the Maryland Communist Party while studying at Johns Hopkins University.[4] Sometimes the reports did not please the KGB and a candidate was dropped.

Feklisov also wrote that even "if these five persons" at a KGB field station "agree to 'approach' the potential recruit," that is not sufficient and "a request is submitted to the director of intelligence [in Moscow] or his assistant, either of whom has the final say."[5] And Moscow's sanction was not automatic or routine. Often the KGB headquarters asked its American station for additional documentation of a candidate's fitness. One case involved Marion Davis, whom the New York KGB wanted to recruit. Davis was working for the Office of Inter-American Affairs in Washington. The field officer report noted that she had earlier worked at the U.S. embassy in Mexico City, where she had had contact with Soviet diplomats. Not only did General Fitin of the KGB request Comintern records on Davis, he refused to sanction her recruitment until he received a confirming report from the head of the KGB station in Mexico City.

Once Moscow sanctioned a recruitment, the actual signing-on usually consisted of a meeting between the candidate and a professional KGB officer or, more rarely, one of the KGB's full-time American agents. The officer who conducted the signing-on then filed a report with Moscow confirming that recruitment was complete. One example is a January 1945 report from Vladimir Pravdin, a KGB officer who worked under the cover of a journalist for the Soviet TASS news agency. He met with Judith Coplon, a U.S. Justice Department employee, whose recruitment had been originally proposed by the New York KGB station in mid-1944. Moscow, however, did not give its permission until December. Pravdin reported that Coplon was a "serious person who is politically well developed and there is no doubt of her sincere desire to help us. She had no doubts about whom she is working for."[6]

Moreover, the Moscow KGB headquarters expected its field officers to provide regular reports on a source's productivity. In most cases Moscow expected the delivery of actual or filmed documents or reports written personally by the source, which were carried to Moscow by diplomatic pouch. When a source failed to deliver material, Moscow demanded an explanation. KGB officers usually could not get by with reporting only information delivered orally; Moscow wanted a justification when a source provided only oral briefings. The head of the KGB station in the United States also periodically shifted responsibility for contact with sources among his field officers. In addition, the heads of the KGB stations in New York, Washington and San Francisco were changed at intervals. With this sort of spy craft in operation, a faked or exaggerated source would surface sooner or later, entailing severe consequences for the offending officer. In the mid-1930s, for example, the KGB station in the United States detected that one of its American sources, a mercenary, was attempting to increase his KGB stipend by inventing fake sub-sources.[7] This incident reinforced the need for a policy, implemented in the 1940s, that a professional KGB officer had to meet directly with a source.

Any system is prey to human incompetence, supervisory inattention, corner cutting and other shortcomings. KGB tradecraft did not guarantee perfect results, but did greatly reduce the possibility that the Venona messages were based on field officers' braggadocio. And certainly, the burden of proof that KGB officers habitually lied or exaggerated ought to be on those historians who question the authenticity of the documents—but they have produced no evidence to back up their doubts.

## A Conspiracy Theory

If some historians toyed with the idea of inflated reports, Victor Navasky went further, depicting the Venona messages as part of a sinister American government project "to enlarge post–cold war intelligence gathering capability at the expense of civil liberty." William Kunstler, a prominent radical lawyer, insisted that the messages should be treated as forgeries because of their derivation from U.S. government agencies. University of Ottawa historian Brian Villa, although acknowledging he had no direct evidence, stated his belief that the U.S. government had lied about when the messages were decoded and that there was a second, still hidden Venona-like project whose disclosure would change the understanding of what had been released. Veteran revisionist writer William Reuben described the new evidence from Russian archives as a "hoax" and a "fraud."[8]

The accusation of fraud, while easily made, is on reflection very implausible. There are cases where U.S. government agencies prepared and distributed forged documents during deception operations in World War II and the Cold War. During wartime, forged documents may be successfully foisted on an enemy when that enemy must make a quick decision, lacks the opportunity to seek corroborative evidence, and is, obviously, denied the perspective brought by the passage of time and hindsight. Successfully forging *historical* documents, however, is much more difficult. Those who authenticate historical documents are not under time pressure, they have opportunity to seek corroborative evidence, and they judge the document in light of how it fits with independently derived historical knowledge. To be sure, historical documents are sometimes forged, but such cases tend to involve documents in very small quantities, often a single document. The reasons are obvious. Avoiding a mistake that would lead to the exposure of even a single document is daunting—errors in formatting, in language and nomenclature, in references to individuals and events, in printing, writing and typefaces, and other telltale anachronisms. Avoiding fatal mistakes if one produces hundreds of documents is close to impossible. For example, in 1983 the West German magazine *Der Stern* created a brief sensation when it announced it had purchased at a very high price a previously unknown set of Adolf Hitler's personal diaries from a memorabilia dealer who stated that they had been hidden in East Germany since the collapse of the Nazi regime. While the dealer had a plausible story, once historians looked at the diaries they found so many mistakes and errors that the tale quickly collapsed. *Der Stern* withdrew its claims, and one of its reporters and the memorabilia dealer went to jail for fraud.

Why, moreover, would the United States government launch a massive forgery operation in 1943, producing at enormous cost documents that falsely implicated hundreds of Americans as spies, and then never use them? If it was part of a government conspiracy to frame innocent people, why not use the documents in court? There are, for example, numerous Venona messages confirming Julius Rosenberg's role as a Soviet spy. Yet the government did *not* use these in the Rosenberg trial or even hint at their existence (wishing to keep the Soviets in the dark about the successful American break into their coded cable traffic). Why keep the forgeries secret for forty years until the Soviet Union was out of business? To discredit hundreds of dead people after the end of the Cold War? Moreover, forgers of historical documents attempt to disguise the documents' origins, to give a deceptive provenance so that potentially critical light will not fall on the forger. In the case of Venona, however, the origins have been openly proclaimed and the identities of the chief cryptanalysts and linguists of the National Security Agency are known. While some are dead, others are still alive and have made themselves available to scholars and the press. Venona could be a forgery only if it was supported by a conspiracy of massive size involving hundreds of people. Many of those who worked on the project are no longer employed by the government and have little incentive to keep silent about any government-sponsored fraud they may have participated in. Such a conspiracy would have to include a remarkably large number of individuals all of whom have remained steadfast for decades.

The decoded Venona messages have been public since 1995, but despite charges of fraud and hoax from Reuben, Kunstler and Navasky, no one advanced a serious argument for their inauthenticity. Professor Bernice Schrank of Memorial University (Canada) put forward the closest thing to a substantive argument in a failed effort to maintain the innocence of Julius Rosenberg. Twenty-one deciphered KGB telegrams discuss in damning detail Julius Rosenberg's role as the head of a Soviet espionage apparatus. Desperate to discredit Venona, Schrank does not claim forgery outright, but uses innuendo to depict the Venona messages as artfully doctored deceptions. In a 2002 article in the Canadian scholarly journal *Labour / Le Travail,* she charges, "The most effective authenticating detail is the reproduction of the material as typescript, the overwhelming majority of which was generated on manual typewriters, revealing all the unevenness of that crude technology. A smoother, neater, right and left hand justified word processed Venona message would not convey the same immediacy and visual authority. Here then, we are left to infer, is the NSA's actual working copy."[9]

Actually one does not need to infer it because the National Security Agency has stated plainly and repeatedly that these are, indeed, photocopies of the last internal working documents at the time the Venona project shut down in 1980 because it was no longer producing information relevant to contemporaneous American intelligence concerns. And the reason that the messages were done on manual typewriters is that *those were the machines actually used by NSA cryptanalysts in the late 1940s and 1950s,* when most of the messages were broken. The word processors that Professor Schrank thinks are normal did not come into

general use in the U.S. government until years after most of the
Venona messages were broken.

Further attempting to throw doubt on the provenance of
the Venona messages, Schrank writes:

> One of the great mysteries of Venona is that, through William
> Weisband, who worked on Venona and was thought to be a Soviet
> agent, and Kim Philby, who was a Soviet agent and, according to
> Benson and Warner [authors of an official CIA/NSA history of
> Venona], "received actual translations and analyses [of the Venona
> material] on a regular basis," the Soviets knew, or ought reason-
> ably to have known, that their codes were broken. So why did they
> continue to use them?[10]

Although Schrank claims to have read several books on Venona,
she appears to have missed the basic point that the ability to read
some enciphered Soviet cables was not a product of conventional
code breaking but a Soviet procedural error in duplicating their
"one-time pads" for a limited period, in 1942. By turning one-
time pads into two-time pads, they made a normally unbreakable coding system vulnerable, but *only* for messages encoded
with the finite number of one-time pads that were duplicated in
1942. Messages generated with nonduplicated one-time pads
remained unbreakable.

As the duplicated one-time pads were used up, Soviet vulnerability disappeared. Thus the number of readable Venona
messages begins in 1942, when the duplicated one-time pads
were first distributed, rising through 1943 and peaking in 1944,
when the duplicated pads were fully distributed and being used.
The number of broken messages then declined rapidly in 1945,
as Soviet cipher officers used up the duplicated pads. By 1946,
so few duplicated pads were still in the Soviet stock that less than
thirty messages in the Soviet-American traffic could be read, compared with several hundred read in 1945 and more than a thousand in 1944. After 1946 no messages to or from the United States
were made with a duplicated pad, and the only remaining breaks
came in a few messages from outlying KGB stations, such as Aus-

tralia, which generated so little traffic that they were still using one of the vulnerable duplicated pads in 1948.

It is important to remember, too, that *none* of these messages were broken until the summer of 1946. The Venona project broke messages several years after they had been sent, again with the exception of a handful of late-1940s Australian messages that were broken shortly after they originated. William Weisband was a Russian language linguist who had no possible association with the Venona project until 1945, when he came to work at the NSA headquarters. It is known that he was consulted about the translation of some of the broken messages in 1946. Kim Philby did not become involved with Venona until 1949, when he arrived in Washington as British intelligence liaison. Consequently, by the time Weisband and Philby learned of the progress the U.S. was making against the duplicated pads, the breakthrough was for all practical purposes irreversible. With only a few exceptions, the vulnerable pads had been used up. What Bernice Schrank sees as a "great mystery" is a figment of her own ignorance.

Schrank also claims that the footnotes in the Venona messages released by the NSA were part of the U.S. government's deception scheme. Let us look at the footnotes. In the Venona messages, Soviet intelligence officers sometimes used the real names of their sources. But more often—almost always for a long-term source—a cover name was employed, partly for security but also as a convenience. A real name had to be laboriously spelled out letter by letter in a special numeric code sequence for the Latin alphabet (Russian uses the Cyrillic alphabet), whereas a cover name could be provided with a simple Russian word. For example, Theodore Hall, one of the Soviet spies at Los Alamos, is identified by his real name in the first deciphered Venona message about him, but thereafter the KGB referred to him with a cover name, "Mlad," Russian for "Youngster." Often the real name behind a cover name could be discerned from the information in the Venona message about where he worked or his residence or travels. The NSA did not have a field investigation staff to pursue the leads, so it brought the FBI into the

Venona project to launch investigations to unearth the real name
behind a cover name.

When the decoded messages were then distributed to American intelligence and security staffs for action, NSA/FBI analysts
added footnotes supplying the real name for a cover name in the
text or noting that the real name had not been identified. For
example, messages where the cover name "Mlad" occurred had
footnotes identifying Mlad as Theodore Hall, whereas messages
with the cover name "Fogel" (Eagle) had footnotes indicating
that Fogel, also a Soviet spy within the atomic bomb project, had
not been identified. Footnotes were also provided to explain
obscure terms. For example, one decoded KGB message reported
that Alfred Sarant (electrical engineer, secret Communist and
spy working for Bell Telephone's Western Electric subsidiary)
"handed over 17 authentic drawings relating to the APQ-7."[11] A
footnote explained that the APQ-7 was a type of airborne radar
developed for the U.S. Army Air Force by MIT and Bell Labora-
tory. Schrank depicts these footnotes as evidence of attempts to
mislead, asserting, "footnotes, sometimes of a length far in excess
of the message, are added to the bottom of the message as if they
flowed automatically from the text instead of being material added
by translators and/or editors." But Schrank's "as if" is absurd. The
footnotes are clearly not part of the original text. Moreover, the
message documents were not produced for the general public
but for intelligence analysts, hardly a group likely to confuse footnotes with original text. Nor, despite Schrank's claims, have any
of the historians who have examined the Venona messages after
their release in 1995 confused the footnotes with the original text.

To reinforce her claim that the messages have been doctored
for dramatic purposes, Schrank also charges, "The releases appear
as if they had just been removed from secret government files.
Albeit crossed out, many still bear the legible notation 'Top
Secret.'"[12] She seems unaware that crossing through a "Top Secret"
stamp on a government document is one of several ways declassi-
fiers show that an American classified document is no longer secret.
No experienced researcher in American archives would think twice

about a crossed-out "Top Secret" anymore than he would think anything unusual about documents of the 1940s, 1950s and 1960s being typed on manual typewriters. Schrank, however, is not an experienced researcher in American government archives or on the subject of espionage and communism; she is a literary scholar who has published one book—on the Irish playwright Sean O'Casey. But in today's politicized academic world, simply to have a strong antipathy to the notion that American Communists spied for the USSR is sufficient qualification to publish an article in a scholarly journal advancing the most feeble of arguments.

Finally, Venona has been corroborated by a massive amount of other evidence. The contents of the decoded messages fit with written and oral testimony by numerous witnesses over many decades. Venona dovetails with voluntary statements by defectors from Soviet intelligence, legally forced testimony by reluctant witnesses, candid remarks gathered by listening devices, as well as information published in scholarly books and articles. The Comintern archive and the KGB archive in Moscow both contain numerous messages and documents that match *exactly* with Venona. For Venona to be a forgery, the American government forgers would have had to have access to top-secret Soviet archives during the 1940s and 1950s.

But for some revisionists, evidence is not terribly important. For example, in 1997 retired KGB officer Aleksandr Feklisov was scheduled to appear on a Discovery Channel television documentary to discuss his role as Julius Rosenberg's Soviet control officer. Aaron Katz, head of the National Committee to Reopen the Rosenberg Case, said he didn't need to hear what Feklisov had to say. He claimed, "Feklisov, supported by CIA, NSA, FBI and far-right forces, is doing what the McCarthyites of the hysterical 1950s were trying to do, branding all Communists and 'Communist-front compatriots' as being 'agents of the Soviet Union.' "[13] In fact, far from being a CIA creation, Feklisov was a much-decorated career Soviet intelligence officer known to Cold War historians as Premier Khrushchev's back-channel communications link to President Kennedy during the Cuban Missile Crisis. And far from being

sympathetic to the United States, Feklisov has written a memoir
in which he proclaims his commitment to the USSR and communism and emphasizes that his purpose is to honor Julius Rosenberg by describing his heroic service to the Communist cause.

The original espionage denier is journalist William Reuben,
who has been maintaining since the early 1950s that reports of
Soviet spying are fraudulent. In a series of articles credited with
first making the convictions of Julius and Ethel Rosenberg a contested issue, Reuben tried to cast doubt on the evidence presented
by the prosecutors. Several years after their execution he wrote
*The Atom Spy Hoax,* not only insisting that there was no evidence
the Rosenbergs "had ever turned over any secrets about anything
to anyone," but also improbably arguing that there were no secrets
of the atomic bomb to be stolen. For the Rosenbergs to be guilty:

> It must be assumed that there is an atom bomb "secret" which
> can be stolen and transmitted by individuals; that without the aid
> of "atom spies" the Soviet Union would not have produced an
> atom bomb so soon as 1949; that Russia's possession of the bomb
> was in some way related to the outbreak of the war in Korea and
> leads to the expectation that she will use the bomb for aggressive
> warfare; that there is an innate relationship between communism
> and Russian espionage.[14]

Reuben made much of scientists' statements that the fundamental principles of physics were not secret, and that the principles
of an atomic reaction were well known to physicists. But the German atomic bomb program, for example, included some of the
most able atomic scientists in the world, yet it worked out solu-
tions to only a few of the immensely daunting engineering problems in constructing a practical weapon and never came close
to building a working bomb. Reuben noted that the U.S. government's publication of the Smyth Report in 1945, with information about the bomb project, revealed a great deal of technical
data. But he neglected to add that key information about the
construction of the bomb remained classified and was not
included in the report. A mass of evidence from Russian archives
and Russian scientists themselves has confirmed that theft of

American secrets sped up Soviet production of an atomic bomb by several years and drastically reduced the cost of the Soviet project. Contrary to Reuben's view, documentary evidence has also confirmed that Stalin's agreement to the invasion of South Korea in 1950 was based in part on the Soviets having successfully tested an atomic bomb in 1949.[15]

But Reuben did not limit his "it never happened" claims to the Rosenbergs. He denied that Igor Gouzenko, a GRU cipher clerk who defected in Canada in 1946, had any real knowledge of espionage and waved away his revelations. Reuben accepted the Soviet accusation that Gouzenko had embezzled money and suggested that he was "paid far more handsomely by the Canadians for the interpretations he gave of what purported to be documents he had taken from the Russians." According to Reuben, even those Canadian defendants who confessed after their arrest were not actually guilty of espionage but had merely committed petty violations of the Official Secrets Act, such as having conversations about innocuous issues with Communist Party leaders or officials at the Soviet embassy. For example, in the case of Dr. Raymond Boyer, who confessed to providing classified information about RDX explosives to senior Canadian Communist Party official Fred Rose, Reuben said that Boyer was merely the victim of "a farcical bit of diplomatic buffoonery."[16]

By Reuben's lights, every post–World War II espionage charge was a fraud. The FBI arrested Judith Coplon in 1949 in the act of handing over Justice Department counterintelligence files to Valentine Gubitchev, a KGB officer working under the cover of an official of the United Nations. Although juries convicted her twice, Reuben stated that she was guilty of nothing: "All that the Coplon case amounts to—according to any evidence ever produced by the government—is that she knew a Russian." Faced with Klaus Fuchs' own confession to espionage, Reuben refused to take yes for an answer. He denied that Fuchs was a Communist because "everything in his entire life—the books he read, ideas he expressed or listened to, people he was friendly with, meetings he attended and activities he engaged in—was completely disassociated with communism." Not even Fuchs' moving to Communist East Germany after his prison term, taking a senior post in the GDR government and becoming a member of the Central Committee of its Communist Party appeared to shake his belief that Fuchs had not been a Communist. In fact, after the collapse of the GDR, newly opened German Communist Party archives showed that Fuchs had joined the party in 1930.[17]

Professor Norman Markowitz is equally disdainful of the new evidence from Moscow and the Venona decryptions on the Rosenberg case. Refusing to evaluate or even discuss the decoded cables, he denounced all of it as "discredited" in *American National Biography,* a highly prestigious reference work that sits on the shelves of hundreds of school libraries.* A reference work like the *ANB* is expected to offer reliable information and reflect the consensus of the best scholarly thinking, not one-sided interpretations. On most matters the *ANB* fulfills this task admirably. But Markowitz was an odd choice to write the Rosenberg entry. Not only a member of the CPUSA who even edits its theoretical/ideological journal, *Political Affairs,* he is also a longtime defender of the Rosenbergs. In 1983, when Ronald Radosh and Joyce Milton published *The Rosenberg File* (which concluded definitely that Julius Rosenberg had been a Soviet spy), Markowitz ignored their evidence and defamed the authors with accusations that they were "apologizing for anti-Semitism" and defending "the capitalist class."[18]

It has been known for decades that both Julius and Ethel Rosenberg were Communists and that Julius was an active figure among student Communists at CCNY. Markowitz's *ANB* entry camouflages this behind a euphemism, admitting merely that

---

*The *ANB,* published in twenty-four volumes in 1999, has been praised by reviewers and received the American Library Association's Dartmouth Medal as the best reference work of the year. Sponsored by the American Council of Learned Societies, the *ANB* replaces the venerable but out-of-date *Dictionary of American Biography,* first issued in 1928 as a standard biographical resource.

Julius was "active in left-wing student circles." Without actually saying so, the entry hints that the two Rosenbergs were religious Jews, stating that both were raised in "orthodox Jewish families" and that "Julius also received religious instruction at Downtown Talmud Torah and Hebrew High School." In truth, both abandoned their youthful Jewish orthodoxy for communism, a loyalty they retained until their execution. The misleading implication of Jewish religiosity and the evasion of their Communist loyalties, however, prop up Markowitz's theme that the case had an "anti-Semitic subtext." A student unfamiliar with the Rosenberg case, exactly the individual most likely to consult a reference book like the *ANB*, will come away from the entry with no knowledge that they actually were Communists but with the definite impression that they were executed because they were Jews.[19]

To promote his notion that the Rosenbergs were innocent Jewish leftists, Markowitz distorts the evidence against them at their trial, portraying it as weak or perjured. He dismisses with a single sentence the most definitive work on the case—*The Rosenberg File* by Radosh and Milton—which conclude they were guilty, while devoting several laudatory paragraphs to writers and books that proclaim their innocence, notably Walter and Miriam Schneir's 1965 book, *Invitation to an Inquest*. However, Markowitz never mentions that in 1995 the Schneirs admitted that new evidence from Venona and elsewhere established that Julius Rosenberg was a Soviet spy. The *ANB* entry demonizes those who concluded that the Rosenbergs committed espionage as "conservatives and anti-Communist or Cold War liberals" for whom "unquestioning belief in the Rosenbergs' guilt" was "a kind of loyalty oath."[20] Deceptive on all counts, the *American National Biography*'s entry on the Rosenbergs will distort the historical understanding of students for several generations to come.

As for Reuben, revisionist historians have not repudiated his fantasies but instead have embraced him as a respected interpreter of the most significant espionage case of the century. The editors of the *Encyclopedia of the American Left* commissioned him to write the entry on "The Hiss Case," a decision akin to choosing a Holocaust denier to contribute to an encyclopedia of Jewish history. And he did not disappoint them. In his essay, Reuben mischaracterized the documents demonstrating Hiss's espionage that Whittaker Chambers had secreted away in the late 1930s and produced as evidence in 1948; omitted any information supportive of Chambers and damaging to Hiss; repeated claims by two psychiatrists that Chambers was a psychopath without mentioning that neither one had actually examined Chambers; and, in the bibliographic note for the entry, simply left out *Perjury,* Allen Weinstein's definitive study of the Hiss case. Not only was Alger Hiss not a spy, according to Reuben, but Whittaker Chambers was never a Communist. Despite the fact that Chambers had been on the staff of the *Daily Worker* in the late 1920s, edited a CPUSA journal, *New Masses,* in 1931 and 1932 and appeared on its masthead, and was known to dozens of Communists and ex-Communists as an active party member, Reuben asserted that "his only verifiable links to the left were four short stories published in the *New Masses* in 1931 and a twenty-line poem in the *Sunday Worker* in 1926."[21]

### The Encyclopedia of Revisionism

Reuben's distortions are symptomatic of the way the editors of the *Encyclopedia of the American Left* dealt with the issues of communism and espionage. The book purports to be a reference work devoted to radicals and radical movements in American history. Published by Oxford University Press, it bears all the paraphernalia of a scholarly enterprise. Its lead editor, Mari Jo Buhle, is a senior "Professor of American Civilization and History" at Brown University. The first edition was selected by *Choice* and *Library Journal* as one of the ten best reference books published in 1990. The second edition, published in 1998, after the opening of Russian archives and the Venona documents, claimed, "Some entries have undergone considerable revision and rewriting to take into account new scholarship."[22] Yet when it came to entries on communism and Soviet espionage, both editions resemble nothing more than a Stalinist effort to pretend that certain unpleasant facts and activities never happened by erasing them from the historical record or creating counterbalancing myths out of thin air. It exemplifies what happens when historians heed the call made by the dean of Communist historians, Herbert Aptheker, in the prestigious *Journal of American History* to abandon "objectivity" and adopt "intense partisanship" as their guide.

Some entries simply omit relevant biographical details that might tarnish a Communist's reputation. Malcolm Sylvers, a radical American historian who is on the history faculty of the University of Venice in Italy, wrote the entry on Earl Browder without mentioning the documentary evidence that Browder cooperated with Soviet intelligence. Sid Resnick, a former Communist, profiled Paul Novick, the longtime editor of the CPUSA's Yiddish-language journal, *Morgen Freiheit,* but never mentioned that one of the charges against the Yiddish writers executed by Stalin in 1952 was that they had turned Soviet secrets over to Novick, falsely alleged to be an American spy. (Loyal Communist that he was, Novick continued to defend the USSR until the late 1950s while his Soviet comrades were being murdered and denounced as "rootless cosmopolitans.")

The choice of contributors for this encyclopedia sometimes borders on the bizarre. A good example is the essay on the *Amerasia* case, the first post–World War II espionage incident involving Communists. In the spring of 1945, with war still raging, the Office of Strategic Services (predecessor to the CIA) launched an emergency investigation of how portions of a secret report had been printed in the journal *Amerasia,* published by Philip Jaffe, a wealthy, pro-Soviet entrepreneur. OSS security officers secretly entered the magazine's offices and discovered hundreds of stolen classified government documents. The FBI later wiretapped and bugged several of the editors and their contacts in Washington. During one overheard conversation, Jaffe told Andrew Roth (one of Jaffe's sources) that Joseph Bernstein, a former *Amerasia* employee, had worked for Soviet intelligence for many years. According to Jaffe, Bernstein had asked him "to give me the dope you get on Chungking out of the Far Eastern Division of the State Department."[23]

Jaffe was willing to help Bernstein but had insisted on checking his *bona fides* as a Soviet agent and paid a visit to Communist Party chief Earl Browder at his home in Yonkers. Although the FBI had observed Jaffe's meetings with Bernstein and Browder, it had not been able to overhear the conversations. But Jaffe later recounted them to Roth with the FBI secretly listening. Browder had advised Jaffe to insist on meeting Bernstein's Soviet contact. If he was genuine, said Browder, "he'll find a way to prove it. If he can't find a way, don't deal with him. It may be that he [Bernstein] is ... on his own, and he just wants to put a feather in his own cap, if he can get a little something. And if it's just personal, nothing doing. Don't touch it."[24]

The FBI arrested Jaffe and several associates on charges of conspiracy to commit espionage. Although the FBI believed Bernstein was a Soviet agent, it never had sufficient evidence to arrest him.[25] The Venona decryptions confirmed that Bernstein worked for the GRU, Soviet Military Intelligence. Venona shows that T. A. Bisson, a member of *Amerasia*'s editorial board, was also a Soviet spy, reporting to the GRU through Bernstein.

To write its essay on the *Amerasia* case, the editors did not turn to a scholar but to Frederick Vanderbilt Field, one of the men who *founded* the journal in the 1930s. Over the years Field had refused to admit that he had been a secret Communist for most of his life, but then, finally, proudly confirmed it in his autobiography, published in 1983.[26] His encyclopedia entry ignored the documentary evidence of the Soviet intelligence connections of those associated with *Amerasia* and claimed that the espionage allegations were a sham.

Choosing committed partisans and cranks to write entries filled with misstatements and errors are the least of the scholarly sins on display in the *Encyclopedia of the American Left*. Several of the entries are notable for their intellectual dishonesty and

determined efforts to whitewash American and Soviet Communist crimes. One was written by one of the editors, Paul Buhle.
The first edition of the *Encyclopedia,* published in 1990, did not
have an entry for "Secret Work," reflecting the decision of its
revisionist editors to ignore the issue. Entries that discussed espionage even tangentially suggested that charges of spying leveled
at American Communists were either smears or frame-ups. By
the time the second edition appeared in 1998, the documentary
evidence supporting such claims could no longer be disregarded,
so Buhle wrote an entry on "Secret Work" that could serve as a
model of how not to write history.[27]

Buhle's first step was to try to exempt rank-and-file Communists from the issue, writing of "espionage efforts apparently
known only at the top levels of the U.S. Communist Party." But
then, knowledge of spying is always limited. By its nature, espionage is secret and only those directly involved know about it.
Communist assistance to Soviet intelligence would not have been
very productive if the fifty thousand or so members of the CPUSA
were in on it. But as Buhle must have been aware, knowledge of
the espionage was hardly confined to one or two top party leaders. We wrote in *The Secret World of American Communism:*

> Participants in the Communist party's secret apparatus came from
> all sectors of the party. In addition to the party's top leaders, the
> documents in this collection tell of a number of other high-rank-
> ing party officials, some of whom quietly retired behind the Iron
> Curtain after World War II. But the apparatus could not have
> functioned without the obscure men and women who were will-
> ing to devote their lives to its service. . . .
>
> And it was these ordinary Communists whose lives demonstrate
> that some rank-and-file members were willing to serve the USSR
> by spying on their own country. There but for the grace of not
> being asked, went other American Communists.[28]

Having admitted that somebody at the "top levels" of the
American Communist Party knew something about some espionage activities, however, Buhle finds a scapegoat: Jay Lovestone,
party leader in the late 1920s until Stalin had him expelled on

suspicion that he held views similar to those of Stalin's rival, Nikolai Bukharin. Lovestone is a handy villain because he certainly
had connections with Soviet intelligence, but chiefly because by
the mid-1930s, several years after leaving the party, he became a
leading *anticommunist* and in the Cold War he covertly assisted
the CIA from his influential position in the American labor movement. In Buhle's account, "A handful of trade union officials—
most prominent among them, Jay Lovestone, former Communist
Party leader and future associate of the Central Intelligence
Agency (CIA)—and some liberal intellectuals apparently traded
secret communications with the Soviet regime in the 1930s, but
the substance of them involved personal information without
any great importance or high-level security connections."

Buhle loathes Lovestone because he became an anticommunist. By implying that the only Communist leader who spied
for the USSR also spied for the United States, he tries to suggest
that the whole issue was one of moral equivalence. But when
Lovestone aided the CIA, of course, he was an American citizen
helping an American security agency, hardly the same thing as
an American citizen assisting a hostile foreign power such as the
Soviet Union.

Nor was Lovestone even the most significant CPUSA leader
who participated in Soviet espionage. Earl Browder and Gene
Dennis, who led the CPUSA from 1930 to 1959, a period during
which the party was far more important than it had been during
Lovestone's brief reign in the 1920s, were closely connected to
Soviet intelligence but they are never mentioned. Buhle never
names the "liberal intellectuals" he says also engaged in Soviet
espionage, possibly because there were none. Nor is it clear why
they or anyone else would use espionage channels to provide, as
he writes, "personal information" to the USSR in a secret form.
The activities of Nicholas Dozenberg, a senior CPUSA official
in the 1920s who worked for Soviet Military Intelligence from
the late 1920s to the late 1930s and later testified about his work,
go unmentioned. Buhle also ignores Whittaker Chambers' story
of a widespread Soviet espionage ring that received a significant

amount of information from secret Communists working for the federal government in the 1930s.

When he turns to the issue of espionage in the 1940s, Buhle first justifies spying and then trivializes it. He confusingly begins by stating that the Office of Strategic Services gave a new dimension to left-wing secret work by hiring radicals and thus "unleashed an unprecedented flurry of left-wing spy activity, some of which inevitably continued into the Cold War era." But he never explains what the "unprecedented" activity consisted of or why it "inevitably" continued. Likewise, he notes that the employment of so many left-wingers on the atomic bomb project meant "virtually ensuring the passage of some highly classified information to a power which at the time was a formal ally." But once again, he eschews any effort to explain who spied or why any left-winger would inevitably be a source of information for the USSR. One possible implication of this ambiguity is that he is attempting to suggest that the American government was in some sense responsible for whatever espionage took place because the atomic bomb project and the OSS hired left-wingers. Buhle does not seem to recognize that his assumption that left-wingers would "inevitably" want to assist the USSR by turning over secret information provides a very powerful rationale for the later Truman administration loyalty-security program that excluded Communists from sensitive government posts.

Regardless of the inevitability of Communists spying for the Soviet Union, Buhle dismisses the significance of the espionage issue. "Such intrigues had almost no role in the day-to-day activities of the American Left, save for the need of Communists to deny the existence of spying by or for the Russians and for anti-Communist socialists to insist upon its central importance to American Communists at large." Why he singles out "anti-Communist socialists" as villains is not clear except perhaps as another expression of the revisionist antagonism toward social democrats and others of the democratic left. But how can what Buhle calls "an unprecedented flurry of left-wing spy activity, some of which inevitably continued into the Cold War era," be irrelevant to historical debates over whether the CPUSA was a legitimate participant in domestic politics during the Cold War era? Further playing down the importance of espionage, he reduces the "secret apparatus" to "rumors circulated within and without the Left concerning possible Russian agents" and adds speculation that "American Communist leaders may have informally assured members that the Russians could penetrate the renowned American security state. . . . [G]arrulous old-timers who had served in the Spanish Civil War and World War II sometimes hinted and even bragged about what they might be able to do in a moment of international crisis."

Immediately after belittling the significance of "such intrigues" on behalf of the Soviets, Buhle creates a counterbalancing myth with an act of historical fiction. He claims that American Communists undertook more "secret work" for Israel than they did for the USSR: "Little was said within the Left or outside it concerning the largest incident of illegal activity: the shipment of arms and assorted war materials to the new state of Israel." There is no documentary support for this fantasy. Neither of the two sources Buhle provides at the end of his entry says a word about the issue. Continuing his fictitious history, he writes: "Among those Americans wounded or killed in battles protecting Israeli gains from Arabs, Communists played a prominent role." Again no evidence is supplied and none exists. The distinguished Israeli historian Yehuda Bauer called the claim "sheer nonsense." The former national president of the American Veterans of Israel, Simon Spiegelman, labeled it "absolutely false," noting that most of the forty Americans and Canadians who died in 1948 were connected to one of the right-wing Zionist political movements. The most thorough account of the Jewish role in the American left does not mention any such volunteers.[29]

Buhle concludes his exercise in damage control and historical myth-making by speculating that the collapse of both the USSR and "the Cold War leadership of the American labor movement" might eventually turn up new "documentation of secret relationships between Americans and either the KGB or the CIA."

Only in the mind of a left-wing extremist who equated Harry Truman with Joseph Stalin could American trade unions assisting an American government agency be equated with American Communists assisting the USSR. Buhle adds, "as of the late 1990s, documents examined in the Soviet Union or reprinted for scholars offered little that was new in regard to illegal or secret work by Soviet sympathizers." In fact, those documents had revealed a great deal that was both new and illuminating to anyone with eyes to see. It is simply that Buhle shut his eyes and pretended nothing was there.

Buhle's fantasies are not the only way the *Encyclopedia* reimagines history. The entry on Finnish American radicals by Michael Karni distorts through selective silence. Much of the essay focuses on the Finnish Workers Federation, an association of radical Finnish immigrants and Finnish Americans who supported the Communist Party. We learn that the federation provided major support for the Central Cooperative Exchange (CCE), whose eighty-odd stores and twenty-five thousand members grossed an impressive $6 million in retail sales by the end of the 1920s. The CCE explicitly espoused radicalism, financially supported Communist causes such as Young Communist League summer camps, the campaign to free Sacco and Vanzetti, and party-led strikes, and its house-brand canned and packaged goods proudly displayed the hammer-and-sickle emblem. In Karni's telling, in 1930, "because of their close association with the American Communist Party, Finnish federation members were driven from Central Cooperative Wholesale at its annual meeting."[30] This sounds as if the unfortunate members of the Finnish Workers Federation were victimized because of their association with communism. The real story is different.

Although nominally an independent organization, the Finnish Workers Federation was an integral part of the CPUSA, one of several foreign-language federations that served as the party's arms for dealing with immigrant members who spoke little English. The Finnish Workers Federation did not merely *support* the CCE: its members *dominated* the CCE and almost all CCE officers were members of the Finnish Workers Federation and the CPUSA. After Moscow ordered the expulsion of most of the CPUSA's leadership in 1929 for ideological deviations, the party encountered fiscal shortages. The new CPUSA leaders requested that the CCE go beyond its usual contributions to Communist causes with a $5,000 loan to the party itself; this was followed by a request for a $1,000 donation to help convert the party's Trade Union Educational League into the more ambitious Trade Union Unity League. When the Finnish American Communists (Eskel Ronn and George Halonen) who controlled the CCE board stalled these requests, Robert Minor of the CPUSA's national secretariat journeyed to the CCE headquarters in Superior, Wisconsin. He directed that the CCE deliver on the requests and plan to provide a future annual contribution to the party of one percent of wholesale transactions, to be carried on the CCE's books as legal fees to a party attorney. Ronn and Halonen still refused to give way, fearing that the demands would eventually destroy the CCE's economic viability. The CPUSA then sent in one of its leading organizers, Carl Reeve, to enforce party demands. A vituperative battle ensued for control of CCE and *Työmies*, the Finnish-language Communist paper also published in Superior. In the end, the Communists kept *Työmies* but lost the CCE at its 1930 convention. CCE delegates from member stores voted by a margin of three to one to back Ronn and Halonen.

In 1931, the CCE renamed itself the Central Cooperative Wholesale (CCW) and dropped its hammer-and-sickle trademark. In later years it grew, prospered and drifted toward the political neutrality that characterized most consumer cooperatives of the era. Communist loyalists retained control of about eighteen stores with about three thousand members. They formed a competing organization, the Workers and Farmers Cooperative Unity Alliance, which loyally followed party leadership for several years. The alliance was never a match for the CCW, however, and eventually it dissolved.

Michael Karni was aware that Finnish American Communists were driven out of the CCE by its membership only after they had attempted to raid its coffers to support the CPUSA. He had described this in his 1975 doctoral dissertation on Finnish American radicalism.[31] Perhaps Karni was not given enough space in the *Encyclopedia* to detail the entire story, but his summary of it distorted the story. Lack of space cannot, however, excuse a more egregious and shocking silence in his entry, the cover-up of the murder of hundreds of Finnish American radicals by the Soviet Union.

Karni's *Encyclopedia* entry blandly explains, "In the early 1930s, in response to Russian requests for aid to develop the timber resources of Soviet Karelia just across the border from Finland, about six thousand to ten thousand Finnish American men, women, and children migrated to Karelia from the United States and Canada." Nothing more is said. If all one knew about this migration was from Karni's entry, one might think these ethnic Finns thrived in the USSR. The truth is far more gruesome.

In the 1920s and early 1930s the USSR sought to strengthen its Karelian republic, which bordered on Finland, as an alternative "Red Finland." Much of the population was ethnically and linguistically Finnish, and many Communist Finns had fled to Karelia after the overthrow of the short-lived Red Finnish government in the Finnish civil war of 1918. Moscow appointed ethnic Finns to head the Karelian government, encouraged the use of the Finnish language and supported Finnish cultural activities. The USSR was also anxious to exploit Karelia's extensive timber resources. Promoting the emigration of American and Canadian Finnish radicals to Karelia served both goals because they were already Communists and many worked in the North American timber industry, regarded as technologically the most advanced in the world. The CPUSA's Finnish Workers Federation and the Finnish Organization of Canada (aligned with the Canadian Communist Party) supported the Soviet Karelian Technical Aid Committee that raised funds and supplies and supervised the recruitment and transportation of North American emigrants. Eager for the opportunity to build a Finnish Communist society, thousands of radical North American Finns volunteered for the venture.

The immigrants found life under Soviet socialism considerably more difficult than most had anticipated. Several hundred who had retained American or Canadian passports returned
to North America. The remainder were not so lucky. One phase
of Stalin's Great Terror of 1937–38 targeted anyone with foreign
contacts. The ethnic Finnish Karelian leaders were arrested and
executed, the public use of the Finnish language prohibited,
Finnish culture suppressed, and a harsh Russification program
instituted. Soviet security police arrested thousands of Karelians,
including many hundred, perhaps a thousand or more, American and Canadian Finnish immigrants (mostly adult males),
accusing them of "bourgeois nationalism," spying for Finland
or some other foreign power, or plotting to detach Karelia from
the Soviet Union and merge it with capitalist Finland. All of these
accusations were fabrications invented by the KGB.

Among the victims were two well-known members of the
American Communist Party: Matti Tenhunen and Oscar Corgan. Tenhunen had led the Soviet Karelian Technical Aid Committee and then joined the exodus himself. For a time he served
as head of the Karelian Council of People's Comissariats Labor
Department and became editor of the Finnish-language *Punainen
Karjala* [*Red Karelia*]. He was arrested in 1937. In 1938 the Communist International privately informed Canadian and American Communists that the Soviet Karelian Technical Aid
Committee had been part of an anti-Soviet conspiracy out to
"flood Soviet Karelia with all sorts of undesirable bourgeois-
nationalist, fascist and Trotskyist agents; in short, under cover of
a working class movement, these people became the advance
agents of fascism aiming at the destruction of socialist economy
in Soviet Karelia and its separation from the USSR." The Comintern stated, "At his trial for diversionist activities ... [Matti Ten-
hunen] was fully exposed as an agent of the Finnish police and
sentenced to a term of imprisonment by the Soviet Courts."[32]
Actually, the KGB murdered Tenhunen on December 28, 1937,
shortly after his arrest, and the charges against him were totally
false.

Oscar Corgan became head of the Soviet Karelian Technical Aid Committee in the United States after Tenhunen's departure for Karelia, and then he too emigrated along with his wife and three American-born children. Corgan, who had once managed the CPUSA's *Työmies* newspaper in Superior, Wisconsin, went to work for a Finnish-language Karelian publishing house. He was arrested on November 4, 1937, and his family was later told that he had received a fifteen-year prison sentence. He never returned from the labor camps, however. In 1956, after Khrushchev's de-Stalinization campaign began, the family received a death certificate showing that Corgan had died of "stomach cancer" in 1940. In 1991, under the Gorbachev reforms, they received a corrected certificate showing that he had been executed two months after his arrest.

In 1997 a Russian organization dedicated to exposing Stalin-era crimes, Memorial, located a KGB burial site near Sandarmokh, one of four it has found in Karelia. The site contains more than nine thousand bodies in approximately three hundred separate burial trenches. The position of the skeletons and other remains suggested that the prisoners had been stripped to their underwear, lined up next to a trench with hands and feet tied, and shot in the back of the head with a pistol. Documents in a regional KGB archive identify about four thousand of the victims as Gulag prison laborers used to build the Belomar canal connecting the Baltic to the White Sea, one thousand as prisoners from the Gulag camp at Solovetskiye, and about three thousand as victims of the Karelian purge. More than six thousand of the dead are listed by name.

Among the victims named are 141 Finnish Americans and 127 Finnish Canadians. They include the two chief organizers of the emigration, Oscar Corgan and Matti Tenhunen. But the list also includes ordinary American workers such as Eino Bjorn, born in Minnesota and shot on February 10, 1938, at age twenty-six; Walter Maki, another Minnesota native who was shot on May 15, 1938; John Siren, born in Duluth, Minnesota, shot on February 11, 1938; Mathew Kaartinen, born in Ironwood, Michigan, and shot by the KGB on December 28, 1937; Andrew Hannula, born in the state of Washington and shot on December 28, 1937; and Enoch Nelson, born in San Francisco and shot on March 5, 1938. Fourteen of the dead were native-born Americans. The rest were immigrants to the United States early in the twentieth century who had then joined the Communist-sponsored emigration to Karelia in the early 1930s. It is unknown how many of the latter were naturalized American citizens. By occupation, the largest group among those murdered by the KGB was loggers, followed by truck drivers and mechanics, then a variety of skilled tradesmen, some factory workers, a few professionals, several actors and musicians, and one hairdresser. Most of the executed were adult males but the list of the dead includes one husband and wife (Niilo and Elvira Filpus of Detroit, Michigan) executed together on January 21, 1938.

Helen Hill, born in Minnesota in 1917, is also listed. Her parents took her to Karelia in 1932 when she was a teenager. She was working as a dispatcher at a lumber camp when she was arrested. A KGB executioner put a pistol to the back of her head and blew her brains out on April 22, 1938, before she was twenty-three years old. According to the KGB her offense was that she "maintained contacts with relatives in the U.S. Collected information in favor of Finland's intelligence service. Praised life in capitalist countries. Spoke of her intentions to cross the border creating a spirit of emigration in the workers."[33]

This saga is depressing, but not surprising to anyone familiar with the history of Stalin's reign. As one of a small group of scholars who have specialized in Finnish American history, Michael Karni certainly knew about the tragic fate of the Finnish American radicals who immigrated to Karelia. The broad outlines of this mass murder have been known since the 1940s, even if the details were still murky. So why did he exclude it from his essay on Finnish American radicalism in the *Encyclopedia of the American Left*? We cannot read his mind nor those of his editors, but this omission is part of a pattern of ignoring, minimizing or obfuscating facts that might put American communism in a poor light.

The *Encyclopedia of the American Left* is not a genuine reference book, although it now sits in the reference section of hundreds of libraries and is used by thousands of unsuspecting students. Rather, like *The Great Soviet Encyclopedia* that similarly misled students, it presents a fake history where unpleasant facts are airbrushed away, crimes against humanity ignored, and smiling workers and peasants march forward to a radiant future in the lockstep of Soviet "socialist realism" art.

Unfortunately, the *Encyclopedia of the American Left* is not alone in ignoring the Americans murdered in Stalin's purge of Karelia. When scholars insist on bringing up the Karelian tragedy, the historical establishment makes clear its distaste for discussing the matter. *The Soviet World of American Communism* reproduced three documents from the RGASPI archive and devoted seventeen pages to the execution of Finnish American Communists in Karelia. Professor James Patterson, holder of the Ford Foundation Chair of American History at Brown University, could not contain his scorn, asserting that there were "questionable conclusions not supported by the documents they print. A case in point concerns a group of Finnish Americans and Finnish Canadians who were recruited by Moscow in the 1930s to help rebuild the Karelia region." He wrote of those Finnish Americans who were "apparently" executed, but stressed his skepticism that any such thing had happened.[34]

There has been no systematic compilation of the number of American radicals and Communists and their family members killed by Stalin's political police, but it is at least five hundred and probably more than a thousand. While Finnish Americans executed in the Karelian purge account for the bulk of the known dead, there are many others. Lovett Fort-Whiteman, a senior black CPUSA official imprisoned for ideological sympathy for Trotskyism, died in the Gulag in 1939. The writer Adam Hochschild gained access to the KGB file of Arthur Talent, executed by the KGB in 1938. Talent's parents were founding members of the American Communist Party. In the 1920s Arthur's father, terminally ill, sent his wife, Elena (who transferred her CPUSA membership to the Communist Party of the Soviet Union), and American-born son to the USSR. She was arrested in 1938 and imprisoned for ten years. Rearrested in 1949, she was jailed until 1954 and died the following year. Arthur, an elevator operator and part-time actor, was also arrested in 1938, at age twenty-one. Under torture, he falsely confessed to being a British and Latvian spy (his parents were originally from Latvia) and part of a KGB-created fantasy of a conspiracy including actors at the Latvian Theater in Moscow to create a "mighty Latvia on the territory of the Soviet Union." The KGB executed Talent and three others named in his confession in 1938.[35]

Alan Cullison of the Associated Press documented the murders of other Americans by Stalin's political police. Alexander Gelver, a native of Oshkosh, Wisconsin, had come to the USSR with his radical parents. He attempted to enter the American embassy in Moscow in 1937; Soviet police arrested him as a spy and executed him on January 1, 1938. Elias Singer moved from New York to Moscow in 1932. He was arrested in 1938 and shot a year later at age fifty-nine. Ivan Dubin, a naturalized American citizen, returned to Russia for a visit, fell in love and got married. Trying to arrange to bring his bride home to America, he visited the U.S. embassy in March 1938, was arrested after he left, accused of espionage and shot. He was twenty-six. Marvin Volat left his native Buffalo, New York, at age twenty to study violin in Moscow. He was arrested after leaving the U.S. embassy in 1938 and charged with counterrevolutionary activity. After two months of interrogation, he confessed, was sentenced to the Gulag and died the next year at age twenty-eight. Julius Hecker, born in Russia, became an American citizen and earned a doctorate at Columbia. In the 1920s he returned to Russia with his American wife and three daughters, gave up his U.S. citizenship, and taught philosophy at Soviet universities. He also wrote several books in defense of communism that circulated widely in the West. Under interrogation he falsely confessed to espionage and was secretly executed in 1938. Arthur Abolin, twenty-eight, and his brother

Carl, both of Boston, were executed together in 1938. Another pair of Boston brothers, Arnold and Walter Preeden, twenty-two and twenty-four years old, was also executed together in 1938. Joseph Sgovio, a CPUSA organizer, was arrested and jailed for a year for disrupting a city council meeting in North Tonawanda, New York, while leading an unemployment demonstration. Deported to the Soviet Union in 1932, he was arrested in 1938 on charges of anti-Soviet activity and spent eleven years in Soviet labor camps. His health broken, he died shortly after his release.[36]

In the appendix of this book is a list of a few of the invisible dead whom the American academic establishment refuses to see and will not discuss. This list, which has never appeared in English, gives the names and biographical data for Finnish American Communists and radicals buried at the secret KGB mass grave as Sandarmokh. Perhaps some day, when the poisonous politicized atmosphere of today's academic world dissipates, American historians will take on the task of a full-scale scholarly study of the American radicals who immigrated to the Soviet Union to build socialism, only to meet the Gulag and Stalin's executioners.[37]

## Premature Antifascism

While a number of the entries in the *Encyclopedia of the American Left* ignore unpleasant facts, the discussion of the role of Americans in the Spanish Civil War casually perpetuates one of the myths so beloved by revisionists about the Abraham Lincoln Brigade. The Lincoln Brigade encompassed the nearly three thousand Americans, mostly Communists, who fought in the Spanish Civil War in the ranks of the Comintern's International Brigades. Samuel Sills, a documentary filmmaker and "oral history worker," wrote the encyclopedia entry on the Abraham Lincoln Brigade, noting that after the Nazis attacked the Soviet Union and the U.S. entered World War II, many of the brigade veterans volunteered for the American armed forces. He then asserts: "In a foreshadowing of the McCarthy period, the armed forces designated the Lincolns 'premature antifascists' and confined them to their bases."[38]

Sills did not simply invent this claim; similar assertions are strewn throughout revisionist works produced in the last thirty years. Ellen Schrecker states that in World War II the Lincoln veterans "were, in the [U.S.] Army's bizarre terminology, 'premature antifascists,' subject to harassment by military intelligence officers and, in many cases, sent to special camps where they were treated almost like prisoners of war." Fraser Ottanelli insists that the veterans "in the witch hunts of the 1950s were disparagingly referred to as 'premature anti-fascists.'" Robin Kelley writes, "Rather than applaud these men and women for risking their lives in a battle America would officially join in 1941, Lincoln Brigade veterans were hounded by the FBI, a variety of 'un-American activities' committees, and labeled 'premature antifascists.'" Southern Illinois University professor Robbie Lieberman writes that the Americans who fought in Spain "faced problems later because of what the government labeled their 'premature antifascist' stance." Another revisionist, Michael Rogin (University of California, Berkeley), refers to "the 'premature antifascists' stigmatized by the US state security apparatus during the thirties Popular Front and World War II." Professor Bernard Knox (Harvard and Yale) states, "'Premature Anti-Fascist' was the label affixed to the dossiers of those Americans who had fought in the Brigades when, after Pearl Harbor (and some of them before) they enlisted in the US Army. It was the signal to assign them to non-combat units or inactive fronts and to deny them the promotion they deserved."[39] One could go on listing many, many more instances of academics putting the term "premature antifascist" in quotation marks and insisting that some sinister government agency had so labeled those idealists who had fought with the International Brigades.

But despite the repeated insistence by persons holding advanced academic degrees and writing in scholarly publications, there is no documentary evidence that "premature antifascist" was a pejorative label created by U.S. government agents and applied to Americans who fought for the International Brigades.

We had noticed the term in the literature but did not question the authenticity of its alleged government origins until the early 1990s when our research took us into FBI, OSS and U.S. Army records including the "dossiers" Knox mentions, dealing with Communists who had fought with the International Brigades and later served in the American armed forces. We examined thousands of pages and did not see the term "premature antifascist" once. Government security agents, we found, did not use code words and certainly nothing as coy as "premature antifascist." Their usual terms were "Communist," "Red," "subversive" and "radical." Our curiosity aroused, we checked the various books that claimed a malevolent government origin for the term but found not a single citation to a specific FBI, U.S. Army or government document. Instead of being cited to a primary source document, the claim was either unsourced, or sourced to secondary work where, upon checking, we found the claim to be unsourced, or cited to an oral history interview of a Lincoln veteran, usually made thirty or more years after the event.

Even the Lincoln Brigade veterans' claims about "premature antifascist" in oral histories were few. One book that promoted the term was entitled *The Premature Antifascists,* published in 1986, based on 130 interviews with American volunteers done between 1979 and 1985. In these interviews a *single* volunteer claimed that when interviewed by military security officers in 1942 "this was the first time that I heard the expression 'premature antifascists.'" Another is quoted as saying, "I realized how much 'the premature antifascists' as we were called, contributed to save the honor of America," but he makes no claim that the volunteers had been so labeled by the government.[40]

If the government did not originate the term, who did? In reviewing the literature and various sources, we found many examples in the 1940s, 1950s and 1960s of Lincoln veterans or those identified with the pro-Communist left applying the term *to themselves* in a proudly sardonic way. In this era there were only a few claims that the term was pejorative and had government origin, and even fewer claims of direct knowledge of government agencies using the term.[41] In the late 1960s, however, claims of government origin increased, and by the 1980s the assertion that the term was a pejorative applied by antagonistic security officials had become something like "common knowledge" among revisionist historians.

In 1994, Dr. Peter Carroll, chair of the Veterans of the Abraham Lincoln Brigade Archives, published *The Odyssey of the Abraham Lincoln Brigade.* One chapter in the book is titled "Premature Anti-Fascists" and on first reading appears to have a single contemporaneous but indirect documentary source for the governmental origins of the term. Carroll discusses the World War II experiences of two Lincoln veterans in the U.S. Army, Milton Wolff and Gerald Cook. Both were assigned to Fort Dix, New Jersey, but inexplicably received no orders to report for basic training. Carroll writes:

> Inquiries about the unusual delay brought mystified responses, until Wolff mentioned to a clerk that they had been in Spain. "Oh, that's a different story!" exclaimed the friendly sergeant, who finally found their records in a special file. A few nights later, Wolff and Cook sneaked into the office and read their papers. Printed on the corners were the letters "P.A." The next day, a clerk explained the initials: "premature anti-fascists." Thus they discovered a euphemism that would become part of anti-Communist rhetoric of the next decade. Service in the Spanish war qualified the Lincolns for that honor.[42]

Although he is a professionally trained historian associated with Stanford University and the author of several widely used college-level American history textbooks, Carroll does not employ the usual scholarly conventions for citing sources, so it is difficult to identify clearly the source for this story. In the book it appears to be based on a letter that Milton Wolff wrote on July 29, 1942, which is cited as being located in a collection of Spanish Civil War correspondence at the University of Illinois at Urbana-Champaign. We wrote to the University of Illinois to obtain a copy of that letter as well as copies of three other letters cited on the same page of Carroll's book. Reference specialists found one of the four but said the other three, including the one that Carroll's text implied had details of the "P.A." incident, were not in the collection. The one letter that was found had no reference to the "P.A." story.[43]

We then wrote to Dr. Carroll. He replied that he had only seen the letter in Milton Wolff's possession and, despite the citation in his book, had just assumed that Wolff had later sent it to the University of Illinois. He also said, "I doubt that these letters include the phrase premature antifascist." He provided no alternative source for the "P.A." story in his book, however, leaving us mystified as to the source of his tale. Later, when the issue was raised on an internet historical discussion list, he offered more details:

> I cannot explain the "missing letters," since I read them before they were sent by Milton Wolff to the University of Illinois. However, I am certain that none of the letters referred specifically to the term "premature antifascist." My source for that reference was my interviews with Wolff himself. As he told me the story about ten years ago, he and another Lincoln veteran, Gerry Cook, were detained at Camp Dix (New Jersey) in June 1942, soon after they had enlisted in the U.S. army. To their dismay, other recruits were routinely being shifted to other camps for basic training, but they remained unassigned. Frustrated by this situation, they entered the camp's office at night and found their names on cards with the initials PA. The next day, they confronted a clerk with that information, and he supposedly said something like "oh, that's why you're not being shipped out." Prompted by the recent flurry of interest in this matter, I reinterviewed Wolff yesterday (May 24, 2000) about this issue. He now told the story differently. Only Cook actually broke into the office, so that Wolff could not, in fact, testify to the authenticity of the PA story. But he was sure that something in their records prompted the clerk's response the next day.

Insofar as documenting the government's use of a pejorative label of "premature antifascist" or "P.A." is concerned, therefore,

Carroll effectively discredited the story he himself had presented in *The Odyssey of the Abraham Lincoln Brigade.* It turns out that the source of the "P.A." story was an interview given forty-eight years after the incident by someone with an interest in being seen as discriminated against because of his politics, and contradicted in a second interview eight years later.[44]

We also placed inquiries in the *Newsletter of the Historians of American Communism* in 1998 and on several internet history discussion lists in 2000 asking for a citation to a specific document proving that the U.S. military, the FBI or some other government security agency had labeled Americans who served in the International Brigades as "premature antifascists." We received many responses, but *none* provided a citation to a specific government document. Brooklyn Polytechnic professor Marvin Gettleman, then executive director of the Abraham Lincoln Brigade Archives and a revisionist historian, responded in 1999 with the comment that while no document has been found, "that may be because the relevant FBI files have not yet become publicly available.... But be assured that the search you call for is underway." In 2002 he posted a message on the ALBA forum indicating that as yet no such document had been located.[45]

What the odd history of "premature antifascist" also shows is that when faced with the revelation that their claims are myths, revisionist historians wave away the need for evidence. When we publicly asked for documentation of the claims advanced about "premature antifascist," Peter Carroll stated, "I am amazed that serious scholars are so exercised about the origins of the term. It seems to me that the important point is that the U.S. Army during World War II did discriminate against Communists or suspected Communists, including Lincoln Brigade veterans.... Does it matter what they called 'them'?"[46] Yes, it does matter. Historians are not free to shade the truth, create dramatic illustrations out of their imagination, or manipulate the evidence in the service of what they believe is some other truth. In the absence of any documentary support, it is an act of scholarly malpractice for a historian to assert that U.S. security agencies commonly labeled or stamped the records of Americans who served in the International Brigades with the term "premature antifascist."

In *The Odyssey of the Abraham Lincoln Brigade,* Peter Carroll also writes that in the spring of 1941 and prior to the German invasion of the USSR on June 22, William Donovan, an adviser to President Roosevelt, arranged a meeting with Lincoln Brigade veteran Milton Wolff through "Dinah Sheean." At the meeting:

> Donovan told Wolff that British intelligence officers, working in the United States, wanted assistance in establishing contact with resident aliens from southern and eastern Europe—Italians, Greeks, Yugoslavs, Austrians, and Hungarians—who would be willing to help the partisan resistance fighters in German-occupied countries. Donovan asked if the Lincoln veterans, particularly those with language skills, would participate in such an operation. Wolff agreed to find out. He knew that before undertaking such work individual volunteers would want the sanction of the Communist party. Steve Nelson [CPUSA official and former Lincoln Brigade political commissar] referred him to Eugene Dennis, an important party official.... Dennis gave his consent and assured Wolff that the party would cooperate, provided the scheme was kept secret. According to Wolff, in other words, the highest level of the American Communist party authorized clandestine operations that violated the avowed noninterventionist line.... The party's acceptance of Donovan's overture to Wolff thus represented an audacious departure from its previous distrust [of the U.S. government].

Carroll goes on to relate that with the CPUSA's "permission granted," Donovan introduced Wolff to two British agents named Bryce and Bailey who asked Wolff to recruit "reliable anti-fascists to place behind enemy lines in Greece, Yugoslavia, and the Balkans." Carroll concludes, "So, at a time when the Communist party officially opposed American involvement in the war, Wolff started a recruitment program on behalf of British intelligence" and was paid a salary plus expenses. After the United States entered the war in December 1941, Donovan asked Wolff to redirect his recruits to the American Office of Strategic Services, headed by Donovan himself. As noted, Wolff later entered the

U.S. Army but subsequently received a commission in the OSS and worked with anti-Nazi partisans in Italy.[47]

Carroll's account is a dramatic refurbishing of the historical image of both the CPUSA and the Veterans of the Abraham Lincoln Brigade (VALB), the organization of those Americans who had fought with the International Brigades. Both had claimed that in the late 1930s, Communists and their allies had been in the forefront of the fight against fascism. Revisionists had agreed, asserting that antifascism, not Stalinism, was at the core of Communist ideology in this period. But this claim shattered on the rock of the Nazi-Soviet Pact. From September 1939 to June 1941, the CPUSA dropped its previous support for an antifascist Popular Front and opposed American alignment with nations opposing Nazi aggression. Instead, it denounced President Roosevelt's aid to Britain and other nations fighting for their lives against Hitler's legions, and attempted to block trade union and liberal support for FDR's reelection in 1940.

The Veterans of the Abraham Lincoln Brigade, led by Milton Wolff, sailed in parallel with the CPUSA and denounced assistance to the anti-Nazi belligerents. After the Nazi attack on the Soviet Union in June 1941, all this changed. The CPUSA once again donned the cloak of antifascism and the VALB called for American intervention in the war. While American Communists were able to regain much of the ground they had lost in the Nazi-Soviet Pact period, serious damage had been done to their standing. Many liberals never again trusted them and readily abandoned them altogether when the CPUSA took up the Soviet cause in the Cold War. And to traditionalist historians, the conduct of the CPUSA during the Nazi-Soviet Pact showed that loyalty to Stalin, not antifascism, was at the core of American communism.

Those who take a benign view of American communism have often passed over the Nazi-Soviet Pact period with silence or a minimal acknowledgement that it was an embarrassing lapse. Carroll, however, is not content with this defensive stance. In his account, Milton Wolff, the last commander of the Lincoln

Brigade in Spain and chief of the VALB, realized the error of the Soviet position and secretly began helping the British *before* the Nazi attack caused Moscow to change its policy. Even more dramatically, Carroll asserts that Gene Dennis, then de facto second in command of the Communist Party, sanctioned Wolff's actions with the support of other party leaders. Thus, prior to June 1941, he claims, "the highest level of the American Communist party" had also seen the error of the Soviet position and possessed sufficient independence from Soviet control that it gave permission for Wolff's work for British intelligence and his recruitment of Communist veterans of the International Brigades into British covert operations.

Carroll's story would be a major historical finding if it were true. But it isn't. Everything that he relates did happen, but *after* June 22, 1941, not before. With CPUSA permission, Wolff agreed to assist British covert operations but only *after* the Nazi invasion of the USSR and only *after* Wolff and the CPUSA concluded that assisting the British was consistent with the post–June 1941 Soviet party line of all-out support for the anti-Nazi war effort.

Carroll based his account on a 1988 interview with Milton Wolff. He claimed it was corroborated by interviews with others, but named only one, an undated interview with Irving Goff, a Lincoln veteran whom Wolff recruited for this covert work. He did not cite a single document, nor did he show how the story fit with the historical context or existing literature about British covert operations.

In *The Secret World of American Communism* we reproduced a document from the Comintern archive, a May 1942 report by Gene Dennis about Wolff's work for British intelligence and the American OSS. The report confirms that *Diana* (not Dinah) Sheean set up a meeting between Donovan and Wolff, that Donovan asked Wolff to recruit International Brigade veterans for the British, that Wolff got CPUSA sanction for the project, and that Wolff set up a recruiting operation funded first by the British and then, after December 1941, by the OSS. However, this document placed the Donovan meeting in *November* 1941, well after the Nazi invasion of the USSR, and not before, as Carroll would have it. The change of date, of course, robs the story of its ability to revise the history of the CPUSA and the VALB during the time of the Nazi-Soviet Pact.[48] This document is corroborated by other 1942 documents in the Comintern archive. The KGB judged that Wolff's recruiting might allow American intelligence insight into Communist networks in the United States and ordered it stopped. In the Comintern archive there is a Comintern directive to the CPUSA to end the recruitment operation and a subsequent report from Dennis that Wolff had shut down his activities as directed.[49]

In a 1989 autobiography the Lincoln veteran Milton Felsen described how in late *November* 1941, Wolff asked him to volunteer for British commando work. Felsen said he was told that British intelligence had approached Wolff through Diana Sheean. In 1982, Maurice Isserman reported that Gene Dennis's widow, Peggy, and the veteran Communist Gilbert Green told him that Gene had met with and furnished Donovan with information on possible recruits for the OSS *after* the Nazi invasion of the Soviet Union. While Carroll reports that Goff corroborated Wolff's pre-invasion dating, this is contradicted by a 1964 Goff interview with the historian Robert Rosenstone where he said that he had been recruited for OSS work shortly before Pearl Harbor and well *after* the Nazi invasion. All of these sources support a fall 1941 date for these activities, not one prior to the June invasion of the Soviet Union.[50]

Wolff's 1988 claim that he worked for the British prior to the Nazi invasion of the Soviet Union is not even supported by his own testimony to the U.S. Subversive Activities Control Board in 1954. Wolff testified as a witness for the Lincoln Brigade veterans contesting the board's proposal to list the VALB as a Communist front organization. Wolff mentioned that he had worked for British intelligence and the OSS in 1941 and 1942. He testified that his work for the British had been at the initiative of William Donovan and that while his memory was unclear on the precise timing, he placed this work in the latter half of 1941, perhaps starting as early as July but still *after* the Nazi invasion of the USSR.[51]

Even more damning, Gene Dennis, who played a central role in the Carroll/Wolff version, was not in the United States during most of this period and could not have met with Wolff when they claimed. The outbreak of war in Europe in September 1939 had disrupted the usual practice of frequent dispatch of high CPUSA officials to Moscow. But in the spring of 1941 the party sent Dennis to Moscow to give a thorough accounting of its activities. The Comintern's archives contain the reports Dennis prepared and personally delivered before the Comintern's leadership in Moscow in April 1941. The earliest is dated April 1, 1941, and the latest June 18, 1941.[52] Given the conditions of wartime travel in 1941, Dennis would have had to leave the United States in mid-March or earlier to reach Moscow by the first of April. Dennis did not return to the United States until *after* the Nazi invasion.

Could Wolff's claimed meeting with Donovan and his consultation with Dennis have occurred prior to Dennis's departure for Moscow in March 1941? No. Carroll is vague about the date of the Wolff/Donovan meeting except that it was prior to the invasion of the Soviet Union and likely in the late spring or early summer. It could not have been earlier than May because in Carroll and Wolff's account, Donovan relayed a British request for aid in recruiting "resident aliens from southern and eastern Europe—Italians, Greeks, Yugoslavs, Austrians, and Hungarians—who would be willing to help the partisan resistance fighters in German-occupied countries." Nazi Germany did not invade Yugoslavia and Greece until April 1941 and the British expeditionary force sent to Greece was not compelled to withdraw until May. Consequently, British plans for organizing partisan forces in Nazi-occupied Yugoslavia and Greece could not have been under way earlier than May and in fact were begun much later.

It was not until August 1941 that the British learned that remnants of the shattered Yugoslav army were regrouping under the command of Colonel Draza Mihailovich, and not until

September had they received reliable information about Communist partisans organizing under Josip Tito. In September 1941, British Special Operations Executive (SOE) sent a small team, Mission Bullseye, into Yugoslavia to contact Mihailovich and Tito and evaluate the possibility of British aid to these forces. Encouraged by the Mission Bullseye report, the British set about preparing SOE units for use in Yugoslavia and other Balkan nations. Because of the availability of recruits with the appropriate language skills and ethnic backgrounds in North America, the SOE decided to recruit and train its Balkan teams in Canada and opened "Camp X" near Toronto in December 1941.[53] This timing fits a Donovan approach to Wolff in the autumn of 1941, not prior to the German invasion of the USSR.

In *The Odyssey of the Abraham Lincoln Brigade,* Carroll maintained that Donovan introduced Wolff to two British intelligence agents, one of whom was named "Bailey." This is S. W. Bailey, who had worked in Yugoslavia prior to World War II and spoke Serb, Croat and several other Balkan dialects. After the decision in the autumn of 1941 to send SOE teams to Yugoslavia, he traveled to North America sometime in *late 1941* to recruit men of Balkan background. His meetings with Canadian Communist Party officials in *early 1942* for recruiting Canadian Communists who had served in the International Brigades have been discussed in histories of the Canadian role in SOE operations.[54] Again, Bailey's story is compatible with a Donovan approach to Wolff in the fall of 1941, *after* the Nazi invasion, not prior to it.

Wolff delivered the keynote address to the Veterans of the Abraham Lincoln Brigade's convention in May 1941. At this point in the war, Nazi Germany had conquered most of Western and Central Europe. Yet the Nazi-Soviet Pact was still in effect and Wolff mentioned Hitler only once, in a sentence that denounced as equally evil "Roosevelt, Hitler, Churchill and Mussolini." The chief target of his speech was FDR's policy of providing assistance to Great Britain, then the only major power fighting Hitler. Wolff told the convention:

Under the dishonest slogan of anti-fascism, he [President Roosevelt] prepares the red-baiting, union-busting, alien-hunting, anti-Negro, anti-Semitic Jingoistic road to fascism in America: we accuse him. Turning with cynical calculation on his own lies and false promises, he drags the American people, despite their repeated expressed opposition, closer and closer to open participation in the imperialist slaughter in which the youth of our country will, if he has his way, join the 1,000 British seamen of the H.M.S. Hood, the 30,0000 German bodies floating in the Mediterranean, the bloody and bloated corpses on battle fields the world over, for the greater glory of foreign trade and the brutal oppression of free people at home and abroad: we accuse him, Franklin Demagogue Roosevelt we accuse; tirelessly and until the people hear and understand, we accuse him.... We fight against the involvement of our country in an imperialist war from which the great majority of the American people can derive only misery, suffering, and death. We stubbornly oppose every move of Roosevelt and the war-mongers in this direction, and call on the American people to organize and make vocal their deep and sincere opposition.[55]

Nor did Wolff confine his support for the Nazi-Soviet Pact to speeches. When a few Americans who had fought in Spain with the International Brigades criticized the Nazi-Soviet Pact, Wolff expelled them from the VALB, never forgave them for contradicting CPUSA policy, and continued to treat them with scorn for the next fifty years.

Wolff's 1988 claim, endorsed by Carroll, that his public adherence to the Nazi-Soviet Pact was feigned is not credible. Equally false is Carroll's claim that prior to the Nazi invasion of the USSR, Gene Dennis and "the highest level of the American Communist party" secretly dissented from the Nazi-Soviet Pact and maneuvered behind the back of the USSR to aid the British. At the time Carroll and Wolff have Dennis in the United States undercutting Moscow's policies, he was actually in Moscow bragging to the Comintern about the enthusiasm and energy of the CPUSA's campaign to subvert Roosevelt's policies of assisting Britain.

Anyone with any doubts about the CPUSA support for the Nazi-Soviet Pact should read *The Yanks Are Not Coming, 1939–1941,* volume six of Bernard K. Johnpoll's *A Documentary History of the Communist Party of the United States,* which reproduces a score of party pamphlets from the period defending the Nazi-Soviet Pact and denouncing any aid to those fighting Hitler in vehement terms. The most remarkable is a 1940 essay by John Gates, a highly successful political commissar in the International Brigades in Spain who returned to the United States marked for high leadership in the American Communist Party. In 1940 he held a senior post in the Young Communist League, and later he edited the party's flagship newspaper, the *Daily Worker,* and served on its national committee. His 1940 article not only defended the Nazi-Soviet Pact, which made the USSR a nonbelligerent ally of Nazi Germany, but also urged party members to be prepared to support a possible next step, a full-scale military alliance between Nazi Germany and the Soviet Union.[56]

### The Two Parties

Assertions that the CPUSA had only casual ties to the Soviet Union and studied ignorance of the new documentary evidence are among the dominant features of the main entry on the Communist Party written for the *Encyclopedia of the American Left* by two of its co-editors, Paul Buhle and Dan Georgakas.[57] While admitting the CPUSA's Soviet connections, they downplay them, emphasizing instead that at its core the party represented an authentic and indigenous American radicalism steeped in American traditions. Their treatment of one of the Soviet Union's baldest interventions into the life of the CPUSA provides a striking example of how revisionists distort even well-established facts.

The CPUSA expelled two groups of activists and leaders in the late 1920s. Both were accused of holding views similar to those of Russian factions opposed to Joseph Stalin. The Trotskyists were unceremoniously booted out in 1928. A year later, much of the party's leadership, including Jay Lovestone and Benjamin Gitlow, was removed from power amid charges they were allied with Nikolai Bukharin, later to be executed by Stalin. Summoned to a hearing in Moscow presided over by Stalin himself, Gitlow and Lovestone reminded the general secretary that they had been chosen leaders of the CPUSA by overwhelming majorities at the recent CPUSA national convention. Stalin gave them a lesson about the source of Communist legitimacy:

> You declare you have a certain majority in the American Communist Party and that you will retain that majority under all circumstances. This is untrue, comrades of the American delegation, absolutely untrue. You had a majority because the American Communist Party until now regarded you as the determined supporters of the Communist International. And it was only because the Party regarded you as the friends of the Comintern that you had a majority in the ranks of the American Communist Party. But what will happen if the American workers learn that you intend to break the unity of the ranks of the Comintern and are thinking of conducting a fight against its executive bodies—that is the question, dear comrades? Do you think that the American workers will follow your lead against the Comintern, that they will prefer the interests of your factional group to the interests of the Comintern? There have been numerous cases in the history of the Comintern when its most popular leaders, who had greater authority than you, found themselves isolated as soon as they raised the banner against the Comintern. Do you think you will fare better than these leaders? A poor hope, comrades! At present you still have a formal majority. But tomorrow you will have no majority and you will find yourselves completely isolated if you attempt to start a fight against the decisions of the Presidium of the Executive Committee of the Comintern.[58]

Stalin was right. In the face of Moscow's demands, the overwhelming support for Lovestone and Gitlow in the CPUSA disappeared. They were stripped of their party offices and, along with anyone unwilling to disown them, expelled. One should also note that Stalin's speech, with its blunt declaration of Comintern supremacy over any national party, was not a secret. So eager was the CPUSA to demonstrate its devotion to Moscow that it printed the speech as a pamphlet and distributed thousands of copies to its members and supporters.

But Buhle and Georgakas cannot bring themselves to say that the expulsions of Lovestone and his supporters were initiated in the Soviet Union. Instead, they write: "Those driven from the Party charged that its basic policies were now being set by the Comintern and that the Comintern reserved the right of final approval of Party leadership. These accusations reinforced popular perceptions of Communism as an inauthentic national movement." It was not an *accusation*, however, but a *fact* that the expulsions reflected Moscow's wishes. And it was not the *perception* that Moscow controlled the CPUSA that the expulsions illustrated, but the *reality* of Stalin's domination.

Some revisionists want to believe that the CPUSA was really two parties—one a multicultural band of brothers and sisters (the good Communist Party at the grassroots), the other a small cadre of bureaucratic dogmatists divorced from American life and oriented towards the Soviet Union (the bad Communist Party isolated on a single floor of a building in New York City). In one of his few efforts to deal with any of the documents unearthed from Russian archives, Buhle admits that one of them depicted "the ham-fisted intervention of a Comintern representative, J. Peters, into the life of the young Communist Party." Apart from the fact that the CPUSA was already thirteen years old (not particularly young) when Peters returned from Moscow to become the leader of the underground, he was *not* a foreign Comintern representative. Peters had immigrated to the United States in 1924 at the age of thirty and became an American Communist Party militant almost immediately. This was a period when the majority of the party was foreign-born. Peters became a full-time CPUSA employee ("cadre" in party jargon) in 1927, and the CPUSA sent him to Moscow for training with the Comintern in the early 1930s. He served briefly as the CPUSA's representative *to* the Comintern in 1932, returned to the United States at the end of 1932 and remained a trusted American party employee until he was deported in 1949. Contrary to the claim of the *Encyclopedia of the American Left*, Peters was never a Comintern representative or a Soviet agent sent to the American party.[59]

Buhle goes on to admit that "demands from the top" were "catastrophic for the real social movement which had depended upon enthusiasms stifled by the conspiracy-minded bureaucracies." The documents "reveal a shameful bureaucratic misrule from what rank-and-filers referred to contemptuously as the Ninth Floor, the Star Chamber of the Party."[60] Typically, Buhle does not document this assertion of widespread rank-and-file contempt for the CPUSA leadership, probably because it did not exist. After the Stalinization of the party in the late 1920s, those contemptuous of the top leadership swiftly became ex-Communists.

The two-party theory is implicit in much revisionist writing, a final fallback position for historian-ideologues who have been beached by the tidal wave of information coming from the newly opened Russian archives. In many revisionist essays or books, individual Communists working on a particular matter are in the forefront while the Communist *Party* remains in the background, often a vague presence. Revisionists have poured out hundreds of essays and books on a broad array of previously neglected topics: Communist influence on folk music, drama and poetry; Communist activity among Jews, Finns, Italians, Blacks, Mexicans and Slavs of various sorts; CPUSA work among Alabama and Arkansas sharecroppers, grain farmers on the Great Plains and dairy farmers in New York; Communist influence on social gospel Protestants, social workers and socially conscious lawyers; even Communist influence in sports; and scores of studies of Communist activities in the labor movement. To revisionism's credit, this body of research demonstrated beyond cavil a significant Communist role in certain areas of American life, a role previously rarely acknowledged in standard histories of the 1930s, 1940s and 1950s.

But most revisionists, like Buhle, are better at asserting rank-and-file autonomy than proving it. Most articles and books have dealt with a limited geographic area, a short time span, a single incident, a specific ethnic or racial group, a particular union, or some other small part of Communist history. Revisionist writers have declared that local Communists habitually disregarded CPUSA orders, but have not presented a broad analysis showing that local autonomy—to the minimal degree that it existed— was typical Communist behavior. One of the most able of the revisionist scholars, Maurice Isserman, while justifying the over- all revisionist approach, recognized the misleading impression that could be conveyed collectively by the multitude of special- ized studies. "It would be a mistake," he remarked, "to regard the Communist Party at any point in its history as if it had been simply a collection of autonomous, overlapping sub-groupings of Jews, Finns, blacks, women, longshoremen, East Bronx ten- ants and baseball fans, who were free to set their own political agenda without reference to Soviet priorities."[61]

Indeed, the CPUSA was not organized on a congregational basis with each local unit free to interpret the gospel as it chose. In its heyday it was highly centralized, rigidly disciplined, and run by a full-time paid bureaucracy controlled by a hierarchy answerable only to a tiny group of top leaders who were them- selves vetted, approved and often picked by Moscow. Too few revisionists have heeded Isserman's sensible stipulation; most continued in the late 1980s and into the 1990s to produce numer- ous articles and dissertations in which American communism appears as an amorphous movement resembling more the chaotic New Left of the late 1960s than the rigid Leninist party it was.

Tony Judt, a scholar of European history, has recently com- mented that this two-party theory of communism:

> has not gained much ground in Eastern Europe, where it runs up against a little too much local knowledge; and for the same reason it is a minority taste in France and Italy. But in Britain and especially in the United States it is enjoying a bit of a vogue.... But we need to learn ... the truth about communism; that it was a singularly dishonest confidence-trick whose consenting victims include its distant apologists in England and America, who enthu- siastically sent others on the road to hell with the very best of

intentions. In the terrifying confusion of the 1930s, in the all-or-nothing choices of Hitler's war, in the looking-glass ethics of the cold war, those who thought they could save the essence of the Communist "dream" by separating it from its rotted Soviet penumbra were, I suppose, useful idiots, if only to that rotted penumbra itself. Today they are just idiots.[62]

# CHAPTER 4

## *Lies about Spies*

Whether they were merely accused of espionage by congressional witnesses or actually convicted in court, those charged with spying for the USSR have found passionate defenders in the United States. From the 1950s onward, their accusers have been derided as liars or fantasists, the substantial physical evidence has been dismissed as fabricated or inconclusive, and the trials have been denounced as unfair and flawed. The counteroffensive on behalf of the spies began with the Communist Party and soon spread outward to the left-wing intellectual elites and, eventually, to the universities. Whether it was Alger Hiss, Nathan Silvermaster, Victor Perlo, Julius Rosenberg, Harry Dexter White or Lauchlin Currie in the dock, some historians found grounds for doubting the charges against each or all of them. But then came important new evidence from the Russian archives and especially the Venona decryptions. Confronted with massive documentation of the guilt of all these individuals, how did revisionist historians respond? By and large, not the way historians should.

No case had a higher profile than that of Alger Hiss. The Hiss case riveted the nation and did more than any other to convince Americans that Soviet spies had infiltrated their government. Whittaker Chambers' 1952 autobiography, *Witness,* a darkly powerful story of his involvement in the Communist underground and Soviet espionage, became a bestseller. Hiss's defenders maintained throughout that he had been framed. Over the

years they have offered numerous explanations to account for
the evidence, ranging from an FBI plot to forge documents with
a faked Hiss family typewriter all the way to claims that the
deranged or vengeful Chambers invented nonexistent spying
because of a psychopathic fixation on Hiss. Then, in 1978, Allen
Weinstein published *Perjury*, a reassessment of the Hiss case based
for the first time on the massive FBI records on the case and uti-
lizing dozens of new interviews with participants. Weinstein
showed that Hiss had taken part in Soviet espionage in a book
that remains to this day the most thorough and comprehensive
examination of the case. (Sam Tanenhaus affirmed and expanded
on Weinstein's findings in his exemplary 1997 biography of
Chambers.)[1]

Hiss's defenders launched a full-scale assault on Weinstein's
methods, data and conclusions that has continued for nearly
twenty years. No one has been more vehement than Victor
Navasky, editor of *The Nation* and a professor at Columbia University, who challenged Weinstein's interpretation and claimed
that he had misused interview material with several witnesses in
a series of articles and essays.[2]*

One of Navasky's major criticisms was that Weinstein had
identified J. Peters as the head of the Communist Party under-
ground in the United States, despite Peters' denials. Apart from
Chambers' claims, Navasky wrote, there was no evidence that
Peters played such a role or was in charge of the Ware group, a
cell of government officials who turned information over to the
CPUSA. Peters, he said, was simply a well-known Communist
Party official. The *Nation* even arranged for a reporter to visit
Peters (deported in 1949 to Communist Hungary) and then fea-
tured Peters' comment that the charge that he did secret work
for the Communist Party was "nonsense."[3]

---

*Weinstein had, in fact, made one error. He had confused Sam Krieger, a Communist
who had used the alias Clarence Miller and who had recruited Chambers into the
Communist Party, with another Clarence Miller, a Communist organizer in North
Carolina, who had jumped bail and fled to the Soviet Union. Although this minor
mixup had nothing to do with Chambers or his story, Hiss's defenders continued to
assert that the mistake undermined Weinstein's veracity.

Navasky also claimed that Weinstein had exaggerated written comments by novelist Josephine Herbst indicating that her ex-husband, John Herrmann, was involved in the underground with Chambers. He accused Weinstein of distorting comments by Czech historian Karel Kaplan, who had examined Czech secret police interrogations of Noel Field in which Field allegedly identified Alger Hiss as a fellow underground Communist agent. Hede Massing, who identified Hiss and Field as spies who knew each other, was untrustworthy, Navasky wrote, because she faced deportation from the United States and had no corroboration. Both Field and Hiss had denied her story. Navasky also sneered at allegations by "the notoriously unreliable Elizabeth Bentley" that Victor Perlo had headed a Soviet spy ring and ridiculed the letter Perlo's ex-wife, Katherine, had written to the government accusing him of Communist subversion by noting that she was mentally disturbed.[4]

Throughout the 1980s and 1990s new evidence steadily undermined Navasky's claims and those of other critics of Weinstein's conclusions. Russian archives and Venona decryptions supported Elizabeth Bentley's testimony. In a posthumous autobiography, John Abt, whom Chambers had named as a member of the Ware group, finally admitted that he had been a secret Communist and a member of the Ware group and that Peters had indeed supervised the group after Harold Ware's death. Although Abt depicted it as a discussion club, he also admitted that its participants, young professionals who worked for various New Deal agencies, provided the CPUSA with information and analysis of government activities. More evidence of this activity came from Elinor Langer, the biographer of Josephine Herbst. She learned that John Herrmann, Herbst's husband at the time, had been connected to the Communist underground:

> From early 1934 until the summer of 1935 he was a paid courier for the Communist Party whose job was to deliver to New York material emanating from the secret cells of sympathetic government employees being cultivated by Harold Ware. There is no doubt that this was an important function. John's superior in the

network was Whittaker Chambers and—the long-standing Nation position on this matter to the contrary—according to his widow, whom I met in 1974, John Herrmann was the man who introduced Chambers to Alger Hiss.[5]

In her 1994 autobiography, Hope Hale Davis described her service in the Washington Communist underground with her then-husband, Hermann Brunck, who passed confidential government Labor Board documents to the CPUSA to assist its union organizers. In addition to confirming J. Peters' role as head of the underground, she identified many of the same people that Katherine Perlo and Whittaker Chambers had accused of being members of the underground in which Victor Perlo had played a key role.[6]

The Russian archives gave even more confirmation. In *The Secret World of American Communism* we reproduced several Russian archival documents regarding Peters and the CPUSA underground. Rudy Baker, who had replaced Peters as head of the underground in June 1938, wrote one of them for the Comintern in early 1939, "Brief on the Work of the CPUSA Secret Apparatus."* The first two sentences could not have been more direct: "The CPUSA secret apparatus has been in existence about four years. Its operations have been directed for that entire period by Com PETERS." This is the party underground organization that Navasky and other Hiss defenders claimed did not exist and was not headed by Peters. We also reproduced two messages from Soviet Military Intelligence (GRU) to the Comintern in 1943 inquiring about Peters' supervision of an American Communist group in Washington engaged in "informational work," a standard term for intelligence gathering. Finally, we included a 1947 biographical summary of Peters' career, prepared by the International Department of the Communist Party of the Soviet

---

*Although the word chosen to translate the Russian is "secret" apparatus, the original text used the word *konspirativnyi*, a cognate of the English word "conspiracy," and the term could as accurately be translated as "conspiratorial apparatus" or "conspiracy apparatus."

Union (heir to the Comintern), that also noted his work for the American party's "secret apparatus" in the 1930s.[7]

The initial reaction of revisionist historians to this confirmation of a part of Chambers' story varied considerably. Maurice Isserman was persuaded: "That J. Peters was involved in a secret party apparatus can no longer be disputed." He was, however, an exception. William Reuben adamantly asserted, "The Moscow archives contain *no* material relating to these key figures in the Cold War 'spy' cases," including J. Peters in his list. Reuben insisted that he had evidence, a letter from the Russian Center for the Preservation and Study of Documents of Recent History, "attesting that the Center has no files on, or relating to, any of the above-named persons."[8]

Reuben's claims are refuted by actual documents relating to Peters from the very archive he says has no such documents. Other American scholars have visited the archive and examined the same documents that we reproduced in *The Secret World*. In addition to those cited in our book, documents by or about Peters can be found in the archive of the Marty Secretariat of the Executive Committee of the Communist International, in the archive of the Dimitrov Secretariat of the Executive Committee of the Communist International, in the archive of the Anglo-American Secretariat of the Executive Committee of the Communist International, and in the archive of the Communist Party USA itself. Further, the archive's collection of Comintern biographical background files contains one devoted exclusively to Peters. Its Russian title reads, in translation, "Peters, John," yet another of the many names that the man best known to historians as "J. Peters," " J. Peter" or "Josef Peters" used in his career. Despite his misrepresentation of archival material, Reuben remains an authoritative source for those defending Hiss and continues to be cited by revisionist historians who ought to know better.[9]

Adamant revisionists not only must pretend that documents on Peters' underground work do not exist in Moscow, they must avert their eyes from those in archives of the former Communist regimes of Central Europe. After his deportation to Budapest in 1949, Peters prepared "The Memoirs of Jozsef Peter," written secretly for the Hungarian Communist Party's Institute for the History of the Party and not available until the collapse of the Communist regime. In it, Peters described how the CPUSA in the early 1930s sent him to Moscow for Comintern training, where he spent his time "studying underground operations" and preparing for "the construction of the secret apparatus." He explained, "The situation demanded the establishment of an apparatus that would enable the Party to work under difficult circumstances. The Party put me in charge of this. The nature of this work demanded that in certain critical periods we had to work and live illegally." He elaborated, "from 1936 I conducted special work for the Party. During this time, between 1936–39, I participated in the organization of all major activities." He then transferred to open party work for a time, but "in 1942 I returned to the underground."[10]

Other evidence from Central European archives corroborating Hiss's role as a Soviet spy involves his relationship with Noel Field. A former U.S. State Department official, Field fled behind the Iron Curtain in 1949 and disappeared. Shortly after his flight, Hede Massing (who earlier used the name Gompertz) testified that in the mid-1930s she had been a KGB agent recruiting sources inside the American government, and that Field was one of them. Massing, a witness at Alger Hiss's trial, corroborated Chambers' testimony that Hiss was a Soviet spy. She stated that in 1936 Hiss, unaware that Field was already cooperating with the KGB, attempted to recruit him for his own GRU-linked apparatus. Instead of declining the offer and leaving Hiss in the dark, Field explained to Hiss that he already worked for the Soviets, thereby entangling two Soviet networks. Massing said that Field later admitted his security slip to her and at a subsequent meeting she and Hiss politely sparred about who would control Field. Because she was a second and independent witness to Hiss's espionage, Massing's testimony gravely damaged him, and Hiss's defenders have long sought to discredit her story as uncorroborated lies.

Meanwhile the unlucky Noel Field discovered that his expected safe haven in the Soviet bloc had become a nightmare. Stalinist security officers, charged with purging the new Communist regimes of Central Europe, seized on him as a way to link leading officials to American intelligence. In the wave of show trials that swept the Soviet bloc, Stalinist prosecutors repeatedly cited Field as an American master spy who had subverted leaders of the underground Communist parties with whom he had had contact as an official of a refugee relief organization operating in Switzerland during World War II. He and his wife were imprisoned in Hungary, his brother in Poland and his stepdaughter in the USSR. Released after Stalin's death, Field was requestioned by Hungarian and Czechoslovak security police as part of the process of rehabilitating Communists victimized by Stalin's purges. Still a loyal soldier, Field publicly reaffirmed his belief in communism after his release from prison, described his imprisonment as an unfortunate mistake that had been corrected, and denied any connection to Soviet intelligence or knowledge of Alger Hiss's espionage. Granted a pension by the Hungarian Communist security police, he spent the rest of his life in Budapest, dying in 1970.

During the Prague Spring of 1968, Czechoslovak historian Karel Kaplan assisted the Dubcek reform Communist government's investigation of the Stalinist purge that had led to the 1952 execution of Rudolf Slánsky, general secretary of the Czechoslovak Communist Party, on the fabricated charge of cooperating with American intelligence. Stalinist prosecutors had cited Noel Field's activities as evidence of betrayal of the Communist cause by Slánsky and his associates. After the Soviet invasion of Czechoslovakia, Kaplan fled west. Allen Weinstein wrote in *Perjury* that Kaplan reported examining secret Czech and Hungarian security police reports on Field's rehabilitation that corroborated Hede Massing's testimony. Hiss's defenders, led by Victor Navasky, accused Weinstein of too quickly accepting and perhaps even distorting Kaplan's report. But in his *Report on the Murder of the General Secretary* (1990), Kaplan noted Field's role in the Stalinist show trials and confirmed that Massing had recruited him as a KGB source in the mid-1930s.[11] Then in 2000 a Czech human rights activist, Karel Skrabek, obtained a copy of the Czechoslovak security police reinvestigation of Field in 1955. The report stated:

> Noel Field said that he was a friend of Hiss at the time he worked at the State Department and that Hiss worked for the USSR as a spy. He knows it, allegedly, from a discussion with him in which Hiss tried to convince him to work with him. Of course, at the time Noel Field already worked for Soviet intelligence through the Massings [Hede and her husband, Paul]. Massing, who later was a traitor [to the USSR], testified about Hiss in front of the Committee on Un-American Activities and Mrs. Massing Gompertz testified against him in front of a New York Federal Jury which convicted Hiss [and sentenced him] to a five-year prison term.[12]

After the collapse of the Hungarian Communist regime, Hungarian historian Maria Schmidt examined the security police files on Field's role in the execution of László Rajk and his close associates. Rajk, a leading Communist Party official and government minister of foreign affairs, was the chief target of the Stalinist purge. Reporting on Field's secret statements during his post-Stalin rehabilitation, Schmidt quoted Field as relating that after his recruitment as a Soviet source by Hede Massing, he initially found his life of deception difficult, but "Finally, I succeeded in surmounting my inhibitions and took on espionage for the Soviet intelligence service. My wife was also [present] at this time.... Even earlier I had become conscious of the fact that the task [of espionage] is an honorable duty." Describing his work, Field stated, "The institution, and consequently, the mentality of the State Department, was rather provincial in my days.... This was evident from the careless manner in which state secrets were managed. The most secret documents, sometimes in multiple copies, circulated from hand to hand. Thus, I saw not merely the telegraph messages, but almost everything concerning the department."[13]

As part of his rehabilitation with Communist security police, Field explained his relationship with Hiss and the difficulty it caused with his KGB contact, Hede Massing, known to him in the 1930s as Hedda Gompertz:

> We made friends with Alger Hiss, one of the top officials of Roo-sevelt's New Deal. Through our gatherings we discovered that we were Communists. In the summer of 1935, Alger Hiss tried to persuade me to render services to the Soviets, which led me to commit the unforgivable indiscretion of telling him he had come too late. At that very moment, I notified Hedda [Gompertz/Mass-ing] about the event. She loaded me with the worst reproaches. She did not know what her boss would say to that, with whom, by the way, I never got acquainted. A little later, she told me that I had done greater damage than I would believe, and that because of me the whole work had to be reorganized. . . . Our misfortune was that not only had the Massings become traitors, but so had Hiss's connection—Chambers.

This documentation is straightforward. Alger Hiss, a Soviet spy, asked Field to join in espionage, just as the much-derided Hede Massing had asserted.[14]

But there is even more evidence that Field was telling the truth about Hiss. Allen Weinstein and Alexander Vassiliev located in Moscow and quoted KGB files that not only corroborated Massing's account of Hiss's attempted recruitment of Field but also explicitly identified Hiss, using his real name rather than a cover name, as a GRU agent. One report Massing wrote to Moscow in 1936 is unambiguous:

> Our friend "Ernst" [Noel Field] the day before his departure to Europe told me the following story. . . . Alger Hiss turned to him approximately a week before "Ernst's" [Field's] departure to Europe. Alger told him that he was a Communist and that he was connected with an organization working for the Soviet Union and that he knew that "Ernst" himself had certain connections. But Alger was afraid that they were not solid enough and that probably his knowledge was being used poorly.
>
> Then he openly suggested that "Ernst" [Field] should make a report to him on London's Conference. According to "Ernst,"

they were close friends; that is why he did not refuse to talk to him about this topic, but told Alger that he already had made a report on that conference. When Alger whom I had met through "Ernst," as you may remember, kept insisting on the report, "Ernst" was forced to tell him that he needed to consult his "connections."

KGB headquarters, irritated that Massing had met the GRU's Hiss, made its displeasure clear by return cable: "We do not understand 'Ryzhaya's' [Massing's] motives in meeting 'Lawyer' [Alger Hiss]. As we understand, it happened after we gave our last directives about 'Lawyer,' after our instruction that 'Lawyer' is the Neighbors' [GRU] agent and needed to be left alone."[15] In a follow-up, Iskhak Akhmerov, a KGB illegal officer in the United States, reported to Moscow: " 'Storm' [J. Peters] let out a secret during one of our conversations: Hiss used to be a member of bratskiy organization [CPUSA underground] who had been implanted into 'Surrogate' [cover name for the State Department] and sent to the Neighbors [GRU] later. He told me about it when I was hunting for Hiss."

But to the determinedly myopic Navasky, the Hungarian material about Field (only summarized here) is "at best, inconclusive." And, he calls Weinstein and Vassiliev's book "methodologically challenged."[16] The former statement is false and the latter is a contrived excuse rather than a real reason to refuse to accept the KGB documents in Weinstein and Vassiliev's book. For this material *not* to incriminate Hiss, Hede Massing and Iskhak Akhmerov, both Soviet agents, had to be *separately* lying about their contacts with Hiss in the 1930s. And Field, the dedicated Communist, had to be lying when explaining himself to his Communist interrogators during his rehabilitation. And the KGB had to be mistaken in identifying Hiss as the agent of Soviet Military Intelligence. What motive would all of them have had to lie to other Communist intelligence officials about Hiss? And why and how could all their accounts coincide in one huge mistake?

Most historians are not as contemptuous about evidence as Reuben or Navasky. Instead, they resort to language that implies the innocence of Hiss (and the Rosenbergs) without actually saying so. The controversial 1994 *National Standards for United States History,* a federally funded classroom guide for grade-school history teachers that has received enthusiastic support from leaders of the historical profession, is typical. It forthrightly and repeatedly condemns McCarthyism as an unmitigated evil, which is appropriate since McCarthy had an overwhelmingly negative impact on public life. But the Hiss-Chambers and Rosenberg cases, the two dominant controversies of the anticommunist era, are described with bland, neutral language crafted to keep from implying guilt while not being quite so foolhardy as to actually assert innocence. While silent on what really happened in the Hiss and Rosenberg cases, *National Standards* urges teachers to show students how the cases "contribute to the rise of McCarthyism" and implies that the cases are part and parcel of the McCarthyite horror.[17] While McCarthy and McCarthyism get mentioned more than a dozen times, there is no mention of the active participation of the American Communist Party in Soviet espionage or of the dozens of hidden Communists in government agencies who spied for the Soviets.

More recently, in 1996, *Grand Expectations: The United States, 1945–1974* appeared to heavy applause in the academic world. Author James Patterson, one of the leaders of the historical establishment, proclaimed neutrality on the case: "whether Hiss was innocent remained a much-disputed fact years later." Patterson also listed Julius Rosenberg among the victims of the "Red Scare" and, while noting that he was executed for espionage, worded his reference to leave the question of Rosenberg's guilt unanswered. In 1998 Ellen Schrecker reluctantly agreed that Julius Rosenberg was a spy but refused to abandon Hiss, concluding, "the case remains problematic in many ways." Her brief summary of the case suggested that the only real evidence against Hiss was Chambers' testimony and erroneously stated, "No further corroboration has surfaced for Chambers' allegations that Hiss gave him information for the Russians." However, in an essay published in 2000 Schrecker, without elaboration, appeared finally to retreat on Hiss as well: "There is now just too much evidence from too many different sources to make it possible for anyone but the most die-hard loyalists to argue convincingly for the innocence of Hiss, Rosenberg, and the others."[18]

In the academic world, alas, there is no lack of "die-hard loyalists" who continue to argue for the innocence of one or another Soviet spy. The continued defense of Julius Rosenberg by Professors Bernice Schrank and Norman Markowitz was discussed earlier. As regards Hiss, no one has been more creative at evading evidence than John Lowenthal, a former Rutgers University and City University of New York law professor. Lowenthal produced and directed a 1979 documentary film, *The Trials of Alger Hiss,* defending him, and served as Hiss's attorney in his final years. In 2000, after Hiss's death, Lowenthal wrote a lengthy article, "Venona and Alger Hiss," denigrating the new evidence for the historical journal *Intelligence and National Security.*[19]

Before dealing with the Venona material on Hiss, Lowenthal first distorts a number of facts about the Hiss-Chambers case. One example is what he says about the stolen State Department documents Chambers had hidden in 1938 and produced in 1949 to support his story, material either in Hiss's handwriting or typed on his own typewriter: "Nor was the content of the papers sensational or sensitive: most of the retyped pages were copied from a report on economic conditions in Manchuria...." In reality the documents dealt with matters of far more significance, including sensitive diplomatic and military issues involving France, Britain, China, the Soviet Union and Japan. The typed or handwritten material Chambers produced summarized sixty-eight different State Department documents that went through Hiss's office. Chambers also produced microfilm made by his espionage network of documents that Hiss had given him in 1938. Lowenthal simply notes, "The film contained photographs of miscellaneous government documents, which Chambers also said Hiss had given him for espionage." What he leaves out is that three of the documents on the film had Hiss's handwritten initials on them and the stamp from the small State Department office where he worked.[20]

Lowenthal also revives the hoary myth (invented by Hiss himself) that the Hiss family Woodstock typewriter introduced as evidence in the trial was an FBI-produced fake. The document examiners who testified at the trial verified that the typed material had been produced on the Hiss typewriter, but they did so by comparing the typed documents with personal correspondence typed by the Hisses *in the 1930s*. Even if the Woodstock typewriter introduced into evidence had never been found, Hiss would still have been linked to the retyped copies of the State Department memos.[21]

But Lowenthal's essay is particularly notable for its silence about numerous issues damaging to Hiss. How does he address Chambers' testimony that Hiss arranged to turn over his automobile to a Communist organizer, a charge supported by the documentary evidence of auto transfer papers signed by Hiss? He doesn't mention it. How does Lowenthal deal with Hiss's claim that he and his family never saw Chambers after 1936 in the face of contradictory testimony from one of Hiss's maids, one of Chambers' housemaids and Hiss's pediatrician? He doesn't address it.

### Hiss and Venona

Much of Lowenthal's essay is devoted to the one incriminating Venona message dealing with Hiss. Before examining this message, it is worth noting that it plays only a minor role in the argument for Hiss having cooperated with Soviet intelligence. Even if Lowenthal were able to demonstrate that the message had nothing to do with Hiss, all the other evidence against him would retain its force. Much of the message's historical significance stems from its 1945 date, speaking to the issue of whether Hiss's cooperation with Soviet espionage continued past the 1930s. Chambers' knowledge of Hiss's espionage extended only to 1938. A number of those who spied for the Soviet Union in the 1930s later quit. Some, like Chambers and Massing, publicly acknowledged their activities. Others quietly dropped out of espionage and remained silent. The Venona message about Hiss indicates that his cooperation with Soviet intelligence agencies continued through World War II.

The message in question is a March 30, 1945, coded cable from the Washington, D.C., station of the KGB to its headquarters in Moscow, signed by Vadim, the cover name of Anatoly Gromov, ostensibly a Soviet diplomat at the USSR embassy but actually chief of KGB operations in the United States. A copy of the cable was intercepted by the American National Security Agency in 1945 and decoded years later. The cable refers to an agent cover-named "Ales" who is identified in a footnote added by the FBI and the NSA as "probably Alger Hiss." A careful examination of the message demonstrates its close fit with what has been known about Hiss.[22]

The message begins by saying: "As a result of A.'s chat with Ales the following has been ascertained: 1. Ales has been working with the Neighbors continuously since 1935." Here "A." is not identified, but taken in concert with other KGB Venona messages, it can reasonably be assumed to refer to "Albert," the cover name of Iskhak Akhmerov, the KGB's chief illegal officer in the United States. "Neighbors" was KGB terminology for the GRU.[23] Ales was thus a Soviet agent working for Soviet Military Intelligence. Whittaker Chambers testified that Hiss entered the CPUSA underground in 1934 and in 1935 became part of a GRU espionage apparatus.

The Venona message notes: "For some years past he [Ales] has been the leader of a small group of the Neighbors' probationers, for the most part consisting of his relations." "Probationers" was standard KGB jargon for agents or active sources. As for Ales/Hiss's "relations," according to Chambers, Priscilla Hiss, Alger's wife, typed many of the documents her husband stole from the State Department. Chambers had also identified Hiss's brother: "Donald Hiss never at any time procured any documents. Nevertheless, he was a member of the apparatus which I headed."[24] Donald Hiss had transferred to the State Department from the Department of Labor in November 1937, less than six months before Chambers dropped out of Soviet espionage.

The message continues: "The group and Ales himself work on obtaining military information only. Materials on the Bank allegedly interest the Neighbors very little and he does not produce them regularly." "Bank" was the KGB's cover name for the State Department, where Hiss was employed. The suggestion that the GRU was pressing Ales to produce military rather than diplomatic information more readily available to someone in the State Department is also significant. When the GRU dominated Soviet foreign intelligence operations in the 1920s and 1930s, its networks sought political and strategic information as well as more narrowly defined military intelligence. But as the KGB established its supremacy in foreign intelligence in the late 1930s, the GRU's jurisdiction was steadily narrowed. It had to get its agents to produce more strictly military information clearly within its jurisdiction or risk losing them to the KGB. Just six months after this cable was sent, Alger Hiss made an extraordinary proposal that the State Department create a new "special assistant for military affairs" linked to his Office of Special Political Affairs. Moreover, when security officers belatedly began to look closely at Hiss in 1946 they discovered that he had used his authority to obtain top secret reports "on atomic energy ... and other matters relating to military intelligence" that were outside the scope of his Office of Special Political Affairs, which dealt largely with United Nations diplomacy.[25]

The next sentence, "All the last few years Ales has been working with Pol who also meets other members of the group occasionally," has not yielded any information because "Pol" is unidentified. There follows, "Recently Ales and his whole group were awarded Soviet decorations," an assertion discussed below in conjunction with additional documentation that has been found in KGB files.

A key sentence in the cable then states that "after the Yalta Conference, when he had gone to Moscow, a Soviet personage in a very responsible position (Ales gave to understand that it was Comrade Vishinski) allegedly got in touch with Ales and at the behest of the Military Neighbors passed on to him their gratitude and so on."

Ales had, therefore, attended the Yalta conference and returned to the United States via Moscow. This message was transmitted only a month after the conference ended and was sent from the United States where "A." had his chat with Ales. Most of the members of the American delegation returned to the U.S. via Iran, bypassing Moscow. A small party of four State Department officials flew to Moscow from Yalta for a brief lay-over to conclude some unfinished business and then proceeded back to Washington. Andrei Vishinski, the Soviet deputy foreign minister, met with this group in Moscow on two occasions, a formal reception and an informal social evening at the Bolshoi Ballet.[26] The list of possible candidates for Ales is small. There has never been any reason to suspect that three of the members of this delegation—Secretary of State Edward Stettinius; H. Freeman Matthews, director of the Office of European Affairs; and Stettinius's press aide, Wilder Foote—were Soviet agents. The fourth official was Alger Hiss.

The most straightforward reading of this message is that Ales was, as the NSA/FBI footnote said, "probably Alger Hiss." Its account of Ales fits Chambers' story of Hiss's espionage activities and is reinforced by Elizabeth Bentley's statement to the FBI in 1945:

> Referring again to Harold Glasser, I recall that after his return from his assignment in Europe, probably in Italy, for the United States Treasury Department, Victor Perlo told me that Glasser had asked him if he would be able to get back in with the Perlo group. I asked Perlo how Glasser happened to leave the group and he explained that Glasser and one or two others had been taken sometime before by some American in some governmental agency in Washington, and that this unidentified American turned Glasser and the others over to some Russian. Perlo declared he did not know the identity of this American, and said that Charley Kramer, so far as he knew, was the only person who had this information. Sometime later I was talking with Kramer in New York City, and brought up this matter to him. At this time Kramer told me that the person who had originally taken Glasser away from Perlo's group was named Hiss and that he was in the U.S. State Department.[27]

Throughout Glasser's career with the government he was an underground Communist and a Soviet source. (A decrypted 1944

Venona message from the New York KGB station said, "Harold Glasser is an old fellow countryman," the standard KGB term for a Communist Party member.) In 1937 he worked with Whittaker Chambers' CPUSA-GRU network. Eleven deciphered Venona messages discuss Glasser's work and role in Soviet espionage under the code name Ruble. Weinstein and Vassiliev quote KGB documents that discuss two Americans with the cover names Ruble and Ales—Glasser and Hiss—who cooperated with Soviet intelligence.[28]

One of the documents is a memo from Pavel Fitin, head of the KGB's foreign intelligence arm, to Vsevolod Merkulov, overall chief of the KGB:

> Our agent Ruble [Glasser], drawn to working for the Soviet Union in May 1937, has been passing (with short breaks caused by business trips) initially through the military "neighbors" and then through our station, valuable information on political and economic issues. Since the beginning of 1945 alone, from reports based on his information and cabled to the station, 34 special reports were sent ... to the "Instance" [Stalin and other top Soviet leaders]. Ruble [Glasser] also gave us talent-spottings on valuable people ... who are now being cultivated by us; communicated data about the trip to the USSR by regular officers of the Office of Strategic Services under cover of the U.S. Embassy in Moscow, etc. He gives much attention and energy to our work [and] is a devoted and disciplined agent.
>
> According to data from Vadim [Gorsky, chief of the KGB station in Washington], the group of agents of the military "neighbors" [GRU] whose member [Glasser] had been earlier, was recently decorated with USSR orders. About this fact, Ruble learned it from his friend Ales who is the leader of the mentioned group. Taking into account Ruble's devoted work for the USSR for 8 years and the fact that as a result of transfer to our station, [KGB], [he] was not decorated together with other members of Ales's group, [we] consider it expedient to recommend him for the decoration with the Order of the Red Star. Ask your consent.[29]

The Fitin to Merkulov memo corroborates Chambers' statement about when Glasser first went to work for Soviet intelligence. It also corroborates Bentley's statement about Glasser leaving Perlo's apparatus to work for a time for one headed by

Hiss. And it confirms the passage saying that Hiss's group had been awarded Soviet decorations. The new evidence, obtained from a Russian archive, dovetails perfectly with Venona cables decrypted by American counterintelligence and stories told by two separate defectors from Soviet intelligence. It all points to one man as Ales: Alger Hiss.

Despite this evidence, John Lowenthal denies that Alger Hiss could be Ales; and other revisionists such as diplomatic historian Scott Lucas quickly cited his analysis as proof that Venona exonerated Hiss.[30] Victor Navasky and Athan Theoharis also put forward variants of Lowenthal's claims, which may form a last line of defense for Hiss partisans. In truth, however, the argument is inaccurate and implausible.

Lowenthal dismisses the parallels with Chambers' account of Hiss's espionage career, asserting, "Ales conducted espionage throughout the 11 years 1935–45 (message paragraph 1), whereas Hiss was accused, and in effect convicted, of having conducted espionage only in the mid-1930s and not later than 1938."[31] Hiss was convicted only on the charge of lying about giving State Department documents to Chambers in 1938. The government said nothing about what happened after 1938 because its chief witness, Chambers, had no knowledge of Hiss's activities after that date. None of the evidence presented at the Hiss trial *precluded* the possibility that Hiss had cooperated with Soviet espionage after 1938.

Lowenthal also writes, "Even if Hiss was the spy that he was in effect convicted of having been, he could not have continued being a spy after 1938, as Ales did, because in that year Hiss would have become too great a risk for any Soviet intelligence agency to use."[32] In the real world, neither Soviet intelligence nor American counterintelligence behaved how Lowenthal thinks they did or should have.

After he dropped out of espionage in 1938, Chambers did not contact the American government to provide an account of his activities. Instead, he reentered mainstream life as a journalist for *Time* under his real name. To discourage retaliation by Soviet intelligence, he sent a letter through Felix Inslerman, the photographer for his espionage apparatus, promising silence but threatening to expose Soviet assets if he or his family were harmed. In 1950 Inslerman confirmed that Chambers had done precisely that and even turned over contemporaneous notes he had made about the letter to the FBI. The Soviets did briefly shut down Chambers' apparatus. J Peters was removed as head of the CPUSA underground in mid-1938, probably in response to Chambers' action. But after his defection there were no government investigations, no surveillance, and no evidence that Chambers had provided names to American counterintelligence.

Soviet sources that were "put on ice" or temporarily left inactive due to the security breach were eventually reactivated after it became apparent that the small and ineffective American counterintelligence forces of that era had little knowledge of Soviet espionage. There are many examples in Soviet espionage history of sources put on ice who were later revived. For example, Morris and Lona Cohen were two American Communists who worked for the KGB for decades but they were deactivated after Gouzenko and Bentley defected in 1945. However, once it was clear that neither had provided information putting the Cohens at risk, they were put back to work in 1947.

Lowenthal writes, "It is a fact that Chambers did denounce Hiss to the US government in 1939, and he continued to do so over the next dozen years. Thus the GRU and Hiss himself, would have been reckless beyond belief to continue for seven years after 1938 the alleged espionage activities that the penitent Chambers could be expected to expose."[33]

But American security agencies—and Chambers, for that matter—*did not* pursue Hiss for years as Lowenthal claims. Chambers dropped out of Soviet espionage in mid-1938 but did not approach government authorities until late August 1939, when the Nazi-Soviet Pact convinced him that the Soviet Union had become a de facto nonbelligerent ally of Nazi Germany and he met with Assistant Secretary of State Adolf Berle. Berle's written notes of the meeting, headed "Underground Espionage Agent," show that Chambers gave him the names and provided short descriptions of twenty-four secret Communists working within the government. Contrary to Lowenthal's claim, Chambers did not target Hiss. Fourteen of the people Chambers named are now known to have cooperated with Soviet espionage. According to Lowenthal's logic, Soviet intelligence would have dropped all of them after 1938 because their association with Chambers would have been deemed too risky. In fact, ten assisted Soviet espionage in the 1940s and most appear in the World War II Venona decryptions as Soviet spies.[34] If Soviet intelligence had operated the way Lowenthal insists it had to, then not only did Hiss not spy in the 1940s, neither did any of these people. But even Lowenthal is not foolish enough to make that claim.

Hiss and the others were able to escape surveillance because no one took Chambers' charges seriously. Berle did not file a report on the interview with the FBI, with either military counterintelligence agency, or even with the State Department's own security office. His diary also shows that not until 1942 did he discuss the matter with one of FDR's secretaries and he did not know if the president was ever informed. Over the years, several sources told FBI agents that Whittaker Chambers had information worth hearing. When the FBI finally interviewed him in May 1942, he told them that he had already given all the information he had to Berle in 1939. The FBI contacted Berle and another year passed until, in June 1943, his notes eventually reached the FBI. Even then the FBI did no serious follow-up investigation due to the higher priority given cases involving German and Japanese espionage. Only in late 1945, with the war over and after the defections of Gouzenko in Canada and Bentley in the United States, did the FBI seriously turn its attention to Soviet espionage. Chambers, meanwhile, was not barraging government agencies with tales of espionage by Hiss or anyone else.[35]

Lowenthal's most audacious maneuver is to deny that Hiss could have received any thanks from Vishinski in Moscow. Government investigators and traditionalist scholars, he contends, have misconstrued the meaning of the cable and incorrectly assumed that Ales was at Yalta and went from there to Moscow.

The sentence in the cable states: "After the Yalta Conference, when he had gone on to Moscow, a Soviet personage in a very responsible position . . . allegedly got in touch with Ales. . . ." The person who went on to Moscow, Lowenthal asserts, was actually Vishinski, not Ales: "a more sensible reading of the cablegram, however, is that it says nothing about Ales being at Yalta, but it does say that about Comrade Vyshinski. Precisely, the person referred to in paragraph 6 as having been at Yalta and gone on to Moscow is not Ales but 'a Soviet personage in a very responsible position', Comrade Vyshinski, the deputy foreign minister."[36] While grammatically possible, Lowenthal's argument is both illogical and physically impossible.

To support his reading, Lowenthal argues that if Ales had been in Moscow, the GRU would not have needed to use Vishinski to contact him. They could have done so directly:

> The whole point of paragraph 6, that the GRU asked Vishinski to get in touch with Ales to convey the GRU's gratitude to Ales, would have been mooted if Ales had been in Moscow, because the GRU could then have contacted Ales in Moscow on its own, without needing Vishinski as an intermediary. But with Ales in the US rather than in Moscow, the GRU would have had good reason to ask the itinerant Vyshinski to get in touch with him to deliver its gratitude.[37]

This misconstrues why Vishinski would have been asked to contact Ales and assumes, with not a scintilla of evidence, that Vishinski could have contacted Ales in the United States. Like the vast majority of Americans who assisted Soviet intelligence in that era, Ales was motivated by ideology and admiration for Soviet communism. American sources often refused financial payments beyond reimbursements for expenses or small gifts. On the other hand, Soviet decorations and other signs of Soviet recognition were highly valued by politically motivated American sources. The KGB awarded Soviet medals to a number of its American spies, including Harold Glasser, Elizabeth Bentley, Gregory Silvermaster and Harry Gold.[38]

The GRU did not need Vishinski as a courier simply to deliver a message in Moscow. It was precisely because he was deputy minister of foreign affairs and a prominent and long-serving Soviet official that the GRU wanted Vishinski to express Soviet gratitude to Ales. Spies in prominent government positions, like Hiss, only rarely met face to face with their Soviet contacts. Most often they dealt through couriers and intermediaries. Even if they did have contact with a Soviet officer, it would have been someone whose public position was relatively minor. By having Vishinski express appreciation the GRU was assuring the highly placed Hiss that his contributions to the Soviet cause were known and valued at the highest levels of the Soviet state.

More importantly, however, Lowenthal also has not done his geography homework. The lesser problem with his argument that the GRU needed Vishinski to deliver a message to Ales in the United States is that the GRU had a number of officers there, including Hiss's regular Soviet controller, and did not need Vishinski's aid. Nor was it usual Soviet practice to use a prominent Soviet diplomat as an espionage courier in a foreign country. The larger problem is that Vishinski *was not in the United States* between Yalta and the time of the Ales Venona message, and the message is from the Washington KGB station reporting on a talk one of its agents had with Ales *in the United States*.[39] Lowenthal's explanation is impossible.

## Wishing Away Archival Evidence

In 1999 Allen Weinstein and Alexander Vassiliev coauthored *The Haunted Wood: Soviet Espionage in America—The Stalin Era*. Based on material from the KGB's own records, the book contains highly valuable information about Soviet intelligence operations against the United States, including damning information on Hiss's espionage in the mid-1930s. But John Lowenthal refuses to accept it as genuine because the KGB archive is not open to all researchers.

The KGB archive was and is closed to research. But in the early 1990s a small window into it opened in the wake of the USSR's collapse. The Russian Intelligence Service (SVR), successor to the foreign intelligence arm of the KGB, shaken by the end of the Soviet order and in need of cash, made a deal with Western publishers to partner a Western author and a Russian with a KGB background to write on certain topics. The Russian coauthor was able to examine the KGB's archives to extract selected documents on specified topics. The KGB veterans' association received a generous payment from the publishers. Four books emerged from this collaboration, including *The Haunted Wood*.[40]

All four books contain information and documents never before available. Would it have been preferable that the SVR fully open the KGB archive for research? Of course. The material in all these books is only a small slice of the evidence and subject to limitations. But it is, nonetheless, far richer evidence than we have ever had before. Historians are used to dealing with partial access and limited availability of documentation. Particularly for twentieth-century material, large sections of government archives are only partially available due to security classifications. The private papers of numerous important people and the records of private organizations are only partially available due to restrictions imposed by donors of these collections. Sometimes historians are allowed access but must agree to donor-imposed restrictions on what or how much can be quoted. Sometimes owners of private papers give exclusive access to authorized biographers or keep access to themselves while writing an autobiography. Historians would prefer that none of the limitations existed, but they have existed in the past, exist now, and will continue to exist. Historians do not ignore an autobiography or authorized biography because the author had preferential access to personal papers.* Nor do historians refuse to take into account information from a collection that is only partially open, as in

---

*For example, access to President Woodrow Wilson's papers was extremely limited for decades. Consequently, until the papers were opened, historians used the documentary information provided in Ray Stannard Baker's three-volume history of Wilson's role in the Versailles peace conference even though Baker was Wilson's authorized biographer and had preferential access to his diplomatic papers.

the case, most obviously, of U.S. government materials obtained under the Freedom of Information Act. They keep these restrictions and limitations on sources in mind, but use what is available. All historical writing is based on information available at the time of writing. More information becomes available as closed collections are opened, new collections are donated to archives, classified material is declassified, and so on. Meanwhile, we use what we have, and it would be foolish to refuse to take into account the material provided by Weinstein and Vassiliev.

Lowenthal's second ostensible reason for rejecting Weinstein and Vassiliev's documents is that he does not believe their linkage of cover names with real names. He triumphantly quotes a Russian Intelligence Service press officer to the effect that none of the cover name identifications should be taken seriously. He fails to consider, however, that by the time *The Haunted Wood* was published, the SVR, recovering from the shock of the USSR's implosion, reconsidered its earlier decision to allow even limited access to its archives and was anxious to discredit the book. The window that had allowed the publication of the four books was firmly closed—so much so that Vassiliev, the Russian coauthor, found it prudent to leave Russia and settle in Great Britain.

There is a more positive reason to accept the reliability of the cover names as well as the authenticity of the documents in *The Haunted Wood,* however. A systematic comparison of its information with the five thousand pages of deciphered Venona cables, written and oral testimony from defectors from Soviet intelligence, wiretaps and previously published information demonstrates a very nice fit. The mutual corroboration is overwhelming.

Finally, Weinstein and Vassiliev note that several of their KGB documents from the 1930s, when Hiss and KGB agent Hede Massing competed to recruit Noel Field, name Hiss as a GRU agent in *plain text,* without a cover name. Since Lowenthal cannot obfuscate the issue by talking about the unreliability of cover names, he solves his dilemma by not mentioning these documents where Hiss's name is stated in the clear without any cover name.

Lowenthal places particular weight on statements by the late Dmitri Volkogonov, a Soviet army general and military historian who lost his faith in communism in the 1980s. After the dissolution of the USSR, Volkogonov advised Boris Yeltsin on military policy, served as the Russian co-chair of a joint Russian-American Commission on Prisoners of War and Missing in Action, and chaired a commission on archival policy before his death in 1995. Lowenthal describes Volkogonov as the "overseer of all the Soviet intelligence archives," but this is another example of his twisting of facts. While Volkogonov advised on archival policy, he never had administrative control of any archive and certainly not the foreign intelligence archives. As a historian, Volkogonov wrote principally on the history of the Red Army, although he is best known in the West for his biographies of Lenin, Trotsky and Stalin. He focused on internal Soviet history and gave little attention to foreign intelligence activities in his research.

In August 1991, John Lowenthal, acting on behalf of Alger Hiss, asked Volkogonov to look into the Hiss case. Volkogonov responded in October 1992 with a letter to Lowenthal that said, "On his and your request, I carefully studied many documents from the archives of the intelligence services of the USSR as well as various information provided for me by the archive staff. On the basis of a very careful analysis of all the information available, I can inform you that Alger Hiss was never an agent of the intelligence services of the Soviet Union." Lowenthal also recorded a video interview with Volkogonov in which he exonerated Hiss on the basis of not having found any documents. "Positively, if he was [a] spy," according to Volkogonov, "I would have found a reflection in various files." Lowenthal was not the only Hiss defender to welcome Volkogonov's statement. Victor Navasky hailed his remarks as total vindication of Hiss, while Professor William Pemberton (University of Wisconsin, La Crosse) wrote in the *Encyclopedia of U.S. Foreign Relations* that Volkogonov's statement was a reason "the Hiss case lingers as one of the mysteries of the Cold War" and the "scholarly community remains divided"[41]

Volkogonov's statements were unpersuasive for several reasons. He said that not only had he been unable to find any documents showing that Hiss had been a spy, but he also hadn't found any indicating that Chambers had ever been involved in Soviet espionage either. Lowenthal insists that this proves that Chambers was "a fantasist, a twentieth-century Titus Oates who invented his story of himself as an espionage agent or courier in order to satisfy his penchant for self-dramatization, his craving for self-importance, and his urge to destroy his victims, notably his erstwhile friends."[42] Of course, this makes Chambers' production of real documents, including ones authenticated as being in Hiss's handwriting and typed on the Hiss family typewriter, as well as microfilm of State Department records from Hiss's office inexplicable. It also turns those Russians and Americans who confirmed that they had worked with Chambers in espionage into liars or co-fantasists. Julian Wadleigh, a State Department official, confessed to having been part of Chambers' apparatus and delivering documents to him. A mathematician at the Army's Aberdeen Proving Grounds, Vincent Reno, confessed that he had furnished government documents to Chambers' apparatus. Felix Inslerman stated under oath that he had been sent to the USSR, trained in photography, and sent back to the U.S. where he worked for the GRU, and specifically functioned as a photographer of stolen government documents for Chambers' espionage network. Nadya Ulanovski, a former GRU officer, confirmed that Chambers had been part of the espionage network that she and her husband supervised in the early 1930s. William Crane confirmed contact with Boris Bykov of the GRU and that he had photographed Treasury and State Department documents for Chambers. Lowenthal's thesis leaves unexplained how Chambers knew about the espionage activities of the people he named to Adolf Berle, the assistant secretary of state—information later corroborated by Venona. Typically, Lowenthal ignores all of this and accepts a self-evidently mistaken statement that was actually withdrawn shortly after it was made.

Even if there *were* no records—and keep in mind that in addition to the material Chambers had hidden in 1938, Weinstein and Vassiliev produced records from the KGB archive about Hiss's espionage—that would prove nothing. The *absence* of a record from an archive is not evidence; it is silence. Evidence can support a positive or a negative proposition, but the *absence* of evidence can do neither. Historians have rejected the notion that the absence of archival documents is evidence *for* something. To take the best-known example, the absence of a direct order from Adolf Hitler sanctioning the mass murder of Jews does not prove that he knew nothing about the Holocaust or that he did not order it, an assertion made repeatedly by Holocaust deniers. If there was a Hitler order, it was destroyed or has not yet been found. Or perhaps there never was a written order. In any case, the other evidence that is available on the nature of decision making in Hitler's regime, the decisions that were made on allocation of resources to the death machinery, and the relationship of those who supervised the Holocaust to Hitler all support Hitler's authorship of the Holocaust.

Additionally, the claim that Volkogonov had searched through the massive Soviet-era archives during a year when he had multiple duties with the Yeltsin government was inherently incredible. Volkogonov later admitted that he spent only two days at the enormous KGB archives, hardly enough time to make any sort of statement about what wasn't to be found. Further, he admitted that he had relied on KGB archivists acting under orders of the SVR's chief to pick what files would be examined. He never inspected GRU files, even though Hiss worked for the GRU. When he was pressed about these issues, Volkogonov swiftly backed away from his unequivocal statements. In the Moscow journal *Neazavisimaya Gazeta* in November 1992 he explained:

> This year I received several fax appeals from Alger Hiss and his lawyer asking for help in elucidating whether this person acted as an agent of Soviet special services in the 1930s and 1940s. Of course, I sent them on to the Foreign Intelligence agency. But the requests continued. When I found out that Hiss was 88 years old and that he only wanted to die peacefully without being branded a "spy," I telephoned Ye. M. Primakov [head of the SVR,

former KGB]. He reasonably said that they give out no information about who is or is not a spy. However, he agreed to help determine the truth of the matter. I was able to visit the foreign intelligence archive [KGB] several times. Its employees on Primakov's instructions, said that A. Hiss was not registered in the documents as a recruited agent.

In December in the *New York Times* Volkogonov retreated further:

> "I was not properly understood," he said in a recent interview. "The Ministry of Defense also has an intelligence service [GRU], which is totally different, and many documents have been destroyed. I only looked through what the K.G.B. had. All I said was that I saw no evidence." ...
>
> General Volkogonov said he was "a bit taken aback" by the commotion his letter caused. He acknowledged that his motive in writing the letter [exonerating Hiss] was "primarily humanitarian," to relieve the anguish of a man approaching death.
>
> "Hiss wrote that he was 88 and would like to die peacefully, and he wanted to prove that he was never a paid, contracted spy," General Volkogonov said. "What I saw gives no basis to claim a full clarification. There's no guarantee that it was not destroyed, that it was not in other channels.
>
> "This was only my personal opinion as a historian," he said. "I never met him, and honestly I was a bit taken aback. His attorney, Lowenthal, pushed me hard to say things of which I was not fully convinced."

While Lowenthal expounded at length about Volkogonov's "exoneration" of Hiss, he buried in a footnote the Russian's backtracking and comments about Lowenthal's own pressure tactics on the issue.[43]

The evidence presented at the Hiss trial was sufficient to convince a jury of his guilt. The evidence also was sufficiently convincing that all of his numerous legal appeals spread over decades failed. New evidence that has appeared from American, Russian, Hungarian and Czechoslovak archives overwhelmingly reinforces the guilty verdict. Those scholars who, against an overwhelming case, continue to insist that Alger Hiss was innocent or even claim agnosticism toward his guilt are blinded by ideological bias.

## The Case of Lauchlin Currie

Lauchlin Currie was among the most highly placed Soviet sources in the American government. A relatively anonymous figure, he never received the notoriety of other prominent individuals accused of espionage. Like Alger Hiss and Harry Dexter White, he appeared before the House Committee on Un-American Activities to deny the charges. But unlike Hiss, he was never tried. Unlike White or Laurence Duggan, he did not dramatically die in the midst of an investigation. Instead, he quietly faded away, leaving the United States and settling in Colombia, where he advised the government and set up a business. Although he periodically returned to the United States, he gave up his American citizenship.

Prior to 1995 there was credible but largely indirect evidence that Currie had consciously assisted Soviet intelligence. The most important witness against him, Elizabeth Bentley, had never met him and could only testify to what other Soviet spies had told her of his work. The opening of Russian archives and the release of the decrypted Venona messages, however, produced damning information. That did not dissuade Currie's biographer, a former student and protégé, Professor Roger Sandilands (University of Strathclyde, Great Britain), from rushing to his mentor's defense in numerous scholarly forums.

Born in Canada and trained as an economist at Harvard, Lauchlin Currie joined the White House staff in 1939 as one of a handful of administrative assistants to the president. That same year, Whittaker Chambers identified him to Adolf Berle as a limited participant in his GRU-CPUSA apparatus: Berle's notes read, "Laughlin Currie: Was a 'Fellow Traveler'—helped various Communists—never went the whole way."[44] As with Hiss, there is no indication that Berle's information reached the FBI until 1943 and little attention was given to it until 1946, by which time Currie had left the government.

Franklin Roosevelt sent Currie to China for several months in 1941 and for several weeks in 1942 to discuss foreign economic aid. In 1943 the Board of Economic Warfare, a section of the Lend-Lease administration, and several other war agencies merged to form the Foreign Economic Administration. The White House detailed Currie to the new agency as deputy administrator and de facto acting head for more than a year. Elizabeth Bentley told the FBI in 1945 that she had been a courier for a group of Soviet spies headed by Nathan Gregory Silvermaster, who was assisted by his wife, Helen, and by William Ullmann. The Silvermasters passed material to Bentley from a diverse group of sources, most of whom she rarely saw and some of whom she never met face to face.[45]

Bentley worked with the Silvermaster group from 1941 to 1944. She described Currie as one of the most cautious members of the ring, although she never met him herself and remembered him only providing oral briefings through Silvermaster and George Silverman. Bentley remembered that Currie had provided a warning that American code breakers were on the verge of breaking the Soviet diplomatic code. The only other specifics she recalled about Currie were that he intervened to assist Silvermaster when he came under suspicion by American security agencies and helped various Soviet intelligence contacts get jobs in the government.

Although he had kept his membership secret, Silvermaster, who was born in Russia, had been active in the Communist Party since its founding, when he was a student at the University of Washington. His 1932 dissertation from the University of California at Berkeley was "Lenin's Economic Thought Prior to the October Revolution." After he moved to Washington, D.C., in the 1930s to work as a government economist, he made no secret of his radicalism among his friends and acquaintances.[46]

When the United States entered World War II, Silvermaster got himself assigned to the newly organized Board of

Economic Warfare while nominally remaining on the employment rolls of the Farm Security Administration. The transfer,
however, triggered objections from the security offices of the
Army and the Navy, which regarded him as a hidden Communist and a security risk. Silvermaster vigorously denied any Communist beliefs and appealed to Under Secretary of War Robert
Patterson. He also called upon friends within the government
to support his cause. Currie personally phoned Patterson and
urged a reconsideration of Silvermaster's case. Harry White,
then assistant to the secretary of the treasury, also contacted Patterson and told him that suspicions about Communist leanings
on the part of Silvermaster were baseless. Patterson deferred to
Currie and White and overruled his counterintelligence agencies. But Silvermaster's security problems did not end in 1942.
He was still officially an employee of the Department of Agriculture. Its personnel office and the Civil Service Commission
were not under Patterson's jurisdiction, and they opened an
inquiry into Silvermaster in 1943, calling in the FBI. Lauchlin
Currie assured the FBI that there was no basis for suspecting that
Silvermaster was a Communist.[47] Currie's protection saved Silvermaster and allowed him to continue to direct the largest Soviet
spy network ever identified inside the U.S. government.

The FBI interviewed Currie in 1947 and asked about one
of the few specifics that Bentley had remembered: that he had
brought word to the Silvermaster network via George Silverman
that American code breakers were close to breaking Soviet codes.
Bentley's statement, while vague about timing, suggested that
Currie provided the warning in the spring of 1943, shortly after
the U.S. Signal Intelligence Service launched what became the
Venona project.[48] While denying all espionage, Currie told the
FBI that he might have talked casually about American code
breaking with Silverman because he was a trusted friend, but he
did not specifically remember discussing the matter. In 1948 Currie shifted his stance in testimony to the House Committee on
Un-American Activities and rejected any possibility that he had
ever talked indiscreetly about code breaking.

But Bentley's report was not the only evidence that Currie had learned about the American attack on the Soviet codes and alerted the Soviets. In 1953 the FBI interviewed William Y. Elliott, who had served as an administrator of the War Production Board from 1942 to 1945 and had worked closely with Currie. Elliott said that sometime in 1944 Currie told him that he had learned that the United States had broken the Soviet diplomatic code. Elliott reported that Currie was upset by America's action and claimed to have "tipped off" the Soviets. Currie defended his actions on the ground that they prevented "the sowing of seeds of distrust between allies."[49]

In addition to denying any knowledge of American code breaking in his 1948 congressional testimony, Currie also denied any suspicions that Silvermaster, Silverman, Ullmann and Glasser—all of whom were close friends and associates, secret members of the Communist Party and Soviet spies—had any Communist sympathies. That Currie, a man of political acumen, could have had no suspicion with regard to Silvermaster, whose Communist sympathies were not well hidden, was not believable. He insisted that he had intervened on behalf of Silvermaster at the request of an official whose name he could not remember and that it was "customary procedure" for senior presidential aides to contact officials at Patterson's level about security investigations of even obscure persons such as Silvermaster. In fact, it was highly unusual.

Currie emerged relatively unscathed from the 1948 Congressional hearings as public attention was riveted on Hiss and Chambers. Convinced of Bentley's reliability, the FBI regarded Currie as a spy, but did not seriously consider prosecuting him because it had no evidence other than her testimony, and even that was second-hand. By 1950 Currie had left the United States; he became a Colombian citizen in 1958.

Roger Sandilands offered the first full-length defense of Lauchlin Currie in 1990, before the release of the Venona messages. Opening his hefty biography of Currie, he clearly stated his biases: "My own association with Currie dates from the time he was my teacher and supervisor, in Canada and Scotland, between 1967 and 1970, and when his Colombian wife, Elvira Wiesner de Currie, taught me Spanish. Subsequently I have worked extensively in Latin America, mainly Colombia, including periods as Currie's assistant at the Colombian National Planning Department and the Colombian Savings and Housing Institute which commissioned me to write this biography."[50]

Sandilands argued not only that Currie was innocent of espionage but also that the charges were based on easily discredited evidence. However, the portions of the biography where he discussed the charges demonstrate a lack of basic knowledge of the case and a casual attitude toward evidence. Consider his account of the 1939 Chambers-Berle meeting, the earliest evidence linking Currie to the Washington Communist underground. According to Sandilands, "[Congressman Karl] Mundt revealed that Isaac Donald Levine (Whittaker Chambers' nephew, in whose house Chambers claimed he had hidden the famous documents that were to lead to the conviction of Alger Hiss for perjury) had testified ..." and "Levine had been present at the meeting with Berle and had later made a note of the names from memory. They included that of 'Lockwood Curry.'"[51]

Instead of using primary sources—Berle, Levine and Chambers had all discussed the meeting—Sandilands described the meeting through the recollection of Representative Mundt of the House Committee on Un-American Activities. In particular, Sandilands never referred to Chambers' account of the meeting in *Witness*. Next, he misidentified Levine in minor and major ways. Levine's name was Isaac *Don* Levine, not Donald. Isaac Don Levine was also *not* the nephew of Whittaker Chambers nor related to him in any fashion. Further, Chambers never hid any documents with Isaac Don Levine. Sandilands confused Isaac Don Levine with *Nathan I. Levine*, Chambers' nephew, who had kept the documents. But this is not merely a confusion of two obscure Levines. Historians knowledgeable in American political history of the 1930s–1950s know Isaac Don Levine as a prominent journalist and author as well as editor of *Plain Talk*, a well-known anticommunist journal of opinion.[52]

By suggesting that the sole source for Currie's name was Levine's memory and noting that Levine had also misspelled it as "Lockwood Curry," Sandilands implied that Chambers perhaps had not even mentioned Currie. The best documentation about the meeting, however, was the four pages of notes that Berle made at the time and later gave to the FBI. Unlike Levine, Berle did not misspell Currie's name. Nor was Sandilands unaware of the Berle material. One of his cited sources is Allen Weinstein's *Perjury*, which not only quoted Berle's notation about Currie but also discussed the differences between his notes and Levine's—on the very same page cited by Sandilands. Weinstein also correctly and clearly differentiates between the two Levines.

Prior to the release of the Venona decryptions, the strongest evidence of Currie's work as a Soviet spy was the testimony of Chambers and Bentley. Currie's own explanations for his actions rang hollow, but there were no documents implicating him. Sandilands' biography essentially dealt with the matter by declaring it all a McCarthyite nightmare, painting Chambers and Bentley as unreliable, and pointing to the absence of corroborating evidence. But the decoded Venona messages, released in 1995, not only confirmed Bentley's overall story, they also corroborated her account of Lauchlin Currie's role.

Nine deciphered Venona messages discuss Currie, who had the cover name "Page." An August 1943 New York KGB cable reports to Moscow that Currie gave Silverman a memorandum on an unspecified political subject that was either from or for the State Department. More significantly, in June 1944 the New York KGB reports that Currie provided information on President Roosevelt's reasons for keeping Charles de Gaulle at arm's length. Currie also told the Soviets that, contrary to his publicly stated position, Roosevelt was willing to accept Stalin's demand that the USSR keep the half of Poland that it had received under the Nazi-Soviet Pact of 1939 and that FDR would put pressure on the Polish government-in-exile to make concessions to the Soviets.[53]

The Venona cables also confirm Bentley's statement that the Soviet Union sought direct contact with Currie. They suggest, however, that she was mistaken when she said that Currie did not turn over documents or that it occurred after she had severed her relationship with the group in 1944. In a March 1945 message the Moscow KGB headquarters notes, "Page [Currie] trusts Robert [Silvermaster], informs him not only orally, but also by handing over documents."[54] The author, General Fitin, head of KGB foreign intelligence, told his New York station that, nonetheless, he wanted more out of Currie, stating:

> Up to now Page's [Currie's] relations with Robert [Silvermaster] were expressed, from our point of view, only in common feelings and personal sympathies. [Unrecovered code groups] question of more profound relations and an understanding by Page of Robert's role. If Robert does not get Page's transfer to our worker, then he [unrecovered code groups] raising with Page the question of Page's closer complicity with Robert.[55]

This March 1945 message was the last one concerning Currie that the National Security Agency deciphered, so we do not know the New York KGB's response. There is other evidence, however, that Moscow's instruction to establish direct contact between Currie and the KGB, bypassing Silverman and Silvermaster, was carried out. FBI surveillance of Bentley's KGB supervisor, Anatoly Gromov, who worked under diplomatic cover in Washington, followed him to several meetings with Currie. Questioned in 1947, Currie told the FBI that he had met Gromov at least four times. He described the meetings as innocent discussions of cultural matters and denied any knowledge that Gromov was a KGB officer.

The KGB documents unearthed by Weinstein and Vassiliev show Currie with the same cover name, Page, as in the Venona decryptions. They confirm that he was initially part of the Silvermaster apparatus and that the KGB wanted him brought into direct contact with their officers. They also make clear that Curried intervened to protect Silvermaster but do not add much to our knowledge of the substance of the information he turned over to the Soviets.

Sandilands responded to this new evidence by committing new errors in a defense of Currie published in 2000 in the journal *History of Political Economy*. Here he condemns use of the Venona decryptions as evidence of espionage but inexplicably retreats from his earlier position and concedes that many of Currie's economist friends were, in fact, Soviet spies: "That Currie was on both professional and social terms with several individuals who certainly were Soviet agents—notably Gregory and Helen Silvermaster, George Silverman, and William Ludwig Ullmann—has never been in question."[56] However, that the Silvermasters, Silverman and Ullmann were Soviet spies, all identified by Elizabeth Bentley, *was* in question for Sandilands in his 1990 biography, in which he scorned Bentley's story as mere "hearsay testimony." But in 2000, suddenly Sandilands agrees that Bentley's statements about Silvermaster and his associates were true—although the same Venona cables that closed the case about them also implicate Currie.

Where he once dismissed Bentley, Sandilands now carefully parses her 108-page typed statement to the FBI in 1945. In it Bentley stated, "To the best of my recollection, Currie did not supply Silverman or the Silvermasters with any documents, but used to inform Silverman orally on various matters."[57] She went on to describe Currie's assistance to the espionage network when its leader, Silvermaster, came under security suspicion, reported his warning about the American attack on Soviet codes, and discussed the dispute between Silvermaster and Akhmerov about whether Currie should be dealt with only via Silvermaster and Silverman or be put in direct touch with a KGB officer. The clear import of the statement is that although Bentley did not deal directly with Currie, she knew of him as a conscious and willing source of the Silvermaster network. She also noted that, unlike the others, Currie, while an ardent admirer of the Soviet Union, was not a CPUSA member, not subject to Communist Party discipline, and thus able to calibrate the extent of his cooperation with Soviet intelligence, occasionally frustrating and annoying the KGB.

Sandilands puts a bizarre spin on Bentley's view of Currie, claiming that she actually meant that she "did not know whether he was a conscious source or only someone who was being used."[58] Bentley, however, never suggested in her FBI statement that Currie was an unknowing dupe. But putting words into her mouth in 1945 enables Sandilands to claim that her 1948 congressional testimony and autobiography, where she made precisely the same charges about Currie, represent an alteration in her story and should not be trusted.

As part of his effort to demonstrate how unbelievable Bentley's congressional testimony was, Sandilands emphasizes that even a member of the House Committee on Un-American Activities, Representative John Rankin of Mississippi, dismissed her second-hand knowledge of Currie as worthless. Rankin told Bentley:

> If you would take the word of any Communist, Silverman or Silvermaster, or both of them, and I believe you named another one, whom you relayed it through, who was also a Communist, if you take that testimony as to what this man Currie, as I said, a Scotchman, has said about the Communists—it just looks to me as if we have gone pretty far afield here to smear this man by remote control, instead of getting someone who heard him or who knew that he had made any statement.[59]

Sandilands used Rankin's remarks in his 1990 defense of Currie, adding only in his more recent article that Rankin was a "far-right member of the House Committee on Un-American Activities."[60] But he still refuses to understand that Rankin's defense of Currie had nothing to do with second-hand testimony and everything to do with Rankin's obsessive hatred of Jews and belief that they were the source of the Communist contagion in American life. In Rankin's eyes, Silverman and Silvermaster, both Jewish, were obviously Communists whose comments to Bentley could not be trusted. Currie's Scottish ancestry insured that when he said he had not been a spy, he was telling the truth.

Sandilands also offers a benign explanation to account for Currie's warning the Soviets that their codes were in danger of compromise. He cannot dismiss Bentley's statement about Currie's warning about the codes because of the independent witness, William Elliott, who remembered Currie discussing the matter with him. Sandilands concocts an imaginary scenario that he calls "more plausible":

> Currie may have mentioned the decision in December 1944 by Secretary of State Edward P. Stettinius, supported by Roosevelt, to order William Donovan of the Office of Strategic Services (OSS) to return some Soviet cryptographic documents that OSS had purchased from émigré Finnish cryptanalysts (Benson and Warner 1996, xviii). Stettinius and Roosevelt did not want to antagonize a distrustful Stalin in his fight against Hitler.

On the basis of this conjured premise Sandilands speculates that in contacting the Soviets, Currie had "acted on authority."[61]

This scenario is "more plausible" only to someone who cannot take the trouble to read the evidence. In late 1944 the OSS had obtained Finnish material about Soviet codes, including a damaged Soviet codebook the Finns had captured in battle. But both Bentley and Elliott independently reported Currie speaking about an *American* attack on the Soviet codes. Nor would it have made much sense for Currie to confide to Elliott that he had privately taken the initiative to inform the Soviets when it had been done by formal presidential authorization after an official State Department request. And why would Currie, when testifying to Congress, have denied speaking about Soviet codes if he had been speaking about the Finnish material, the return of which was not secret? If there was any truth to Sandilands' speculation that Currie had acted on presidential authority, why did Currie not simply say so to the FBI or Congress?

Even more damning to Sandilands' scenario is that his "more plausible explanation" fails because *the dates are wrong*. The State Department initiated the return of the Finnish material in

December 1944. Elliott stated that he thought his conversation with Currie about Soviet codes took place in the spring of 1944 but could have occurred as late as the fall. With some straining, Sandilands might be able to stretch Elliott's timing to assume that Currie told him in December 1944 about the Finnish matter. But Bentley's account wrecks the scenario; she recalled that the issue came up in 1943. And there is conclusive independent evidence that she could not have heard the story in late 1944. The KGB removed Bentley from contact with the Silvermaster apparatus and she had no contact with the group after September of 1944. Her account to the FBI and in congressional testimony *could not* have resulted from hearing a garbled account of the Finnish episode in December 1944.

In addition to his implausible scenario on Currie and code breaking, Sandilands must explain away the incriminating Venona decryptions. At various points in his article in *History of Political Economy* he describes what he has done as "fanciful, but not completely implausible, conjecture" and "a sympathetic reading."[62] What his interpretation lacks is evidence and common sense.

When one decoded Venona message reports the KGB receiving sensitive information from Currie on FDR's private attitudes on French and Polish diplomatic matters, Sandilands speculates that Currie had been "indiscreet" when speaking with Silvermaster or Silverman.[63] Actually, had Currie provided this information to either of his friends, unaware that they were Soviet agents, the cable would have said so.

Later, however, Sandilands advances a second theory that on President Roosevelt's orders, Currie had briefed Oscar Lange on the president's private foreign policy views. Lange, a pro-Soviet Polish American, traveled to Moscow in 1944 to meet with Stalin and on his return urged the United States to accommodate Soviet policies toward Poland. Starting from the fact that FDR asked Currie to interview Lange to hear what Stalin had told him, Sandilands states, "The possibility cannot be ruled out that Currie was authorized—even told—to reveal to Lange (who had close KGB contacts) Roosevelt's own attitude toward the

Polish border issue." Still later Sandilands converts that "possibility" to a probability.[64] Such fanciful conjectures, however, have no connection to the content of the Venona message, which doesn't mention Lange at all. Additionally, it is farfetched to suggest that FDR instructed Currie to talk to Lange about the Polish diplomacy and, by the way, let him know the president's private thoughts on French diplomacy as well.

Another Venona message reports Currie meeting with Silvermaster, Silverman and Iskhak Akhmerov, the KGB officer who posed as an immigrant clothing dealer. How does Sandilands deal with a meeting between Currie, two friends who were Soviet spies and the KGB's chief illegal officer in the United States? It was innocent, he says, because "it would have been possible for Silvermaster to invite the Curries and the Akhmerovs to dinner."[65] Can one really imagine a professional Soviet intelligence officer operating under a false identity and without diplomatic cover allowing two of his American sources to invite him to dinner with a high American official who was an unknowing dupe of his two spies?

Sandilands has to rewrite not only the Venona messages, but also the KGB documents uncovered by Weinstein and Vassiliev, including a November 1945 order sent by Moscow to its Washington station after Bentley's defection. She had defected in September, but the KGB didn't learn about it until November. It is worth quoting the message to see how Sandilands strains to try to make its reference to Currie benign:

> 1. To cease connection with "Ruble" [Harold Glasser], "Mole" [Charles Kramer], "Izra" [Donald Wheeler], "Raid" [Victor Perlo], "Sid" [Allen Rosenberg], "Tan" [Harry Magdoff], "Page" [Currie], "Gore" [unknown], "Muse" [Helen Tenney], "Hare" [Maurice Halperin], "Adam" [Eva Getsov], "Arena" [unknown] and "X" [Joseph Katz].
> 2. To communicate to "X" [Katz], "Mole" [Kramer], "Ruble" [Glasser], "Raid" [Perlo] and "Adam" [Getsov] under strict secrecy that halting all contact was caused by [Bentley's] betrayal. To warn them that, if American counterintelligence summoned them or took measures against them (interrogation, threats, arrest, etc.)

they should deny their secret connections with [Bentley], stating that her testimony was a lie and provocation by the authorities. As counterintelligence may have arranged some meetings with [Bentley], they shouldn't deny simply being acquainted with her.

3. The aforementioned sources should cease all connections with their subsources; [but] should not inform them about the real reason for halting contact. Mention, instead, intensified counterintelligence activity against Communists and progressive elements in the U.S.

4. Documents from American government institutions [and] other documents and notes which could compromise agents and their subsources should not have been kept at their homes. If they existed, they should be destroyed immediately. Personal meetings should be minimized.[66]

The obvious way to read this document is that in the first paragraph Moscow instructed its officers to cut connections with thirteen sources about whom Bentley knew. In the second paragraph the KGB headquarters provided special instructions for five of the thirteen. Bentley had worked closely with them and Moscow feared they had met with Bentley before her defection had been detected and that the FBI had observed the meetings. Consequently, if questioned, these vulnerable people should not deny having met with Bentley but say only that no espionage was involved.

The obvious and logical reading of the message presents a major problem for Sandilands because it identifies Currie as a Soviet source. He offers an exculpatory variant: "This message appears to differentiate between the Soviets' principal agents or 'sources' (Katz, Kramer, Wheeler, Perlo, and Getsov) and 'subsources' from whom information was obtained. Currie is evidently a 'subsource,' but not evidently a conscious one, and not one of those 'sources' who were to be confided in."[67] Once again, Sandilands makes logical leaps that convert an implausibility to an "evidently." Although he never specifies his grounds, he seems to be arguing that the statement in the third paragraph, "the aforementioned sources should cease all connections with their subsources," means that the people in the second paragraph are all sources, the people in the first paragraph are all subsources, and the subsources are not "conscious."

This tortured reading creates a multitude of problems. The "aforementioned" in the third paragraph, on its face, takes in all those previously mentioned. Everyone in the second paragraph was already named in the first one; how could they be both sources and subsources? If all those in the first paragraph were unconscious subsources, how does Sandilands account for the fact that Maurice Halperin, Helen Tenney, Donald Wheeler and Harry Magdoff had the same exact status as Currie? All of them were conscious, active Soviet sources about whom there is ample evidence.

Sandilands has averted his eyes from genuine documents, evaded the plain meaning of texts and testimony, invented fanciful conjectures, and placed himself in the front ranks of the deniers of Soviet espionage. His efforts earned him praise from Scott Lucas and John Lowenthal.[68] What he has not done, however, is exculpate Lauchlin Currie.

### Harry White

Just as Sandilands, Schrank, Lowenthal, Theoharis and Navasky maneuvered desperately to avoid facing the new evidence confirming the guilt of Julius Rosenberg, Alger Hiss and Lauchlin Currie, so James Boughton (former Indiana University professor and official historian of the International Monetary Fund) has manipulated the truth in an attempt to rescue Harry Dexter White, assistant secretary of the Treasury and the most highly placed government official known to have consciously assisted Soviet espionage. After he joined the Treasury in 1934, his combination of technical competence, policy vision and ability to explain complex issues to policy makers without technical training soon made White one of the department's most influential officials. He became director of monetary research in 1938, assistant to the secretary of the Treasury in 1941, and assistant secretary of the Treasury in 1945. Along with John Maynard Keynes, he was one of the two chief architects of the historic Bretton Woods monetary agreement in 1944 that structured international monetary policy for decades to come. In 1946 President Truman appointed him as the American director of the International Monetary Fund, one of the pillars of the postwar international economic order.

Whittaker Chambers stated that in the mid-1930s White was a source for his GRU-CPUSA network. At that time the Treasury was not involved in issues of much interest to the Soviets, and White was valued more for his talent and potential than for his actual productivity. White was not a CPUSA member but ardently sympathized with the Soviet Union; he cooperated with the Communist underground on his own terms and was not under party discipline. He did, however, provide information both in oral briefings and in written summaries, one of which Chambers hid in 1938 and produced in 1948 along with his material implicating Alger Hiss. The White memorandum consisted of four sheets of letter-sized yellow paper, handwritten in pencil in White's own hand. Three pages were written on two sides and the fourth on only one, with material dated from January 10 to February 15, 1938. There was no single theme but notes and summaries on a wide variety of issues, ranging from Secretary Morgenthau's attitudes on various Treasury issues, his reading habits, and conversations with President Roosevelt on economic policy toward Japan as well as State Department reports about Swiss financing of Japanese economic projects in Manchuria and European tensions, the bomb-proofing of Japanese oil storage sites, and American diplomatic reports of a possible French alliance with the USSR against Germany. As Allen Weinstein has written, "It is difficult to fathom any purpose in the line of official duties for which White could have put together this disparate collection of news in a single memo."[69]

White assisted Soviet espionage by sponsoring or facilitating government employment of a number of Soviet sources. During his tenure in the Treasury Department at least nine Soviet sources also worked there: Frank Coe, Harold Glasser, Ludwig

Ullmann, Sonia Gold, Gregory Silvermaster, George Silverman, Irving Kaplan, William Taylor and Solomon Adler.[70] They assisted each other's careers and protected each other's reputations. For example, one Treasury economist, Harold Glasser, had been an active member of the Washington Communist underground, aiding Soviet intelligence since the mid-1930s. At various times in his Treasury career, fellow Communists Frank Coe and William Ullmann, who reported to Harry Dexter White, determined Glasser's promotions and job ratings. This hidden network also helped him when security officers first ran across evidence of his Communist background. In December 1941 the Secret Service, the Treasury Department's investigative arm, forwarded a report indicating that it had evidence of Glasser's involvement in Communist activities. But because the report went to Harry White, nothing happened, and Glasser was able to continue his espionage.[71]

White also intervened to assist Gregory Silvermaster when he faced security scrutiny in 1942 after transferring from the Department of Agriculture's Farm Security Administration to the Board of Economic Warfare. Neither agency came under the jurisdiction of White's Treasury Department and Silvermaster was an obscure midlevel economist without any outstanding achievements, but White nonetheless contacted Under Secretary of War Robert Patterson and told him that suspicions about Silvermaster's Communist leanings were baseless. With pressure from White and Lauchlin Currie, Patterson overruled military counterintelligence and allowed Silvermaster to take the job at the Board of Economic Warfare.[72] In 1944 Silvermaster's tenure at the Board of Economic Warfare (then merged into the Foreign Economic Administration) ended and he sought to return to the Department of Agriculture. Although no adverse action had been taken against him in two security probes, there was a security cloud about him. White again intervened on behalf of someone with whom he had no official connection. Under Secretary of Agriculture Paul Appleby sent a memo to his subordinates that stated:

The other day when Harry White, of the Treasury Department, was in to see me on other business, he lingered to ask whether or not I could do anything about placing Gregory Silvermaster, who has been in Farm Security Administration for some years.... Silvermaster has been under some attack by the Dies committee, I believe, principally or exclusively because he happens to have been born in Russia and has been engaged most of his life as an economist and more particularly a labor economist. He is a highly intelligent person and is very close both to Harry White and to Lauch Currie. There is no reason to question his loyalty and good citizenship.

Silvermaster organized a Soviet espionage network of extraordinarily large size, and his ability to retain his position in the government and supervise the apparatus he created would not have been possible without the protection provided to him by Lauchlin Currie and Harry White.[73]

After Elizabeth Bentley named him as a member of the Silvermaster network, White appeared before the House Committee on Un-American Activities to rebut Bentley's charges. He acknowledged knowing the people identified as members of the Silvermaster group, denied any suspicion that any of his friends had Communist sympathies, and indignantly denied being a Soviet source. Three days later he died of a heart attack. Those who believed that Bentley and Chambers were liars also believed that the Red Scare killed Harry Dexter White.

In her 1944 letter to President Roosevelt and later statement to the FBI, Katherine Perlo included White among her ex-husband Victor's associates in the Washington Communist underground in the 1930s. Likewise, in her statement to the FBI in late 1945 and later in testimony, Elizabeth Bentley identified White as a highly valued source and protector of the Silvermaster network in the period from 1942 to 1944. Decrypted Venona messages and Weinstein and Vassiliev's KGB material corroborate White's assistance to Soviet intelligence. Weinstein and Vassiliev, for example, quote from a KGB document of the 1940s noting that White had been a GRU source in the mid-1930s, which exactly fits Chambers' story: Chambers' network, of which White was a part, reported to the GRU.

None of this evidence convinces James Boughton, who wrote "The Case against Harry Dexter White: Still Not Proven," published first as a paper by the International Monetary Fund and then in the academic journal *History of Political Economy*.[74] Despite the title, Boughton is anything but agnostic about White's case. He believes not only that there is no credible evidence implicating White in espionage but that he never consciously assisted Communists in any fashion. To make his case, Boughton misuses evidence, confuses facts and ignores inconvenient data.

Consider, for example, Boughton's treatment of those expensive Oriental rugs given to White and three other Soviet sources by Chambers in late 1936. Boughton cannot even set the stage accurately: "Colonel Boris Bykov was in regular contact with Whittaker Chambers, who at the time was an active member of the American Communist Party." Since Chambers had been in the party's underground after 1932 and was working for Soviet intelligence, he was *not* active in the CPUSA: rather, he was a spy. Boughton also misidentifies Bykov as a KGB officer: he worked for the GRU. Nor does Boughton do much better when he gets to the simplest and most uncontroversial details: he has Bykov giving Chambers $600 to purchase the rugs. The sources he cites, however, give a higher figure.[75]

Boughton surmises, "Since, by Chambers's own account, Bykov's only knowledge of White at that time was through Chambers, it is clear that the attempt to give money to White was not in return for services but was aimed at securing future information." This is not "clear" at all. Certainly the rugs were intended in part to promote future help, but Chambers stated that Bykov chiefly wanted to reward the "sources" for their past work. Chambers recollected Bykov telling him: "You will buy four rugs, big, expensive rugs. You will give White, Silverman, Wadleigh and *Der Advokat* [Hiss] each one a rug. You will tell them that it is a gift from the Soviet people *in gratitude for their help.*" (Emphasis added.)[76]

Finally, Boughton claims, "no direct or even circumstantial evidence supports the allegations that White knew that the rug was intended as a bribe from the KGB or that he ever did anything in return for it." He rests this assertion on George Silverman's veracity: "Silverman later testified under oath that Chambers had told him that he had obtained the rugs from a 'connection' in the trade. He in turn gave one of the rugs to the Whites as a personal gift, in thanks for their having let him live rent-free in their home for two months." Boughton here described Silverman as "an economist who had been a friend of White's for many years and who had introduced White to Chambers." If Silverman were a reputable source, his testimony would have weight. But Chambers, Bentley, Katherine Perlo, numerous Venona messages, and Weinstein and Vassiliev's KGB documents all identify Silverman not as a friendly economist but as a Soviet spy. Even Boughton later in his essay admits that he was a spy, stating first that Silverman "may have actively engaged in espionage activities," and later noting, "Silverman was known by both Bentley and Chambers as a Soviet agent, a charge corroborated by several Venona cables." But if Silverman was a secret Communist and a Soviet spy, he had every reason to lie about the rugs to protect White. Boughton advances two incompatible explanations for White's receiving a rug: either Chambers gave the rug to White as an inducement to *future* espionage; or Silverman gave the rug to White out of friendship, and Chambers' only connection was selling the rug to Silverman and there was no inducement of any sort. Both explanations cannot be true at the same time. But Boughton doesn't care which one you believe; his attitude is, if one defense of White won't do, another might.[77]

Boughton's explanation of the 1938 White memorandum is an exercise in obfuscation:

> White drafted several pages of notes on a variety of international issues, some of which involved confidential information and some of which was merely speculative. The notes appear to record his thoughts and impressions from meetings or readings over a period of time, as they do not form a connected narrative or convey

information in any organized manner. Chambers testified that White gave these notes to him in 1938, and that he (Chambers) gave a copy to a Soviet contact and hid the original. Chambers gave the papers to the Justice Department a decade later, in 1948. Whether White or someone else with access to White's office really gave them to Chambers is not known. If White gave them to him, the seemingly random structure and content of the notes make the purpose of the gesture difficult to fathom.[78]

That is all. No examination of the specifics of the notes: nothing, for example, about White summarizing information on the bomb-proofing of Japanese oil storage facilities or French diplomatic attitudes toward an alliance with the USSR, matters far afield from his duties at the time in Treasury's Division of Monetary Research. As to how Chambers got these notes, that is a mystery to Boughton. It is very difficult to construct a credible benign explanation for these notes; so to Boughton, the less said, the better.

If Boughton cannot explain away Chambers' evidence against White, he largely ignores what Elizabeth Bentley said, noting merely that his name happened to be included in "a long list of names" she gave the FBI. But she gave the FBI a great deal more than a list of names. Her November 30, 1945, signed statement of 108 typed pages described in considerable detail her experiences as the contact between the KGB and the Silvermaster network, the Perlo apparatus, and a number of singleton agents. Her allegations were corroborated by the deciphered Venona messages, material in the Comintern archives, Weinstein and Vassiliev's KGB documents, and KGB documents obtained by Jerrold and Leona Schecter.[79]

But it is when he turns to the Venona messages implicating White that Boughton's hidden agenda is brought into the open. The release of the Venona messages settled the issue of White's relationship with Soviet intelligence. He was discussed in fifteen deciphered KGB messages during 1944 and 1945. Several report on the information he had provided to Soviet intelligence officers, including how far the Soviets could push the United States to abandon the anticommunist Polish government-in-exile and assuring the Soviets that despite their public opposition, American policy makers would acquiesce to the USSR's 1939 annexation of Latvia, Estonia and Lithuania. But what others see as espionage merely demonstrates to Boughton that "White was indiscreet in discussing policy issues with the Soviets" during meetings that "were a regular and important part of White's official duties at the U.S. Treasury throughout the wartime period."[80]

For example, in March 1945, the Moscow KGB headquarters sent a message to the New York KGB station. It ordered Iskhak Akhmerov to use his sources, in particular the Silvermaster network to which White belonged, to obtain information about the composition of the American delegation to the founding conference of the United Nations in San Francisco in May 1945, their negotiating tactics, the nations expected to support American positions, and the extent of American coordination with Great Britain.[81] White was in a perfect position to fulfill this Moscow order because he was a senior adviser to the U.S. delegation.

Deciphered Venona messages show that at the San Francisco conference White met with Vladimir Pravdin, a senior KGB officer working as a Soviet TASS correspondent. White advised Pravdin that "Truman and Stettinius want to achieve the success of the conference at any price," and that if Soviet diplomats held firm to their demand that the USSR obtain a veto power over U.N. actions, the U.S. "will agree." He offered other tactical advice on how the Soviets might defeat or water down positions being advanced by his own government. A reasonable reading of this message is that it reports espionage. But Boughton sees no espionage, merely that the deciphered messages show "frank discussions with a Russian journalist (who was actually a KGB agent)."[82]

Several deciphered Venona messages report information from White on sensitive discussions among American government officials about a proposed American loan to the USSR in early 1945. The U.S. State Department opposed discussing the matter with the Soviet Union at the time as ill advised, Roosevelt agreed with the State Department, and the issue was deferred. If the loan proposal had moved to the point of serious negotiations, the Soviets would have been in the enviable position of having covert communications with a leading member of the American negotiating team who was their secret partisan. A betrayal of U.S. confidential information? Not to Boughton. He dismisses White's informing Moscow as routine: "For him [White] to keep his Soviet contacts apprised of the progress of that effort would have been consistent with his usual working habits."[83] In Boughton's telling, this sounds as if White were simply keeping Soviet diplomats informed. The Venona message, however, reports White telling the Soviets about the matter not through diplomatic channels but through Gregory Silvermaster, an American government official who was a secret Communist and head of a Soviet espionage network.

As part of its program of reorganizing the Silvermaster network by removing first Bentley and then Silvermaster himself as intermediaries, the KGB pressed for direct Soviet contact with important sources such as Harry White. The KGB had an elaborate system for recruitment of sensitive sources. In most cases, the final step was a face-to-face meeting between the prospective spy and a KGB officer. Describing this policy, retired KGB officer Aleksandr Feklisov added that on some occasions, when there was a risk of exposure to counterintelligence or some other hazard, a resident KGB field officer was not used for conducting the "signing-on." He wrote, "To avoid such a negative result, should the outcome of an attempt to recruit be in doubt, a special recruiter is generally brought in from overseas to handle the approach. In case of failure, he would be able to leave without compromising the Rezidentura [local station]."[84]

Because of White's prominence and the possibility of political embarrassment should something go wrong, establishing direct contact with him appears to have been treated by the KGB as such a special case. An August 1944 deciphered cable reported on a July meeting between Kolstov, the cover name of an unidentified KGB officer, and Jurist, White's cover name

at the time. Kolstov does not appear to have been a regular officer of the KGB stations in New York or Washington, but a vis-
itor to the United States from Moscow, probably posing as a
diplomat in a Soviet delegation who could meet with a man of
White's standing without attracting security attention. Kolstov's
report reads:

> As regards the technique of further work with us Jurist [White]
> said that his wife was ready for any self-sacrifice; he himself did
> not think about his personal security, but a compromise would
> lead to a political scandal and the discredit of all supporters of
> the new course,* therefore he would have to be very cautious. He
> asked whether he should [unrecovered code groups] his work
> with us. I replied that he should refrain. Jurist has no suitable
> apartment for a permanent meeting place; all his friends are fam-
> ily people.** Meetings could be held at their houses in such a
> way that one meeting devolved on each every 4–5 months. He
> proposes infrequent conversations lasting up to half an hour
> while driving in his automobile.

To any reasonable reader, this passage describes espionage. The
KGB field officer reported that White understood the risks of
his relationship with Soviet intelligence but was committed to
the task. To minimize the risk, White and the KGB considered
two ways to meet covertly, either to use his friends' residences as
safe houses or to report while driving around Washington in a
car. Boughton, however, believes that White's rendezvous with
Kolstov and discussion of safe houses and covert conversations
in moving automobiles were nothing more than a "means of
keeping an ally informed of pertinent developments."[85]

The evidence of the cooperation of Alger Hiss, Julius Rosenberg, Lauchlin Currie and Harry Dexter White with Soviet espionage is not ambiguous: it is convincing and substantial from

---

*The "new course" refers to a policy of American accommodation of Soviet foreign
policy goals.
*"Family people" was KGB jargon for Communists and those close to the Communist
movement. Here it refers to the number of White's close friends, such as the Silvermasters, George Silverman and Frank Coe, who were secret Communists.

multiple sources that corroborate each other. Yet too many revisionist historians disregard the evidence and continue to insist that these people were innocent or at least that their guilt is still unproven. Academic journals have a responsibility to insure that articles meet basic scholarly standards. But when it comes to defending Hiss or the others, too many academic gatekeepers abandon minimal requirements of logic or fidelity to fact, and publish essays that ignore evidence and offer fanciful conjecture as reasoned argument.

# CHAPTER 5

# *From Denial to Justification*

FTER ALL THE EVASIONS, averted eyes, tortured logic, improbable scenarios, denials and falsehoods, the hard evidence of the Venona cables and the Moscow archives continues to bedevil revisionist historians. A few have adopted a traditionalist perspective, and some have sought to engage the new evidence and modify the revisionist interpretation. Far too many, however, either remain in denial or, at this late date, shift to putting forward justifications for American Communists' betrayal of the United States.

The work of Maurice Isserman, one of the most prominent revisionists, shows someone honestly trying to deal with the new evidence. Initially he expected that the revelations from the Russian archives required only limited modification of the revisionist stance. "For my own part," he wrote, "what has always interested me in the history of the C.P.U.S.A. had been the *conflict* between the 'democratic, populist, and revolutionary' beliefs of individual Communists, and its decidedly undemocratic purposes and conduct imposed on the party from abroad." (Emphasis in original.) Reviewing *The Secret World of American Communism* in 1995, Isserman thought it demonstrated only "ad hoc, amateurish and sporadic" participation in Soviet espionage by American Communists and believed that we had confused the party's clandestine efforts to protect itself from government infiltrators with espionage. But as more information appeared, Isserman adjusted his views, and in 1999 he noted that previously there had been "sufficient ambiguities and blank spots in the available evidence to offer a last ditch in which the remaining defenders of Alger Hiss and Julius Rosenberg could take their stand," but "with the publication of . . . [Weinstein and Vassiliev's] *The Haunted Wood* . . . that ditch just disappeared."[1] By this he still didn't mean he was adopting the traditionalist position. Rather, he indicated that:

> The "new" history of American Communism and what might be called the new history of Communist espionage need not be mutually exclusive, let alone antagonistic, historical inquiries. If this reviewer were to rewrite "Which Side Were You On?" today, it would certainly be influenced by the revelations contained in books like "Venona" and "The Haunted Wood." By the same token, some of the concerns and themes raised by the new history of American Communism are not irrelevant to those who seek to decipher the mixture of faith and breach of faith that created a romance of the clandestine among some American Communists during World War II.[2]

Taking his own advice, Isserman wrote an essay entitled "Disloyalty as a Principle: Why Communists Spied." Coming as this did from a historian whose book on American Communists in World War II had virtually nothing on espionage, it represented a genuine and admirable attempt to grapple with the evidence. Isserman noted that the newly opened Russian archives and Venona "provided evidence that confirms the guilt of many of those previously accused of espionage, and have revealed the names of scores of other individuals who were either active participants in Soviet espionage, or at the least compromised by their contacts with Soviet agents in the 1930s and 1940s." He sketched out two different types of Communist loyalties that provided motives for spying, represented respectively by Peggy Dennis and Walter Bernstein. Dennis, a lifelong Communist militant and wife of Gene Dennis (head of the party from 1945 to 1959), was never a spy. But her commitment to the USSR was typical of one kind of Communist, as Isserman wrote: "the Soviet Union was her real homeland, while life in the United States was a kind of unfortunate exile she had to endure until the great day came when American workers overthrew their own oppressors." Isserman illustrated a second type of Communist loyalty with a quotation from screenwriter and party member Walter Bernstein: "I believed in antifascism and international solidarity and brotherhood and the liberation of man, and the Soviet Union stood for all of these. . . . I was in the grip of a new kind of patriotism, one that transcended borders and unified disparate peoples." Isserman was inclined to think that most of those recruited to espionage were motivated by such a "romantic anti-fascism."[3]

Reading people's motives is never easy, and whatever the motive, it does not mitigate or make less reprehensible espionage against the United States. The people of the United States had a right to expect that those entrusted with the nation's secrets were loyal to America and not to some vague internationalist idea that sanctioned passing American secrets to foreign intelligence services. And one cannot but feel a metaphysical lurch at the idea that someone would believe that the "liberation of man" was embodied in Stalinism or take seriously a "romantic anti-fascism" that could swallow the Nazi-Soviet Pact.[4]

Unfortunately, most revisionists, faced with the new evidence, have stopped denying that Soviet espionage took place and have begun justifying or excusing those who engaged in it. Victor Navasky, for instance, continues to deny that Alger Hiss was guilty of spying for the USSR while still managing to suggest that if such spying occurred, it was not a betrayal of the United States:

> There were a lot of exchanges of information among people of good will [Navasky writes], many of whom were Marxists, some of whom were Communists, some of whom were critical of US government policy and most of whom were patriots. Most of these exchanges were innocent and were within the law. Some were innocent but nevertheless were in technical violation of the law. And there undoubtedly were bona fide espionage agents—on both sides.[5]

Navasky's claim that those who cooperated with Soviet intelligence were "patriots" destroys any coherent meaning of the word.

These people sought the replacement of America's constitutional democracy and free market economy with a system based on Communist collectivism and Stalinist political monopoly. Even in the mid-1930s, the heyday of American communism, new members of the CPUSA recited a pledge to "defend the Soviet Union, the land of victorious Socialism" and to bring about "the triumph of Soviet Power in the United States."[6] The problem was that these Communist patriots kept their pledges to the Soviet Union and Soviet Power but broke pledges they made when in U.S. government service to bear true faith and allegiance to the American Constitution.

In addition, Professor Navasky, while nominally maintaining that people like Alger Hiss were not providing information to the Soviet Union, insists that even if they were, what they were doing was not espionage and, besides, the United States was doing the same thing. This ethically incoherent moral equivalence is also practiced by Professor Athan Theoharis:

> Both U.S. and Soviet intelligence operatives paid the sources they recruited, and both also looked for recruits who for ideological reasons were willing to betray their country's secrets—whether they were committed American Communists and Communist sympathizers (for the Soviets) or disaffected Soviet Communists (for the United States).

Along the same line, Professor Bernice Schrank writes, "If the Soviets were spying on the Americans, the Americans were most assuredly spying on the Soviets."[7]

To point out that these remarks are ahistorical is probably not the worst thing that could be said about them. During the 1930s and World War II, the period under question, the United States did not have or even attempt any significant espionage penetration of the USSR.[8] In truth, there was nothing remotely resembling the scores of professional Soviet KGB and GRU officers operating within the United States in the 1930s and early 1940s, supervising hundreds of American sources, couriers, recruiters, safe houses and photographers. Nor was there any

American-oriented equivalent of the American Communist Party operating as a fifth column within the USSR and providing American intelligence with a willing auxiliary arm. Only after the Cold War got under way in the late 1940s did the United States make espionage against the USSR a priority—two decades after the Soviet intelligence assault on the United States had begun. To claim that "both sides" were doing the same thing is simply lame.

Professor Schrank tries to pretend that America's passive interception of cable traffic *across its own borders,* something all nations did in wartime, was an offensive intelligence assault on the Soviet Union. Indeed, Schrank is indignant that others have expressed "no interest in how these intercepts [the Venona messages] came into the possession of the United States government at a time when the Soviet Union was its ally in World War II." The nerve of the Americans to have uncovered Soviet espionage inside the United States! She goes on to hope for more academic research to expose "American efforts at subversion in the former Soviet Union" during the Cold War.[9]

In his most recent book, *Chasing Spies,* Athan Theoharis offers another mitigating factor about Soviet espionage: it was frivolous. He allows, "KGB and Venona records document ... political intelligence operations: reports on the plans and objectives of Democratic and Republican officials; operations directed against Communist political adversaries—Trotskyites, Russian Monarchists, Social Democrats, Russian Orthodox prelates, and anti-Russian Polish Americans." All of this Theoharis dismisses as "silly" and swiftly passes on to other subjects. Professor Theoharis has made a career out of deploring in extravagantly sinister terms FBI monitoring of domestic radicals and others suspected of being engaged in espionage and political subversion. It is also the principal theme of the very book in which he casually brushes aside political intelligence activities of the KGB as not worthy of examination. Theoharis is particularly indignant that during World War II the FBI monitored the activities of German exiles in the United States. But when the Soviet KGB, with the assistance of American Communists, reached into the

United States to track the actions of American Trotskyists and exiled Russians, Poles and Ukrainians, monitored Eastern Orthodox clergy in America for anti-Soviet sermons, infiltrated Zionist and American Jewish organizations, kidnapped Russian seamen who jumped ship in American ports to escape tyranny, infiltrated the American Socialist Workers Party, and with the assistance of American Communists slipped an assassin into Leon Trotsky's residence in Mexico, killed an American who was guarding Trotsky, and aided an unsuccessful attempt to free Trotsky's murderer from prison, Professor Theoharis is not even mildly indignant.[10]

In *Chasing Spies,* Theoharis does agree that some Soviet espionage was aimed at American technological and military secrets. But in another intellectual contortion, he goes on to suggest that the theft of these secrets was *in America's interest:* "The information about U.S. industrial productivity and military strength provided by the Silvermaster group—the numbers being overwhelming—might have deterred Soviet officials from pursuing an aggressive negotiating strategy."[11] The KGB awarded Silvermaster a Soviet medal in 1944 in recognition of his espionage against the United States; in light of Theoharis's analysis, the U.S. should retroactively do the same. But no historian, and certainly not Professor Theoharis, has had access to the Soviet files showing that Stalin was restrained by what his spies told him.

While Navasky, Theoharis, Schrank and others have tried to surround the issue of Communist espionage with a fog of moral equivalence and dismissive ambiguity, Walter and Miriam Schneir, longtime defenders of the Rosenbergs, have reacted to the new evidence with a confused mixture of denial, acceptance and defiance. In *Invitation to an Inquest* (1965) they argued that the FBI had forged the evidence used to convict Julius and Ethel Rosenberg, that the confessions of Harry Gold and David Greenglass were false, and that other prosecution witnesses had committed perjury. Ronald Radosh and Joyce Milton's seminal book demonstrating with extensive documentation that Julius had run a spy ring did not move the Schneirs. In a raucous public debate in New York in October 1983 they vociferously asserted the Rosenbergs' total innocence and denounced Radosh and Milton for becoming part of the government's hoax—to the delight of screaming crowds of leftists who packed the meeting.

As each new item of evidence of the Rosenbergs' guilt emerged from Russia, they stood firm. In 1990, transcripts of a secret taped memoir by Nikita Khrushchev appeared in which the former Soviet leader said that he "heard from both Stalin and Molotov that the Rosenbergs provided very significant help in accelerating the production of our atom bomb." Walter Schneir insisted that the transcript was probably fake: "What can be said with certainty about the Rosenberg tape is that its provenance is shadowy, its authenticity dubious and its content fabricated in the book by patching two diverse passages in the recording—and perhaps by far worse." In 1994 a retired senior KGB officer, Pavel Sudoplatov, who had once supervised Soviet atomic espionage, also confirmed that Julius Rosenberg had been a spy. Again, the Schneirs would have none of it and denounced this claim also as false.[12]*

The Venona messages, however, were too much even for the Schneirs. Twenty-one deciphered KGB cables discuss Julius Rosenberg under the cover name "Antenna" and, later, "Liberal." The first, May 5, 1944, and the second, May 22, 1944, show that the Rosenberg apparatus was already so productive that the KGB station chief in New York sought Moscow's permission to allow Rosenberg to film the stolen documents to reduce the workload on Soviet intelligence officers. After the decoded Venona messages were made public, Alexander Feklisov, the KGB

---

*Scholars today overwhelmingly accept the authenticity of the Khrushchev tapes. In further confirmation is a volume of reminiscences published in 1991 by Vyacheslav Molotov, a veteran Stalin aide who supervised the Soviet atomic bomb program for a period. Molotov spoke of the major contribution of Soviet espionage to the Soviet bomb program and remarked, "The Rosenberg couple ... I think they were connected with our intelligence effort." Feliks Ivanovich Chuev and Vyacheslav Mikhaylovich Molotov, *Molotov Remembers: Inside Kremlin Politics: Conversations with Felix Chuev*, ed. Albert Resis (Chicago: I. R. Dee, 1993), 56. This is a translated and edited edition of *Sto sorok besed s Molotovym: Izdnevnika F. Chuyeva* (Moscow: Terra, 1991).

supervisor of the Rosenberg apparatus, commented that by 1946 the group had delivered more than twenty thousand pages of military technology documents to the USSR, including the design plans and technical drawings for the F-80, America's first operational jet fighter.[13]

A deciphered KGB message of July 26, 1944, allowed the identification of Julius Rosenberg as the man behind the cover name Antenna. In this message the New York KGB reported that Antenna had been to Washington to explore recruitment of a new source. The cable named the candidate for recruitment as Max Elitcher, described him as an old friend of Antenna's and an electrical engineering graduate of CCNY, adding that both Elitcher and his wife were Communists. It noted that she worked for the War Department while he headed a section of the U.S. Bureau of Standards working on a fire control system for heavy naval guns, prompting Antenna to explain, "he has access to extremely valuable materials."[14]

When the NSA's cryptanalysts broke this message, neither they nor the FBI knew who Antenna was. But Elitcher's name was in clear text. The FBI confronted Elitcher in 1950 and he broke, admitting he had been a Communist and saying that in 1944 Julius Rosenberg had visited him in Washington and asked him to spy for the Soviet Union. Elitcher said he had declined to make a decision at the time and Rosenberg had repeated the appeal periodically. He also said that his friend Morton Sobell, another engineering colleague, was already a member of Rosenberg's network.

In the face of the Venona documents, the Schneirs finally threw in the towel, at least part way. They admitted, "no reasonable person who examines all the relevant documents can doubt, for example, that in World War II Washington some employees of government agencies were passing information that went to the Russians, that the American Communist Party provided recruits for Soviet intelligence work or that VENONA yielded clues that put investigators on the trail of Klaus Fuchs, Harry Gold, David Greenglass, Julius Rosenberg and others." And they conceded, "What these message show, briefly, is that Julius Rosenberg was the head of a spy ring gathering and passing on non-atomic defense information." They also agreed that the messages "implicate the American Communist Party in recruitment of party members for espionage." Illogically, however, the Schneirs continued to insist that "the messages do not confirm key elements of the atomic spying charges against him. They indicate that Ethel Rosenberg was not a Soviet agent."[15]

Drafted for military duty, Ethel's younger brother, David Greenglass, a skilled machinist by training, had been assigned to Los Alamos and in August began work in a facility that machined models of the high-technology bomb parts being tested by various scientific teams; specifically, he worked on models of the key implosion detonators being developed for the plutonium bomb. Through phone calls and letters David let his wife, Ruth, know something about his work. She, in turn, informed Ethel and her husband, Julius. Although they didn't know the details, both of the Greenglasses were aware that Julius was involved in secret work with concealed Communist engineers. Julius immediately understood the importance of the project on which David was working and reported to the KGB in September 1944 that his brother-in-law was at work on the atomic bomb project.

The Rosenbergs suggested to the Greenglasses that David should put the information to which he was privy to the service of the Soviet Union. David worked under secure conditions at Los Alamos, so the initial approach used guarded language in phone calls and letters. Then David Greenglass got five days of leave, and Ruth prepared to visit him in New Mexico. She testified that she had dinner with the Rosenbergs just before she left, and that Julius and Ethel both pushed her to press David to take part in espionage. According to those who always believed in the Rosenbergs' innocence, a key article of faith was that Ruth's testimony was phony and there had been no such discussion. However, among the Venona cables is a KGB message dated 14 November 1944, devoted entirely to the work of Julius Rosenberg, reporting, among other matters, that Ruth Greenglass had

agreed to assist in "drawing in" David, and that Julius would brief
her before she left for New Mexico.[16] Later cables fill out the
story of David Greenglass's recruitment by Julius Rosenberg.

The Schneirs concede that Greenglass was a spy but somehow balk at calling him an atomic spy. But if what he was doing
at Los Alamos wasn't *atomic* espionage, what was it? The Schneirs
admit that Harry Gold, Alfred Sarant, Joel Barr, William Perl and
others were spies in Julius's network—the network that for
decades they insisted was a fantasy. In their grudging efforts to
accommodate the new evidence, nowhere do they deal with their
earlier flat assertions that Greenglass was a liar, Gold a fantasist,
the Khrushchev tapes a forgery, and Radosh and Milton accom-
plices to a government hoax. In this they resemble other revisionists who have come to acknowledge Soviet espionage, Soviet
subsidies to the CPUSA, or other unpleasant aspects of Communist history that they once denied. There is no self-examination,
reflection and admission of error among most revisionist historians about what in their historical interpretative framework led
them to such horribly wrong conclusions on these matters. The
truth they prefer not to confront is that too many of them
regarded these historical questions as matters of ideology, not
matters of fact. Even when it turns out that they got the facts
wrong, they are still convinced that they got the ideology right,
which makes for the unresolved intellectual muddle in which
they find themselves.

Not only do they not reflect on why they got the facts wrong,
neither do the Schneirs withdraw their earlier intemperate language or admit that others were right. Instead, they talk of the
new evidence as "sad" and "painful." Far from retracting their
smears of historians who were correct when they were mistaken,
they proclaim "No Regrets. No Apologies" and renew their attacks
with fresh vitriol, denouncing those scholars who see the new evidence from Russian archives as a vindication of anticommunism.[17]

But the Schneirs' new position is nonetheless an acceptance, however partial, of the power of the new evidence and a
recognition that their old positions cannot stand. For moving

that distance, at least, they demonstrate some responsiveness to historical data. Other, more prominent, historians who ought to know better have not yet come even this far.

Professor Eric Foner is a prime example. He made his reputation in nineteenth-century U.S. history but has never hesitated to intervene in historical debates far afield from his specialization when myths of the pro-communist left were challenged. After Radosh and Milton published *The Rosenberg File* (1983) detailing the convincing evidence that Julius Rosenberg had spied for Stalin, Foner leaped forward to condemn the book and the proposition that the Rosenbergs might have participated in espionage. A few years later he again dismissed their book and enthusiastically endorsed the revisionists' benign interpretation of American Communist history. While the release of the Venona documents confirming Julius Rosenberg's espionage prompted longtime defenders of the Rosenbergs such as the Schneirs to acknowledge his guilt, albeit reluctantly, Eric Foner has stood fast.[18]

Professor Gerda Lerner also established her scholarly reputation in an area, women's history, far afield from the history of Soviet espionage and the CPUSA. But she too has not hesitated to use her prestige as a senior scholar to proclaim the innocence of the Rosenbergs. In a book published in 2002, without providing any documentary analysis, she announced that the new evidence regarding the Rosenbergs was "conflicting," and said, "I am still convinced of the Rosenbergs' innocence—Ethel's, because there was not a shred of evidence against her except the self-serving recollections of the Greenglasses. I believe in Julius's innocence because, if he has been a spy, he would have recanted and named names. There is no single case history in the cold war when actual spies, once confronted with evidence against them and faced with the prospect of decades in jail, did not admit their guilt."[19]

Nothing in Lerner's statement is accurate. First, "not a shred of evidence" regarding Ethel, aside from the Greenglasses' testimony? A deciphered September 1944 cable from the New York KGB to Moscow stated:

Liberal [Julius Rosenberg] recommended the wife of his wife's brother, Ruth Greenglass, with a safe flat in view. She is 21 years old, a Townswoman [U.S. citizen], Gymnast [Young Communist]. Liberal and wife [Ethel Rosenberg] recommend her as an intelligent and clever girl.... Ruth learned that her husband was called up by the army but he was not sent to the front. He is a mechanical engineer and is now working at the Enormous [atomic bomb project] plant in Santa Fe, New Mexico.[20]

In this message the New York KGB station credited *Ethel* for recommending to the KGB the reliability of her sister-in-law for espionage work. Another decoded New York KGB cable, from November 1944, stated:

Information on Liberal's [Julius Rosenberg's] wife. Surname that of her husband, first name Ethel, 29 years old. Married five years. Finished secondary school. A Fellowcountryman [CPUSA member] since 1938. Sufficiently well developed politically. Knows about her husband's work and the role of Meter [Joel Barr] and Nil [unidentified agent]. In view of delicate health does not work. Is characterized positively and as a devoted person.[21]

At bare minimum, these two messages qualify as a "shred" of evidence. How does Lerner deal with their implication? By ignoring the messages altogether.

Lerner's second point is that there is "No single case history in the cold war when actual spies, once confronted with evidence against them and faced with the prospect of decades in jail, did not admit their guilt." This statement is a complete historical falsehood. A partial list of Communist and East Bloc spies convicted and sentenced to long prison terms, all the while insisting on their innocence, includes Alger Hiss (convicted in the U.S., 1950), Morton Sobell (convicted in the U.S., 1951), William Remington (convicted in the U.S., 1951), Rudolf Abel/Vilyam Fisher (convicted in the U.S., 1955), Mark Zborowski (convicted in the U.S., 1958), Morris Cohen (an American convicted in Great Britain, 1961), Lona Cohen (an American convicted in Great Britain, 1961), Robert Soblen (convicted in the U.S., 1961), Marian Zacharski (convicted in the U.S., 1981), Clyde Conrad (an American convicted in the Federal Republic of Germany, 1990), Kurt Stand (convicted in the U.S., 1998), Theresa Squillacote (convicted in the U.S., 1998) and George Trofimoff (convicted in the U.S., 2001).[22]

Lerner is not the only revisionist scholar to demonstrate ignorance of the subject with sweeping and inaccurate declarations about those convicted of espionage-related crimes. In her analysis of the Rosenberg case, Bernice Schrank makes the astonishing statement, "With the exception of the Rosenbergs and Sobell there were no other Americans convicted of espionage (or conspiracy to commit espionage) in the 1950s." But those convicted in the 1950s of espionage (or perjury as a substitute for an espionage charge) include Alger Hiss, Harry Gold, David Greenglass, William Remington, Mark Zborowski, Jack Soble and Myra Soble.[23]

The new evidence has also caused dissension in the ranks. Berating her fellow revisionists in a historical journal, Professor Schrank accuses the Schneirs of "premature capitulation" and a "failure of nerve, inexplicable except in terms of the right-wing drift of American politics, which encourages even sophisticated critics of American domestic policy to read indeterminate texts of unverified provenance as proof positive of extensive Cold War Communist subversion." Schrank regards the Schneirs' retreat as "inexplicable" because, using the techniques of textual deconstruction, she claims it is possible to depict the Venona documents as benign. Pretending that "the guilt of Julius now hinges on nineteen Venona messages," and reading them in isolation, Schrank then uses her imagination to devise possible benign readings for each. She disparages reading Venona cables in the light of other evidence as playing "connect the dots." But connecting the dots is exactly what historians do. Documents are not read in isolation but in context and in light of other documents and evidence to find an explanation that makes the most sense out of the totality of the evidence. The guilt of Julius Rosenberg does not hinge on nineteen Venona messages but on the entire body of evidence, of which the Venona messages are an important part, but only a part.[24]

Professor Schrank is still in denial about Soviet espionage in America. Looking toward a happier tomorrow when the bothersome evidence will vanish, she asserts that the "revisionist approach" is only "temporarily muted by an increasingly noisy right-wing counter-revisionism."[25]

### Nuanced Positions

Like the Schneirs dealing with the Rosenbergs, Ellen Schrecker has taken a half-step, conceding, "it is clear that some kind of espionage took place during the 1930s and 1940s" and "as the evidence accumulates, it does seem as if many of the alleged spies had, indeed, helped the Russians."[26] But then Schrecker wonders aloud:

> Were these activities so awful? Was the espionage, which unquestionably occurred, such a serious threat to the nation's security that it required the development of a politically repressive internal security system? It may be useful to take a more nuanced position and go beyond the question of guilt or innocence to ascertain not only how dangerous the transmission of unauthorized information was, but also why it occurred. Because espionage is an issue that carries such heavy emotional freight, it is usually treated in a monolithic way that overlooks distinctions between different types of spying and different types of spies.[27]

Schrecker then praises the motives of Communist spies:

> The men and women who gave information to Moscow in the 1930s and 1940s did so for political, not pecuniary reasons. They were already committed to Communism and they viewed what they were doing as their contribution to the cause ... [and] it is important to realize that as Communists these people did not subscribe to traditional forms of patriotism; they were internationalists whose political allegiances transcended national boundaries. They thought they were "building ... a better world for the masses," not betraying their country.[28]

Schrecker does not seem to consider that her rationale for Communist sedition justifies the suspicion with which security officials regarded Communists who worked in sensitive positions. No one who wanted to protect American secrets would trust someone whose "political allegiances transcended national boundaries," who "did not subscribe to traditional forms of patriotism," or who regarded giving secrets to the USSR as "not betraying their country" but as "building ... a better world for the masses." Yet Schrecker regards these motives as exculpatory: if there were Communists who spied for Stalin, they at least spied for what they thought was a good cause. On the other hand, she regards any attempt to stop Communist espionage as part and parcel of vile McCarthyism. For example, although Schrecker agrees that Julius Rosenberg was engaged in espionage, she labels his firing from a defense plant on security grounds an example of "inquisitorial" tactics by American authorities. When describing Alger Hiss, the Rosenbergs and others who spied for the Soviet Union and lied about it under oath, her tone is never critical, often admiring and always respectful. Toward those who ceased spying and assisted the United States, however, her attitude is entirely different. Despite having admitted that the charges regarding Soviet espionage made by Elizabeth Bentley in 1945 have been largely confirmed by the new evidence, Schrecker describes Bentley as "not a reliable informant," "unstable, and alcoholic," and "slightly hysterical."[29] She is equally contemptuous of Whittaker Chambers. Soviet spies who lied are admirable; defectors who told the truth are reprehensible.

Historian Bruce Craig also believes that those who spied for Stalin did so for good reasons: "For many, it was a desire to humanize the American social system that first attracted them. Others sought merely to work for world peace, and still others sought to assist the Soviet Union in, what was perceived during the 1930s, as that nation's lonely effort to fight fascism." Like Schrecker, Craig finds their motives exculpatory. In his study of the Harry Dexter White case, he comments: "How American Communist party members and fellow travelers managed to reconcile their soaring idealism with the monstrous evil of Stalin's totalitarian regime is a topic ripe for further study."[30] But this topic is not ripe; it is overripe. It has been studied and discussed for decades and is central to the matter of how to evaluate American Communists and those who spied for Stalin. The dirty little secret of much revisionist writing about Soviet spying is that many of its proponents applaud, albeit sometimes in camouflaged language, the assistance that American Communists gave to Stalin. In their view the "evil empire" was the USA, not the USSR, and any means were—and are—justified in bringing America to heel.

Professor Michael E. Parrish is not quite so bold. But he argues that those who spied for Stalin helped achieve world peace by restraining a dangerous America:

> Ted Hall believes his espionage that helped to break the atomic monopoly, was "in the best interests of the Americans, even if it meant breaking American law." Who is to say that Hall's decision and those of Fuchs, Morris Cohen, Rosenberg, and the others who gave atomic secrets to the Soviets did not contribute significantly to what John Lewis Gaddis has called "the long peace" that followed World War II? Would the United States have been as prudent in times of crisis in the absence of Soviet nuclear weapons? The world has not been a kinder and gentler place since the collapse of the Soviet Union and the dismantling of its sphere of influence in Eastern Europe.[31]

The post–Cold War world may be neither kind nor gentle, but it is hard to share Parrish's nostalgia for forty years during which NATO and Warsaw Pact armies, both wielding conventional arms with firepower several times that of the armies that reduced Europe to ruin in World War II, faced each other along the inter-German border with thousands of ready-to-launch nuclear weapons that threatened a civilization-destroying nuclear war. For decades, millions of men were trained for World War III and many trillions of dollars were spent on weaponry that could have gone for other purposes. And although World War III never did break out, despite several close calls, the Cold War was hardly peaceful: several *million* men, women and children died in Korea, Vietnam, Cambodia, Afghanistan and other small hot wars waged by the superpowers directly or through proxies. Parrish wants to return to *that?*[32]

Parrish's implicit support of espionage on the grounds that it restrained American power has been echoed by others who exult that the release of the Venona decryptions finally relieved the far left from having to argue for the innocence of the accused spies. After all, if Alger Hiss or Julius Rosenberg had not spied, they would have capitulated to American hegemony. Doesn't their guilt give them a greater dignity as committed idealists and models for a new generation of far-left activists? Joan Hall, the wife of spy Theodore Hall, cited America's "scheming the whole while to use the atomic bomb as a threat to hold over the heads of the rest of the world" as justification for her husband's "humanitarian act" of handing American atomic secrets to Stalin. Hall's daughter, Ruth, elaborated:

> We've seen the U.S. feeling that it could just trample all over the world because there was no one to stop it. We've seen it using depleted uranium in the Gulf, in Kosovo, whereas before with the Soviet Union it felt that it had to think twice before using what amount to nuclear weapons. Now, with the death of the Soviet Union, there's no powerful state to stand up to them. Cuba tries to stand up, but it's very small, and there are youth with stones in Palestine, there are revolutions in South America, but there's no state. I think that does make a difference.

Presenting her father's espionage as a model, she called for a new generation of scientists "who dare to come forward as he did...."[33]

The New York Historical Society took a slightly different tack in an exhibit it opened in October 2001 entitled "The Rosenbergs Reconsidered: The Death Penalty in the Cold War Era."[34] Admitting that the Rosenbergs were spies, it presented their treachery as a normal and mundane part of political life. Of Julius Rosenberg and his network, the New York Historical Society said: "They imbibed the values of the Communist left that were prevalent in New York City politics at the time and eventually were recruited by the Soviet Union to fight fascism and help the cause of beleaguered workers." But while New York City was, indeed, the center of American communism and the CPUSA played a significant role in the city's politics through its influence in the American Labor Party, it is historically illiterate to credit the Communist left with being "prevalent in New York City politics" or to assert that the KGB used Rosenberg and his colleagues to assist "beleaguered workers" when what the KGB actually did was to conduct a massive espionage assault on the United States.

The exhibit added, "Those concerned with nuclear technology as a looming threat to human civilization felt that some other power should counterbalance America's control of the most devastating weapon known to humanity." Once more, a malevolent and aggressive America has been conjured up to justify service to Joseph Stalin. Further, while Julius Rosenberg did participate in atomic espionage, most of his work for the USSR involved theft of nonatomic military technology, principally radar and advanced military aircraft design. Apparently the United States couldn't be trusted with radar and jet planes either. And, demonstrating that it cannot get even minor historical details correct, the Historical Society erred in claiming that America had a nuclear monopoly. Great Britain had been a partner in the American atomic bomb project; the British could and did build a bomb as soon after the war as possible. But in the minds of revisionist historians, nuclear weapons in the hands of Great Britain would not counterbalance American weapons. The *only* remedy was a Red bomb.

In the academic world, the movement to honor Soviet spies and Stalinist acolytes had long been under way. Bard College, an elite liberal arts school in New York, created the "Alger Hiss Professor of Social Studies" in honor of one of the most highly placed Soviet spies ever to betray the American people. The longtime holder of the Alger Hiss professorship is Joel Kovel, who has fittingly written that the United States is the "enemy of humanity." Kovel dedicated his book *Red Hunting in the Promised Land* not merely to one Soviet spy, Hiss, but also to a second, Harry Magdoff.[35]

Similarly, Columbia University, one of the nation's most prestigious schools, created the "Corliss Lamont Chair of Civil Liberties." Lamont was not a spy, but he was one of America's leading public defenders of Stalinist tyranny. He spent most of his adult life and a good portion of his considerable personal fortune on defending Communist totalitarianism as morally justifiable because in the end it would bring about socialism. There was no Stalinist crime, no matter how gruesome—from the coercive collectivization of the peasantry to Stalin's Great Terror—that Lamont could not find grounds to excuse, explain, justify or minimize. He was equally enthusiastic about Mao's China, Castro's Cuba and Ho Chi Minh's Vietnam. That the name of someone who justified tyranny in all its Communist guises adorns a chair of "civil liberties" shows that important sections of the academic world are without shame.[36]

The University of Washington, meanwhile, created the "Harry Bridges Center for Labor Studies." Harry Bridges made the International Longshoremen's and Warehousemen's Union (ILWU) into a power in the West Coast maritime industry and politics in the mid-1930s and dominated the union until his death in 1990. Given his standing as a major West Coast trade union leader, the impulse to honor Bridges is not surprising, but it ignores what he stood for. In 1950 the CIO expelled the ILWU for its subordination to Communist direction. Bridges, however, always denied being a Communist during testimony under oath in several court appearances. Many scholars had believed Bridges' staunch denials until our research in Moscow produced documentary proof that he had not only been a secret party member but served on the CPUSA national Central Committee under a pseudonym. And the University of Washington center named for him not only promotes the study of labor history but also glorifies the achievements of American Communists. Its "Communism in Washington State—History and Memory Project" makes a few perfunctory bows to objectivity, but the overwhelming bulk of its material constitutes a celebration of Communists in Washington history as well as a condemnation of anyone who dared to criticize communism.[37]

The most sophisticated and detailed effort to justify Soviet espionage is "Treasonable Doubt," Bruce Craig's doctoral dissertation on Harry Dexter White, completed in 1999 and forthcoming as a book. Soon after receiving his Ph.D., Craig became the director of the National Coordinating Committee for the Promotion of History, the governmental affairs arm of the American Historical Association, the Organization of American Historians, the Society for Historians of American Foreign Relations and other scholarly organizations. Like many revisionist historians, Craig proclaims a formal position of moral equivalence between America and the USSR, but actually places most of the blame for the Cold War squarely on the former: "The United States and Soviet Union both share partial responsibility for creating international conflict during the Cold War era. Tensions rose, in particular when President Truman's administration shifted away from the Roosevelt administration's policy of 'accommodation and cooperation' with the Soviets toward a new position of what historian Melvyn Leffler characterizes as 'preponderant power.' "[38]

The first portion of Craig's study presents Harry White as a moral and political paragon while depicting his accusers as liars and psychopaths. But the evidence is too overwhelming, and Craig reluctantly writes:

> Based on the totality of evidence, there remains little doubt that Harry Dexter White was involved in ... "a species of espionage." ... White undoubtedly passed oral information, perhaps written summaries, and possibly even sensitive documents to "the collectors." He knowingly met with NKVD underground contacts in 1944.... Not only does the gist of Chambers' story about White to the FBI and congressional subcommittees stand up under scrutiny, but documentary corroboration also suggests White's complicity in intelligence-gathering activities in 1938 if not earlier.... The [Venona] decrypts also corroborate the general thrust (though not all the relevant details) of Elizabeth Bentley's story relating to Harry Dexter White.[39]

Craig's dissertation displays extensive research in original sources, and he is a far more skilled and sophisticated historian than James Boughton, the White defender discussed earlier. Craig sees that the evidence is too powerful and concedes in the end what an espionage denier like Boughton was reluctant to admit: Harry Dexter White consciously provided information to Soviet intelligence. But Craig then moves to a new defensive line: justification. He insists, "before branding him a 'spy,' as ... others have done, let us first seek to answer several unsettled questions and address other remaining issues before passing final judgment." And, not so surprisingly, Craig is not inclined to regard Communist espionage as spying, stating that the Venona decrypts merely "establish that some 'FELLOWCOUNTRY-MEN'—the codename for members of the American Communist Party—had extensive contacts with the NKVD, and certain Party members were recruited for *what have come to be considered* 'spy' operations." (Emphasis added.)[40]

Craig is also not alone in suggesting that handing American secrets to the KGB should be called something other than spying. Professor Bernice Schrank writes that Julius Rosenberg was "not necessarily [involved] in espionage" but in what she calls "unauthorized technological transfer." Speaking of the atomic espionage of Klaus Fuchs and Theodore Hall, Robert Meeropol (eldest son of the Rosenbergs) refers to it as "sharing information with their Soviet counterparts," which some called "spying" but others regarded as "international cooperation." Along similar lines, Joan Hall insists that her husband, Theodore, "wasn't a spy ... he was a scientist with a conscience who shared knowledge with the Soviets that he felt needed to be shared with them." Victor Navasky of Columbia prefers "exchanges of information among people of good will."[41] (These supposed "exchanges" of information were actually one-way. No one can point to any Soviet scientists who shared Soviet secrets with the United States.)

Craig offers a variety of excuses to absolve White and his associates of espionage. One is to depict the information turned over as insignificant. He says, "In many instances the information secured by them possessed little if any significant intelligence value." Other revisionists have invoked a similar claim. Athan Theoharis, for example, insists that "the majority of the reported information did not compromise U.S. security interests" since it involved "reports on the plans of foreign (non-U.S.) officials, simple political intelligence, and the monitoring of Trotskyites and Russian émigrés." Later he elaborates: "American spies may have aimed to further Soviet interests and betray their own nation, but the effect of their actions compromised neither long-term nor immediate U.S. security interests."[42]

With only a few exceptions, however, American scholars have not seen the actual information furnished to the Soviets by their spies in the United States. The Venona material consisted of telegrams with brief texts in which KGB officers and their superiors in Moscow briefly discussed meetings, recruitment or time-sensitive problems, and summaries of the espionage product being sent to the USSR by diplomatic pouch—but not the actual material passed along. Theoharis and Craig have no idea of exactly what documents White and his fellow spies turned over to the KGB, and it is disingenuous of them to pretend that they do.

The espionage product not yet seen by historians is considerable. The productivity of the CPUSA-based networks is illustrated by KGB records of the numbers of reels of microfilm of U.S. government documents delivered to Moscow by Iskhak Akhmerov's network: 59 in 1942, 211 in 1943, 600 in 1944, and 1,896 in 1945.[43] The Leica cameras favored by Soviet intelligence typically held 36 frames. If each frame recorded one page, Akhmerov's sources, only a fraction of the total number of Soviet spies, provided 2,124 pages of material (reports and documents) in 1942, 7,596 pages in 1943, 21,600 pages in 1944, and 68,256 pages in 1945. We have not read those 90,000+ pages, or the many hundreds of thousands of pages from other KGB and GRU networks in America, and neither has Craig, Theoharis or any other scholar. Consequently Craig's declaration that "the information secured by them possessed little if any significant intelligence value" and Theoharis's confident claim that "the majority of the reported information did not compromise U.S. security interests" are baseless.

Moreover, they are quite likely wrong. Some of the Soviet spies were supplying low-grade information but others were turning over most of the key technical secrets of constructing both a uranium and a plutonium nuclear bomb, with profound consequences for American security. Joel Barr and Alfred Sarant furnished information on advanced military radar, while William Perl provided information on the design of America's first jet aircraft. Julius Rosenberg is credited with stealing a working sample of the proximity fuse, a key American advance for artillery. As for sensitive diplomatic information, the list of subjects of U.S. diplomatic cables stolen by Maurice Halperin alone is impressive.[44]

Another of Craig's exculpatory lines is that in turning over information to the KGB, White was only carrying out Franklin Roosevelt's foreign policy of friendship with the Soviet Union. In this view "President Roosevelt, indeed the American foreign-policy aristocracy, like White, opted to focus their attention on the broader foreign-policy objectives that necessitated Soviet-American friendship and cooperation." Soviet-American friendship is one thing, but surely espionage is another. Not in Craig's argument, however:

> As the end of World War II drew near, White became even more committed to the cause of international monetary reform and Soviet/American partnership. In his mind he could justify transmitting oral information to the NKVD (provided it advanced the 'new course') and, based on the assumption the information he was providing did not harm American interests, he was willing to give his handlers his personal opinions and observations on the future course of American politics.

Peering into White's mind, Craig judges: "He probably believed that by answering questions posed by representatives of the Soviet underground he would be able to provide America's present and future friend with an insider's view of the American bureaucracy and thereby advance the goal of Soviet/American partnership"[45]

In Craig's reading of the history, Harry Truman comes off as the knave who destroyed world peace: "On 12 April 1945, Franklin Roosevelt died and with him the dreams of a Rooseveltian internationalist approach to world peace.... Unlike Franklin Roosevelt, Harry Truman assumed a hard-line approach toward the Soviets early in his presidency. Within weeks of taking office the possibilities of postwar cooperation with Russia had already begun to disintegrate." Truman subverted the idealistic international institutions that FDR and Harry White had created (the World Bank and the IMF) and changed them into agencies that "advanced an economic program that guaranteed economic American dominance in the postwar world." White recognized that the Marshall Plan economic aid which assisted the rebuilding of Western Europe after World War II was actually "an institution that served American hegemonic objectives in Europe," writes Craig.[46]

There was a "Rooseveltian internationalism" embodied in Roosevelt's "Four Freedoms" speech, the Atlantic Charter and the "Declaration of Liberated Europe" that envisioned a postwar Europe rebuilt on the basis of free and independent nations whose governments respected democratic liberties and were freely chosen by their citizens. But to Craig, as to most revisionists, Rooseveltian internationalism came down to a single point: "America could not afford to let anything block the program of wartime cooperation and aid to Russia." With that distortion of Roosevelt's war aims as a premise, Craig treats President Truman's demands that the USSR live up to its wartime promises to allow the peoples of Eastern Europe to choose their own governments freely as a betrayal of FDR's internationalism and justification for White's action. Craig explains that in 1946,

> During his last months in Treasury, White worked to expedite multilateral trading regimes which culminated in a $6 billion loan to Britain, an action that cemented Britain's commitment to the Bretton Woods institutions. To his dismay, though, he was unable to convince his superiors of the necessity to approve a similar loan for the Soviet Union. Already the mood in Congress toward

Soviet Russia had begun to shift, and the atmosphere of "cooperation" that had existed during the war was in rapid decline.
Though White knew, "the international situation has deteriorated
sharply" since FDR's death, nevertheless, he remained confident
that it was still possible "to change the trend of affairs." ...
  Perhaps White rationalized his meeting with NKVD officials
because he believed the Rooseveltian vision of economic cooperation with the great powers was endangered.

Craig further explains, "It was during this era of upheaval and
stress ... that, through secret meetings with Soviet officials, White
took direct action and met with NKVD officials in an effort to
advance closer Soviet and American ties." But Craig also makes
an unexplained passing remark that this period of stress began
"around the time of Bretton Woods (July 1944)." This date, however, was well before Roosevelt's death, well before Truman came
to the presidency, and well before any deterioration in Ameri-
can-Soviet relations. Additionally, Harry White's active cooperation with Soviet espionage, Craig agrees, did not begin in 1946,
or even 1944, but in *1938,* seven years prior to Truman's administration and long before any of the issues of postwar Soviet-
American cooperation were glimmers in anyone's eye. Craig's
suggestion that Truman's initiation of the Cold War drove White
to espionage is not only a misjudgment about the Cold War but
chronologically impossible.[47]
  Having invented a motive for spying that could not exist,
Craig in "Treasonable Doubt" drifts into a starry-eyed daze, writing that White was not merely advancing Soviet-American partnership, but pursuing something far, far greater: "Harry Dexter
White's brand of internationalism was rooted in a deep personal
conviction [of] ... a utopian vision of world peace." White
believed in "collective action of the world community," and "in
the final analysis, White's loyalties transcended any that he may
have felt for his ancestral homeland of mother Russia or for the
country of his birth."[48]
  Craig is so intent on demonstrating that White's assistance
to the KGB was undertaken with a pure heart that he justifies all

that came with it, including lying under oath and traducing those who tell the truth. Indeed, Craig has White lying for peace, for the Democratic Party, for Rooseveltian internationalism and for his friends:

> When Harry White appeared before HUAC to defend his actions and those of other birds of a feather, he knew that telling the truth would do nothing to bolster the cause of world peace. In fact, if someone of his prestige and influence told the whole truth, any remaining chance for peaceful coexistence with the Soviets could evaporate. His confession would have placed the Democrats in a quagmire, as well as jeopardized the very existence of the International Monetary Fund and the World Bank if not the United Nations itself. Though he had little in common with the new Democratic leadership then in power, nevertheless, White maintained a high sense of loyalty to his friends, associates, and Democratic Party co-workers. He would not turn his back on them and become an informer. In defense of the Rooseveltian internationalist agenda and in deference to his friends, when called to testify, he was prepared to and did lie.[49]

Here Craig has White lying to a congressional committee in 1948 to help the Democratic Party, but actually White had already abandoned the Democratic Party and shifted his support to Henry Wallace's Progressive Party, a body secretly dominated by the Communist Party. And he certainly was not loyal to his immediate superior, Treasury Secretary Henry Morgenthau, or Presidents Roosevelt and Truman, who had trusted his integrity and loyalty.

The American people, through the Constitution and under laws enacted by the Congress, invested in Presidents Roosevelt and Truman authority to share or not share the nation's secrets with our allies. They did not invest that authority in Harry White, Theodore Hall, Alger Hiss or Lauchlin Currie. These men never went before American voters to ask for this authority or to account for their actions, but arrogated to themselves the right to give secrets to a foreign power. They betrayed the American people and the Constitution. Moreover, not one of them had the courage to admit what he had done and accept the consequences. Why admire and apologize for them?

## The Question of the Barn Door

WHEN REVISIONIST HISTORIANS were secure in the idea that those accused of espionage were both innocent and admirable figures, they simultaneously advanced the argument that the government's loyalty-security program was a monstrous betrayal of American democratic principles. In fact, the two ideas reinforced each other. If there were no spies, wasn't the ceaseless search for "Reds under the beds" a symptom of paranoia and a nightmarish witch hunt for nonexistent witches?

But once the existence of significant Soviet espionage and its connection with the CPUSA is admitted, the question of whether an aggressive loyalty-security program was justified becomes a pressing problem. Some revisionist historians have abandoned the earlier view that Elizabeth Bentley and Igor Gouzenko were frauds and conceded that there was a great deal of Soviet espionage and that the CPUSA was part of it. How, then, to continue to portray postwar anticommunism as a mistake? Revisionists cite Weinstein and Vassiliev's documents in *The Haunted Wood* to show the severe disruption of Soviet espionage networks in the years after Bentley and Gouzenko defected. These documents suggest, for example, that by 1951 the Washington KGB station was down to a single active source, and in a report to the Soviet leadership, the KGB itself acknowledged "the lack of agents in the State Department, intelligence service, counterintelligence service, and the other most important U.S. government institutions."[50]

Fearing exposure and controversy in the wake of the Bentley and Gouzenko defections, the argument goes, the KGB and the GRU withdrew their experienced offices from the United States and ended the practice of using the CPUSA as an auxiliary espionage arm and recruiting ground for spies. Therefore, by the early 1950s the federal government's scrutiny of the party and its members was unjustified and the entire domestic anticommunist campaign of the late 1940s and early 1950s was an unnecessary assault on basic liberties.

Several revisionists have turned the old revisionist thesis inside out. No longer is it a matter of witch hunting for imaginary witches; now it is a counterproductive closing of the barn door after the horse was stolen. Ellen Schrecker has allowed, "Soviet intelligence recruited about sixty US citizens, most of them Communists," and they "provided Moscow with an abundance of secret political and military information." But, she concludes, "whatever threat to the United States such espionage may have posed, it was gone by the time it became the main justification for the McCarthy-era purges." She then suggests that the greater sin was not betrayal of the United States by American Communists but anticommunists using that betrayal as "a rationalization for the most widespread and the longest-lasting episode of political repression in our nation's history."[51]

Professor Schrecker's arithmetic on the number of Americans who assisted the KGB is off by a considerable number. Her more significant point, moreover, is also far from established. It is quite true that Bentley's and Gouzenko's defections, Chambers' testimony and the ongoing decryption of the Venona cables severely damaged and disrupted Soviet espionage rings in the last half of the 1940s and the early 1950s. While the high thresholds of the American criminal justice system limited prosecutions to only a few spies, scores of others were identified, removed from their government posts and neutralized. Others who functioned as support personnel for Soviet espionage networks (couriers, recruiters, hosts of safe houses, and providers of false identities and sham jobs) were identified, questioned and frightened into inactivity.[52] The developing Cold War and a hot war in Korea reduced both government and public toleration of Communists and Communist sympathizers. In response to political pressures from Republicans and ethnic Democrats, many of whom had familial and religious ties to Eastern European countries under Stalinist tyranny, the Truman administration adopted a more vigorous legal assault on communism, culminating in Smith Act prosecutions of party leaders and a loyalty-security program removing Communists and security risks from government service.

Within the Democratic Party itself a vigorous left-liberal anticommunist movement, centered on Americans for Democratic Action, fought to isolate and delegitimize Communists at the same time as the labor movement ousted Communist-dominated unions. Documents from Russian archives clearly indicate that Soviet espionage rings took a battering from all these shocks.

It is an exaggeration, however, to conclude that all of the Soviets' sources were compromised. Bentley dealt with only a few dozen people. While many other sources were urged to lie low until the furor blew over, we know only bits and pieces about what happened to Soviet espionage in the postwar world. Morris and Lona Cohen, who had worked for the KGB as recruiters and couriers for sources, were "put on ice" in late 1945. Theodore Hall, who had spied for the Soviets at Los Alamos, went inactive after he left the atomic bomb project at the end of 1945 and resumed his physics studies. Similarly, his close friend Saville Sax also appears to have been inactive. But in 1948, the KGB contacted and reactivated Hall, Sax and the Cohens. In this period Hall recruited two new sources inside the American atomic weapons program for the Soviets. Vasili Mitrokhin, a recent KGB defector, has confirmed that the Cohens and Hall were part of a spy network supervised by a Soviet illegal officer, Vilyam Fisher (Rudolf Abel), that included at least three other Americans.[53]

Nor were they all the Soviet spies who remained active even after Bentley's defection. Judith Coplon, a Soviet spy working in a counterintelligence office in the U.S. Justice Department, was in a position to monitor FBI progress in uncovering Soviet espionage. She was never deactivated. When deciphered Venona messages identified her as a Soviet agent, FBI surveillance soon showed that she was in contact with the Soviets, and she was arrested in early 1949 in the act of delivering counterintelligence files to a Soviet intelligence officer who posed as a United Nations diplomat. Coplon's ability to warn the Soviets about the direction of FBI investigations also helps to explain why some suspected spies were able to suspend contact with Soviet controllers when the FBI became interested in them.

During World War II, Alfred Sarant and Joel Barr, who worked on high-tech military radar and electronic systems, were active sources in Julius Rosenberg's network of Communist engineers. After the war, they set up an engineering firm that sought U.S. defense contracts, but the venture failed to prosper. Sarant moved in 1946 to Ithaca, New York, where he worked in the physics laboratories at Cornell University, then engaged in atomic research. Barr worked on secret military radar systems for Sperry Gyroscope Company in late 1946, but lost his job a year later when the Air Force denied him a security clearance. We know that Sarant and Barr were active spies as late as 1945. Were they also active after that time? We don't know, but the ease with which they escaped behind the Iron Curtain in 1950 after the FBI opened inquiries on them suggests they remained in close contact with the KGB. Similarly, William Perl, who supplied the Soviets with sensitive information about aircraft design, continued to engage in secret high-technology research after World War II. When the FBI first realized that Perl might be a spy in 1950, he was under consideration for an appointment to a sensitive scientific post with the Atomic Energy Commission. Had he been put on ice in the wake of the Gouzenko and Bentley defections? The Soviets thought Perl's intelligence highly significant and had financed a husband-and-wife team, Ann and Michael Sidorovich, who were devoted solely to the task of liaison with him. It would seem unlikely that Perl would have been kept in an inactive status unless there was a significant risk of his exposure, and he was too remote from either Bentley or Gouzenko to be threatened.[54]

Some of the agents with whom the Soviets cut contact as a consequence of the defections probably were not revived as sources because after the end of World War II they no longer held positions with access to information of interest. Others, too closely identified with the CPUSA, would have been too hazardous to revive given the government's increasing scrutiny of American Communists as security risks. Some may have been contacted but declined to reenlist because in the new postwar context they feared that spying for the USSR was far more dangerous than it had been earlier; some may even have developed ethical qualms. Although there are no known cases of such reservations, Laurence Duggan committed suicide in 1948 while the KGB was attempting to revive him at the same time the FBI was quizzing him about accusations he had spied for the Soviets in the past. A KGB network run by Jack Soble continued in operation during the late 1940s and into the 1950s, although with limited effectiveness because one of its members, Boris Morros, was secretly cooperating with the FBI. In addition to Morros and Jack Soble, this network included Myra Soble, Robert Soblen, Jacob Albam, Henry and Beatrice Spitz, Jane Foster Zlatowski and George Zlatowski. Alfred Stern and Martha Dodd Stern, Mark Zborowski, Floyd Miller, Lucy Booker, Johanna Beker and Ilya Wolston had all worked with the Soble network during World War II, but the extent of their postwar activities is unclear.

It also appears that when Soviet intelligence rebuilt its espionage networks in the 1950s, it changed key elements of the methods used in earlier years. The CPUSA was largely, although not entirely, abandoned as too risky as a base for recruitment and running of spies. The KGB remained in covert contact with senior officials of the CPUSA and there is evidence that Communist Party officials acted on an ad hoc basis as talent spotters of potential sources and assisted KGB disinformation operations. Even as late as the 1980s the KGB couriered millions of dollars of secret Soviet cash subsidies to the American Communist Party. By and large, however, active Soviet agents and sources were separated from Communist political activity, and recruitment of sources with radical sympathies was often, although not always, avoided if their radicalism was too public and likely to attract counterintelligence suspicion. In the 1930s and early 1940s most Americans who assisted the Soviets were ideologically motivated, but by the 1950s the KGB was forced to rely increasingly on money, cultivation of personal resentments and blackmail to recruit sources.

In 1999 Ellen Schrecker published a new edition of *Many Are the Crimes*. She added a new two-page preface, stating that in light of the new evidence, "If I could revise my text, I would. I would acknowledge more conclusively than I did that American Communists spied for the former Soviet Union." But, she insists, "the defection of several key agents and the normal security procedures of the FBI effectively wiped out the KGB's underground apparatus within the federal government" while "the onset of the Cold War and the decline of American Communism ensured that it would never be reconstituted." Therefore, "the recent disclosures from the archives of the former Soviet Union reinforce the main thesis of this book—that the political repression it describes was unnecessary." She then suggests that those who criticize her interpretation demonstrate "that the political agendas that fueled McCarthyism still resonate today."[55]

What Ellen Schrecker is still unable to understand is that American communism declined *because* of the determined campaign by anticommunists of every political hue. If Bentley and Chambers, among the villains of *Many Are the Crimes,* had not defected and testified, there would have been little concern about Communist infiltration of the government. If President Truman, another object of Schrecker's ire, had not established a government employee loyalty-security program that sought to remove Communists and Communist sympathizers from positions of trust; if the FBI (savagely denounced by Schrecker) and other government authorities had not infiltrated, harassed and prosecuted the CPUSA; if labor unions and liberal political bodies (depicted as liberal McCarthyites in *Many Are the Crimes)* and other civic and private groups had not made Communists unwelcome in their institutions, then the KGB and the GRU would not have changed their methods of operation. They abandoned use of the CPUSA not because they had developed ethical objections to this strategy or because the CPUSA had developed moral objections to it. Soviet intelligence abandoned use of the CPUSA for espionage *because it had become risky.* Had the U.S. government and the American public not adopted anticommunist policies, the KGB, GRU and CPUSA would have happily continued as before.

The popular anticommunist temper of the late 1940s and the government's prosecution of the CPUSA's leadership crippled Soviet intelligence in the early years of the Cold War. KGB officer Vilyam Fisher came to the United States in 1948 to create new sources and agents as well as revive the spy networks that had been "put on ice" in 1946 in the wake of the Bentley and Gouzenko defections. Fisher operated undetected for nearly a decade and was later joined by several assistants. He was exposed only when one of the assistants defected. While he revived some inactive spies and recruited a few new ones, his accomplishments were not impressive compared with those of his predecessors such as Iskhak Akhmerov. After the collapse of the USSR, a KGB officer, Vasili Mitrokhin, defected to the British Secret Intelligence Service with a trove of notes and copied excerpts from KGB archival material, chiefly about KGB operations in Western Europe but some on North American operations as well. After a review of Mitrokhin's KGB archival notes on Fisher's work, the British historian Christopher Andrew commented, "unlike Akhmerov ... he did not have the active and enthusiastic assistance of a well-organized American Communist Party (CPUSA) to act as talent-spotters and assistance. Part of the reason for Fisher's lack of success was the post-war decline and persecution of the CPUSA."[56]

Most of the Communist parties of Western Europe and Canada were not subjected to the civic ostracism and official scrutiny encountered by the CPUSA. As a consequence, Mitrokhin's documents show that the KGB *continued* to make extensive use of the Canadian, French, Italian and other European Communist parties for espionage purposes throughout the Cold War. For example, Mitrokhin's material shows that when foreign Communist leaders were in Moscow in 1971 for the twenty-fourth congress of the Communist Party of the Soviet Union, senior KGB officers met with the leaders of six foreign parties to arrange their assistance in placing a new group of illegal KGB officers in the West.[57] And, unlike the situation in America, the continued existence of influential Communist parties in Western Europe also meant that Marxist ideology remained a major KGB tool for recruiting Soviet spies in Europe during the later decades of the Cold War.

It ought to be clear that in light of what actually happened, the anticommunist policies of the late 1940s did not represent closing the barn door after the horse had bolted. To follow the cliché to its logical end, there were more horses in the barn and if the door had not been closed, more would have gotten out. This is not to say that American internal security policies of the late 1940s and 1950s were always well designed and skillfully executed and continued only as long as needed, or that anticommunist attitudes did not sometimes mask ugly motives or result in injustices. For all its shortcomings, however, the anticommunism of the postwar era was a rational and understandable response to a real danger to American democracy.

CONCLUSION

# Constructing a Myth
# of a Lost Cause

In recent decades, the study of American communism has even seen the advent of the history of what never happened. Revisionist historians have offered up visions of what America would have been had American Communists not been frustrated by the malign influence of anticommunism. Ellen Schrecker wrote, "At a time when most of their fellow citizens were ignorant and uninterested, Communists knew about the world and cared about it. They belonged to an international movement that alerted them to what was going on in places like South Africa and Vietnam and helped them do something about it." Consequently, "we are looking at a lost moment of opportunity, when in the immediate aftermath of World War II the left-labor coalition that McCarthyism destroyed might have offered an alternative to the rigid pursuit of the Cold War and provided the basis for an expanded welfare state." From this premise she launched into a reverie where "we encounter a world of things that did not happen: reforms that were never implemented, unions that were never organized, movements that never started, books that were never published, films that were never produced. And questions that were never asked."[1]

Among the "things that did not happen" was a very different and, in revisionists' eyes, a very much better civil rights movement. The actual civil rights movement that did happen developed in the mid-1950s and was one of the most powerful forces in American life in the latter half of the twentieth century, profoundly changing the nation. In revisionist history, that wasn't good enough. Writing in the *Journal of American History,* Robert Korstad (Duke University) and Nelson Lichtenstein (University of California, Santa Barbara) offered a vision of the "autonomous labor-oriented civil rights movement" *that should have been.* It was a Popular Front fantasy of black and white workers marching side by side behind the banners of the left-led [i.e. Communist] CIO unions to transform not merely American race relations but its economic system as well by implementation of an egalitarian welfare state. But the "window of opportunity" was lost because "the employer offensive of the late 1940s put all labor on the defensive. Conservatives used the Communist issue to attack New Deal and Fair Deal reforms, a strategy that isolated Communist-oriented black leaders and helped destroy what was left of the Popular Front."[2] The essay has some excellent substantive information on several CIO union locals in which Communists were key to the development of short-lived black-white coalitions, but the overall theme is a dream of a movement that did not happen. It is not history, but radical-left wish projection.

Professor George Lipsitz (University of California, San Diego) presented a book-length radicalized version of Korstad and Lichtenstein's revisionist daydream. In *Class and Culture in Cold War America: A Rainbow at Midnight,* America at the end of World War II was on the verge of a left-led social upheaval with a black-white worker coalition supported by small businessmen, clergy and local politicians ready to take on the corporations and transform America. Alas, laments Lipsitz, big business, government and conservative labor union elites started the Cold War, enacted Taft-Hartley, and used anticommunism to suppress the popular revolt that lay just beneath the surface of postwar America.[3]

Revisionists are intent on creating a grand version of a Communist "Lost Cause" myth much like that which governed too much of the historical writing about the American South until the mid-twentieth century. The myth of a genteel, magnolia-scented pastorale in the South was not harmless romanticism. It was part of the ideological rationale that racist white Southerners used to "redeem" the South from Reconstruction and to establish a system of legal racial segregation that consigned black Southerners to a subordinate status. It nursed a sense of historical grievance against the North and gave white Southerners confidence in the ethical rightness of segregation and the unworthiness of Northern criticism. Even many non-Southerners became enamored with the cavalier image of the antebellum South carried into popular culture by the phenomenally popular novel and film *Gone with the Wind*. The Southern Lost Cause helped to maintain segregation until it gave way to legal and social assault during the civil rights campaigns of the 1950s and 1960s.

Nor is the revisionist myth of American communism a harmless phenomenon. True, unlike the slavocracy, American Communists never controlled any American territory. But they were allied with and swore fealty to a powerful regime as murderous as any that has ever existed. Quite aside from the errors that flow from any misunderstanding of the past, there is a political dimension to this issue that cannot be ignored. Just as advocates of the Lost Cause of the Confederacy were using nostalgia to impose and perpetuate a racist status quo, so many revisionists see their teaching and writing as educating a new generation of radicals to the necessity of overthrowing American capitalism. Some of the revisionist fantasies are driven by an extremist politics, such as underlies Professor Robin Kelley's call for "civil war" and "class war," or Professor Alan Wald's self-identification with the "radical cultural workers" whose academic task is a contribution to the "construction of an effective oppositional movement" to the "absolute horrors" of "United States capitalism and imperialism."[4] To ignore or fail to respond to the revisionist distortion of the past endangers not only our ability to understand what has happened but also our ability to respond to what *might* happen.

In his 1928 epic poem *John Brown's Body*, Stephen Vincent Benét tells the story of the American Civil War. *John Brown's Body*

is poetry, not history, but it is poetry by a man who steeped himself in the scholarship of that conflict. Benét used his poem to
deflate the very powerful Lost Cause illusions of the white South.
At points his characters offer up not what was true for the time,
but what the white South had come to insist had been true.

One of the poem's characters, Clay Wingate, represents
the white South's cavalier image. Wingate prepares to join the
Confederate cavalry and ponders why he and the South are going
to war. Was he going to war to preserve slavery? Wingate says
firmly:

> It wasn't slavery,
> That stale red-herring of Yankee knavery.

(One can almost hear an echo in which revisionists denounce
bringing up Stalin as the "stale red-baiting of anticommunist
knavery.") And what did Wingate say he was fighting for?

> Something so dim that it must be holy.
> A voice, a fragrance, a taste of wine,
> A face half-seen in old candleshine.
> . . . . . . . . . . . . . . . . . .
> Something beyond you that you must trust,
> Something so shrouded it must be great.

Wingate's flowery explanation sounds very noble, and much
like revisionists' insistence that Communists were fighting not
for Marxism-Leninism but for noble though vague causes such
as "social justice" and "antifascism." Benét rejects Wingate's self-
deception and tells the white South that the dimly seen object
of Wingate's veneration in reality was "the sick magnolias of a
false romance," a rhetorical camouflaging and forgetting of the
centrality of slavery to the war. Benét also speaks to the Lost
Cause myth of the kind slave master with contented slaves. He
allows that perhaps there were rare individuals who took slavery
and "tamed [it] into mercy, being wise," but even these "could
not starve the tiger from its eyes, / Or make it feed where beasts
of mercy feed." And he concluded by urging white Southerners
to acknowledge slavery's evil and to:

> Bury this destiny unmanifest,
> This system broken underneath the test,
> . . . . . . . . . . . . . . . . . .
> Bury the whip, bury the branding-bars,
> Bury the unjust thing. . . .
> . . . . . . . . . . . . . . . . . .
> And with these things, bury the purple dream
> Of the America we have not been.

One can no more starve Stalin out of the eyes of American communism and make it feed where beasts of freedom feed than the white South could make slavery into a benign institution. And the time has come for historians to bury the crimson dream of a benign American communism that never was and noble spies who never were.

### "Bluntness Is Presently a Therapeutic Necessity"

Far too much academic writing about communism, anticommunism and espionage is marked by dishonesty, evasion, special pleading and moral squalor. Like Holocaust deniers, some historians of American communism have evaded and avoided facing a preeminent evil—in this case the evil of Stalinism. Too many revisionists present a view of history in which the wrong side won the Cold War and in which American Communists and the CPUSA represent the forces of good and right in American history. Most new dissertations written in the field still reflect a benign view of communism, a loathing for anticommunism, and hostility toward America's actions in the Cold War. Many American historians hold America to a moral standard from which they exempt the Soviet Union and practice a crude form of moral equivalence.

Like Holocaust deniers, too many revisionists deny the plain meaning of documents, invent fanciful benign explanations for damning evidence, and ignore witnesses and testimony that is inconvenient. In the face of clear and compelling evidence of Soviet espionage, they see nothing. When the bodies of more than a hundred former American Communists murdered by Stalin's police are discovered in a mass grave in Karelia, they will not look. Confronted with documents and trails of evidence leading where they do not wish to go, they mutter darkly about conspiracies and forgeries and invent incidents for which there is no documentation. Some brazenly offer confident exegeses of documents they admit they have not seen or condemn books they admit they have not read. They confidently propose chronological impossibilities as probabilities and brazenly situate people in places they could not have been at times they could not have been there. It is not entirely clear how to classify such intellectual activity. But it is certainly not history.

Despite all of the new archival evidence of Soviet espionage and American spies, revisionism still dominates the academy and the historical establishment. The leading journals of the historical profession do not print essays that are critical of the CPUSA or cast a favorable light on domestic anticommunism.[5] In these journals there is no debate about American communism and Soviet espionage; revisionism reigns without challenge. Revisionist history continues to be exempt from the standards of scholarly accuracy applied to other fields. Scholarly reference books that contain distortions and lies about Soviet espionage go unchallenged and the conventional wisdom of the academic world continues to accept pro-communist disinformation ploys as authentic. Elementary standards of proof and logic are ignored and political commitment is allowed to trump factual accuracy.

This is an intellectually sick situation. Writing about revisionist accounts of Soviet communism, the historian Martin Malia observes:

> Western revisionism overall developed within what was basically a Soviet, or at least a Marxist, perspective. Putting matters this bluntly, however, was until recently impossible in academic discourse, especially in America. Down through the failure of Gorbachev's perestroika, any allusion to these obvious facts was met with protestation from the revisionists that they were not Marxists but merely positivists whose "social science" ... was a strictly non-political, "value-free" enterprise. Or they might revert to the countercharge of "McCarthyism."[6]

Malia's strictures are just as relevant to the revisionist account of American history as of Soviet communism. American democracy vanquished two dangerous totalitarian foes in the twentieth century. No reputable historian laments the collapse of Nazism or seeks to redeem the historical reputation of its domestic adherents. It would be a tragedy if academic historians rehabilitated American communism through shoddy, error-filled and intellectually compromised scholarship. Malia is right in remarking that "bluntness is presently a therapeutic necessity."[7]

# Appendix

# The Invisible Dead:

## American Communists and Radicals Executed by Soviet Political Police and Buried at Sandarmokh

A list of the names, biographical data, and dates of execution of 141 Finnish Americans executed and buried in a secret KGB mass grave at Sandarmokh in the Karelian Republic of the Russian Federation. Fourteen victims were American citizens by birth. It is unknown how many of the others, who immigrated to the United States early in the twentieth century, were naturalized citizens at the time of their move from the United States to the Soviet Union in the early 1930s.[1]

*Aaltio, Toimi Kallevich*     born 1913, Red Granite, Wisconsin; emigrated from the USA in 1931; driver, Vilga machine station; executed 11 February 1938.

*Bjorklund, Adolf Leanderovich*     born 1878, Finland; emigrated from Wisconsin in 1932; logger; executed 22 April 1938.

*Bjorn, Eino Antonovich*     born 1912, Angora, Minnesota; emigrated from the USA in 1932; driver, mechanic, Vilga machine station; executed 10 February 1938.

*Corgan, Oskar Fredrik Karlovitsh*     born 1887, Sweden; emigrated from the USA in 1934; book shop director; executed 9 January 1938.

*Ekholm, Arvid Oskarovich*     born 1908, Finland; emigrated from Baltimore, Maryland, in 1931; driver; executed 21 January 1938.

*Elo, Johan Gustavovich*     born 1889, Finland; emigrated from Quincy, Massachusetts, in 1931; blacksmith; executed 21 January 1938.

*Erkkilä, Eino Fridrihovich*     born 1908, Finland; emigrated from Detroit, Michigan, in 1932; blacksmith; executed 3 April 1938.

*Ernest, Kalle Oskarovich*     born 1895, Finland; emigrated from Sebeka, Minnesota, in 1931; logger; executed 22 April 1938.

*Eskola, Samuel Ivanovich (Juho)*     born 1882, Finland; emigrated from Massachusetts in 1931; driver; executed 28 December 1937.

*Eskolin, August Einar Augustovich*     born 1894, Finland; emigrated from Brooklyn, New York, in 1931; motor operator; executed 28 April 1938.

*Filpus, Elvira Karlovna*     born 1888, Finland; emigrated from Detroit, Michigan, in 1933; housewife; executed 21 January 1938.

*Filpus, Niilo Ollivich*     born 1880, Finland; emigrated from Detroit, Michigan, in 1933; metal worker at Lososina car depot; executed 21 January 1938.

*Finberg, Väinö Karlovich*     born 1892, Finland; emigrated from Superior, Wisconsin, in 1931; journalist; executed 10 February 1938.

*Fors, Antti Matvejevich (Matti)*     born 1878, Finland; emigrated from the USA in the late 1920s; carpenter; executed 10 February 1938.

*Goldberg, Juho Ivanovich (Juho)*     born 1891, Finland; emigrated from Astoria, Oregon, in 1931; carpenter; executed 8 May 1938.

*Grandel (Ruohisto), Toivo Viktorovich*     born 1898, Finland; emigrated from Detroit, Michigan, in 1933; metal worker; executed 9 January 1938.

*Hakkarainen, August Olavich (Olavi)*     born 1901, Finland; emigrated from the USA in 1932; carpenter; executed 28 December 1937.

*Halonen, Vaino Fridanovich (Fritjof) Oskarovich*     born 1891, Finland; emigrated from the USA in 1924; metal worker, timber floating site in Karelia; executed 9 January 1938.

*Halme, Iivari Iisakovich*    born 1885, Finland; emigrated
from Newberry, Michigan, in 1932; logger; executed 20
January 1938.

*Hannula, Andrew Osvaldovich*    born 1913, Washington
State; emigrated from the USA in 1932; electrician,
Petrozavodsk power plant; executed 28 December 1937.

*Hannula, Nikolai Matvejevich (Matti)*    born 1902, Finland;
emigrated from Angora, Minnesota, in 1931; mechanic at
sawmill; executed 10 February 1938.

*Heikanen, Jaakko Matveevich (Matti)*    born 1895, Finland;
emigrated from the USA in 1932; tractor driver; executed
20 January 1938.

*Heikkila, Artur Matveevich (Matti)*    born 1892, Finland; emigrated from the USA in 1932; metal worker, Kolodozero
logging center; executed 8 May 1938.

*Heikkinen, Vaino Erikovich*    born 1908, Finland; emigrated
from Phelps, Wisconsin, in 1931; logger; executed 21
January 1938.

*Heino, Frank (Frans Luther) Ivanovich (Juho)*    born 1887,
Finland; emigrated from Menagha, Minnesota; paper
mill worker; executed 22 April 1938.

*Helander, Yrjo Niilo Andreevich (Antti)*    born 1899, Finland;
emigrated from the USA in 1932; naturalized American
citizen; construction mechanic; executed 20 January 1938.

*Helin, Evert Stepanovich (Teppo)*    born 1888, Finland; emigrated from Chicago, Illinois, in 1932; carpenter; executed 28 December 1938.

*Heimonen, Edvard Juho Abelevich*    born 1887, Finland; emigrated from the USA in 1931; dock laborer; executed 20
January 1938.

*Hendriksson, Stepan Stepanovich (Aleksanteri Akseli)*    born 1893,
Finland; emigrated from Brooklyn, New York, in 1932;
foreman at printing house; executed 10 February 1938.

*Hendriksson, Juho Matveevich (Matti)*    born 1886, Finland;
emigrated from the USA in 1932; metal worker; executed
10 February 1938.

*Henell, Benjamin Jakovlevich (Jaakko)* born 1905, Finland; emigrated from the USA in 1932; culture worker, Kiestinki house of culture; executed 9 January 1938.

*Herrala, Erkki Antonovich* born 1896, Finland; emigrated from Spencer, New York, in 1932; carpenter, Solomennoye power plant; executed 3 April 1938.

*Hill, (Maki) Helen Oskarovna* born 1917, Minnesota; emigrated from the USA in 1932; logging dispatcher; executed 22 April 1938.

*Hill (Mäki), Oskar Henrikovich* born 1888, Finland; emigrated from Minnesota in 1931; logger; executed 15 May 1938.

*Hill, Otto Matveevich (Matti)* born 1890, Finland; emigrated from the USA in 1933; logger; executed 21 April 1938.

*Hiltunen, Jaakko Ivanovich (Juho)* born 1881, Finland; emigrated from the USA in 1922 to Knosas fishing commune; executed 21 January 1938.

*Honkanen, William Johannesvich* born 1903, St. Petersburg, Russia; emigrated from the USA in 1932; logger and secretary of local Soviet Communist Party unit; executed 9 January 1938.

*Huuki, Karl (Kalle) Karlovich* born 1898, Finland; emigrated from Ohio in 1931; carpenter; executed 28 December 1938.

*Huttunen, David Simovich* born 1884, Finland; emigrated from the USA in 1922; worker, Suontale brick factory; executed 21 April 1938.

*Isaakson, Tuomas Tuomasovich* born 1894, Rock Springs, Wyoming; emigrated from Canada in 1931; mechanic; executed 3 April 1938.

*Jääskeläinen, Juho Davidovich* born 1884, Finland; emigrated from Gardner, Massachusetts, in 1934; logger; executed 8 May 1938.

*Jarvenpaa, Eero Matvejevich (Matti)* born 1905, Finland; emigrated from the USA in 1931; sawmill worker; executed 20 January 1938.

*Jokela, Johan Erikovitsh*    born 1883, Finland; emigrated from the USA in 1931; school carpenter; executed 20 January 1938.

*Jormalainen, Alpo Heikkivich*    born 1910, Finland; emigrated from the USA in 1932; post office driver; executed 20 January 1938.

*Kaartinen, Eino Anttivich*    born 1912, Finland; emigrated from the USA in 1932; logger; executed 21 April 1938.

*Kaartinen, Mathew Alfredovich*    born 1907, Ironwood, Michigan; emigrated from the USA in 1931; mechanic; executed 28 December 1937.

*Kaipainen, Johan Ivanovitsh (Juho)*    born 1887, Finland; emigrated from the USA in 1932; deputy director of construction agency; executed 21 January 1938.

*Kajander, Niilo Davidovich*    born 1901, Finland; emigrated from the USA in 1932; logger; executed 22 April 1938.

*Kallio, Arvid Valentinovich*    born 1888, Finland; emigrated from the USA in 1932; logger; executed 11 February 1938.

*Kallio, Julius Andreevich (Antti)*    born 1891, Finland; emigrated from the USA in 1931; actor, Petrozavodsk national theater; executed 10 February 1938.

*Kangas, Matti Erikovich*    born 1904, Finland; emigrated from the USA in 1931; logger; executed 3 April 1938.

*Karlson, Karl Augustovich*    born 1894, Finland; emigrated from the USA in 1932; turner for Sunastroi; executed 8 May 1938.

*Karlstedt, Viktor Maurivich*    born 1892, Finland; emigrated from the USA in 1931; driver; executed 10 February 1938.

*Kemppainen, Valdemar Ivanovich (Juho)*    born 1883, Finland; emigrated from the USA in 1931; driver; executed 20 January 1938.

*Ketola, Eino Vilhovich*    born 1891, Finland; emigrated from the USA in 1932; carpenter in cooperative for the disabled; executed 10 February 1938.

*Kivistö, Karl Ivanovich (Juho)* born 1896, Finland; emigrated from the USA in 1931; carpenter; executed 6 March 1938.

*Koivu, Onni Aleksandrovich* born 1914, USA; emigrated from the USA in 1931; tractor driver; executed January 20, 1938.

*Koivulehto (Kinnunen), Otto Nikolaevich* born 1894, Finland; emigrated from Aurora, Minnesota, in 1932; sawfitter, Santala tractor station; executed 21 January 1938.

*Koivuluoma, Jaakko Ionovitsh (Johan, Joonas?)* born 1897, Finland; emigrated from Maine in 1931; logger; executed 22 April 1938.

*Korpi, Arvo Ivanovich (Juho)* born 1892, Finland; emigrated from the USA in 1931; driver; executed 20 January 1938.

*Korpi, Jaakko Ionosovich (Joonas)* born 1898, Finland; emigrated from the USA in 1932; logger; executed 3 April 1938.

*Korpi, Oskar Aleksandrovich* born 1891, Finland; emigrated from Quincy, Massachusetts, in 1932; mechanic; executed 20 January 1938.

*Kortes (Lähdeskorpi), Viktor Maurivich* born 1892, Finland; emigrated from Michigan in 1931; driver, construction company; executed 10 February 1938.

*Koskelainen, Aleksandr Ivanovich (Juho)* born 1899, Finland; emigrated from Aberdeen, Washington, in 1928; foreman and mechanic; executed 11 February 1938.

*Koski, Kalle Villevich* born 1888, Finland; emigrated from the USA in 1934; logger; executed 10 February 1938.

*Kuusela, (Kakkonen)Antti Jakovlevich (Jaakko)* born 1893, Finland; emigrated from the USA in 1932; logger, Padozero-Vidany tractor station; executed 6 March 1938.

*Laakso, Toivo Osipovich (Jooseppi)* born 1892, Finland; emigrated from the USA in 1932; factory worker; executed 21 April 1938.

*Laakso, Uuno (Niva Einari) Ionovich (Joonas)* born 1900, Finland; emigrated from Frederick, South Dakota, in

1931; member of the Soviet Communist Party (VKP/b) and taught Communist Party history at party school, Petrozavodsk; executed 11 February 1938.

*Laine, Vilho Enoch Vilgemovitsh*     born 1901, Finland; emigrated from Pennsylvania in 1933; instructor at lumbering site; executed 20 January 1938.

*Laitinen, Martti Alfredovich*     born 1902, Finland; emigrated from the USA in 1931; painter at hospital; executed 9 January 1938.

*Laukkanen, Antti Albinovich*     born 1891, Finland; emigrated from Rock, Michigan, in 1932; carpenter; executed 5 March 1938.

*Lehto, Väinö*     born 1904, Finland; emigrated from Detroit, Michigan, in 1932; electrician at Solomennoye hydropower station; executed 3 April 1938.

*Lehtola, Vaino Andreevich (Antti)*     born 1912, Finland; emigrated from the USA in 1932; logger; executed 28 April 1938.

*Leinonen, Vilho Matveevich (Matti)*     born 1891, Finland; emigrated from the USA in 1932; sawmill worker; executed 11 January 1938.

*Leivo, Hugo Germanovich (Herman)*     born 1888, Finland; emigrated from the USA in 1931; road builder; executed 3 April 1938.

*Levanen, Abel Aleksandrovich*     born 1883, Finland; emigrated from Hancock, Michigan, in 1931; metal worker, Kondopoga paper mill; executed 28 April 1938.

*Lindkvist, Otto Gustavovich*     born 1887, Finland; emigrated from Massachusetts in 1931; worker, Uhtua machine and tractor station; executed 5 March 1938.

*Lumio, Toivo Davidovich*     born 1886, Finland; emigrated from the USA in 1932; painter for Karelstroi; executed 3 April 1938.

*Luoma, Lauri Ludvig Mihailovich (Mikko)*     born 1895, Finland; emigrated from the USA in 1931; foreman for Karelstroi; executed 6 March 1938.

*Maki, Juho Matveevich (Matti)*     born 1879, Finland; emigrated from Pennsylvania in 1932; mechanic, Vilga machine station; executed 11 February 1938.

*Maki, Walter Walterovich*     born 1907, Minnesota; emigrated from the USA in 1931; carpenter; executed 15 May 1938.

*Maki, George (Yrjo) Karpovich*     born 1888, Finland; emigrated from the USA in 1934; logger; executed 22 April 1938.

*Makkonen, Karl Ivanovich (Juho)*     born 1899, Finland; emigrated from the USA in 1932; logger; executed 6 March 1938.

*Mantyla, Toivo Mihailovich (Mikko)*     born 1911, Finland; emigrated from Gardner, Massachusetts, in 1932; tractor driver, electrician; executed 8 May 1938.

*Matson, Eino Walfredovich*     born 1909, Finland; emigrated from Queen Village, Illinois, in 1931; plumber; executed 11 February 1938.

*Matson, Henry (Heikki) Henrikovich*     born 1891, Finland; emigrated from Massachusetts in 1932; metal worker, Central Repair Works; executed 8 May 1938.

*Merilä, Leo (Leonard) Stepanovich (Teppo)*     born 1886, Finland; emigrated from Grand Rapids, Michigan, in 1931; carpenter; executed 20 January 1938.

*Moisio, Jaakko Ioganovich (Johannes)*     born 1877, Finland; emigrated from the USA in 1931; carpenter; executed 6 March 1938.

*Multimäki, Ivan Ivanovich (Johan Juhovich)*     born 1880, Finland; emigrated from Rhode Island in 1932; logger; executed 22 April 1938.

*Myllari, Otto Karlovich*     born 1898, Finland; emigrated from Ohio in 1932; sawfitter; executed 6 March 1938.

*Nahkala Juho Fedorovich (Heikki)*     born 1884, Finland; emigrated from the USA in 1931; metal worker at a paper mill; executed 22 April 1938.

*Nelson (Poukkula), Enoch Jakovlevich (Jaakko)*     born 1897, San Francisco, California; emigrated from the USA in 1921;

member of the Soviet Communist Party (VKP/b); director of industrial enterprise, Uhtua; executed 5 March 1938.[2]

*Niemi, Andrei Ioganovitsh (Antti Johannesovich)* born 1886, Finland; emigrated from New York in 1931; carpenter, city hall, Petrozavodsk; executed 6 March 1938.

*Nikander, Svante Gustavovich, Korila (Karila?)* born 1882, Finland; emigrated from the USA in 1931; logger, Vilga machine station; executed 10 February 1938.

*Niva, Emil Nikodimusovich (Nikodemus)* born 1882, Finland; emigrated from the USA in 1931; carpenter; executed 11 February 1938.

*Oinonen, Eino Ottovich* born 1906, Finland; emigrated from the USA in 1932; tinsmith; executed 10 February 1938.

*Oja, Aleksi Viktorovich* born 1892, Finland; emigrated from Minnesota in 1931; metal worker; executed 3 April 1938.

*Oksanen-Porvali, Anna Mihailovna (Mikko)* born 1897, Finland; emigrated from Gardner, Massachusetts, in 1932; housewife, Petrozavodsk; executed 21 April 1938.

*Olkinuora, Armas Andreevich (Antti)* born 1902, Finland; emigrated from the USA in 1931; mechanic; executed 11 February 1938.

*Paakkonen, Matti Petrovich (Pekka)* born 1898, Finland; emigrated from the USA in 1930; handicraft worker, Kustprommetal cooperative; executed 11 February 1938.

*Paju, Emil Matveevich (Matti)* born 1878, Finland; emigrated from Cleveland, Ohio, in 1931; stove/fireplace mason; executed 10 February 1938.

*Paju, Viktor Emilevich* born 1908, Finland; emigrated from the USA in 1931; worker at ink-making shop; executed 20 January 1938.

*Peltonen, Kaarlo Kaarlovich* born 1886, Finland; emigrated from Astoria, Oregon, in 1930; blacksmith; executed 28 April 1938.

*Pesonen, Feliks Emelianovitsh (Emil)* born 1895, Finland; emigrated from New York in 1931; club manager, Lososina lumbering site; executed 10 February 1938.

*Pietilä, Alfred Ivanovich*  born 1911, Washington State; emigrated from Aberdeen, Washington, in 1923 to "Sower" commune; then driver, Petrozavodsk; executed 6 March 1938.

*Pyykkö, Mihail Matveevich (Mikko Mattivich)*  born 1884, Finland; emigrated from the USA in 1931; carpenter; executed 10 February 1938.

*Rantala, Toivo Isakovich*  born 1904, Finland; emigrated from Oregon in 1932; worker at Onega tractor factory; executed 3 April 1938.

*Rantaniemi, Toivo Ivanovich (Juho)*  born 1906, Finland; emigrated from the USA in 1934; carpenter; executed 3 April 1938.

*Rautio, Antti Uunovich*  born 1909, Finland; emigrated from the USA in 1931; driver, Vilga machine station; executed 11 February 1938.

*Ruuskanen, Uuno Pavlovich (Paavo)*  born 1908, Finland; emigrated from Minnesota in 1931; driver; executed 9 January 1938.

*Saarenpaa, Solomon Mihailovich (Mikko)*  born 1881, Finland; emigrated from Marshfield, Oregon, in 1932; mechanic; executed 9 January 1938.

*Saastamoinen, Robert Robertovich*  born 1888, Finland; emigrated from Ishpeming, Michigan, in 1933; logger; executed 10 January 1938.

*Salmi, Kalle Rihardovich*  born 1897, Finland; emigrated from Chicago, Illinois, in 1931; logger; executed 21 January 1938.

*Salminen, Eino Gustavovich (Kustaa)*  born 1906, Finland; emigrated from the USA in 1931; actor, Uhtua National Theater; executed 22 April 1938.

*Salminen, Eino Karlovitsh*  born 1901, Finland; emigrated from Chicago, Illinois, in 1931; mechanic; executed 20 January 1938.

*Salminen, Richard Nikolaevich*  born 1883, Finland; emigrated from New York in 1930; school janitor; executed 11 February 1938.

*Salo, Simo Jegorovich (Yrjo)*     born 1890 Finland; emigrated from the USA in 1931; foreman for Karelstroi; executed 6 March 1938.

*Salo, Yrjo Petrovich (Pekka)*     born 1898, Finland; emigrated from Ishpeming, Michigan, in 1932; carpenter, Vilga machine station; executed 11 February 1938.

*Salonen, Toivo Gustavovich (Kustaa)*     born 1904, Finland; emigrated from the USA in 1931; set painter at Uhtua National Theater; executed 21 January 1938.

*Saviniemi, Elis Fedorovich (Heikki)*     born 1898, Finland; emigrated from the USA in 1931; logger; executed 8 May 1938.

*Silvan, Rafael Vainovich*     born 1916, New York; emigrated from the USA in 1933; mechanic, car repair shop; executed 5 March 1938.

*Siren (Kari), John Ioganovich (Johan)*     born 1915, Duluth, Minnesota; emigrated from the USA in 1932; paper mill electrician; executed 11 February 1938.

*Solkela, Severi (Seth) Yakovlevich (Jaakko)*     born 1902, Chassel, Michigan; emigrated from the USA in 1930; accordian player, Kiestenga club; executed 9 January 1938.

*Tabell, Isaak Eino Isaakovich*     born 1904, Finland; emigrated from the USA in 1932; borer, Samoilovich mine; executed 21 January 1938.

*Tamminen, Toivo Fritovich (Frithof)*     born 1887, Finland; emigrated from the USA (or Canada, records unclear) in 1931; construction worker; executed 6 March 1938.

*Tenhunen, Matti Petrovich (Pekka)*     born 1883, Finland; emigrated from the USA in 1931; head of the Karelian Council of People's Comissariats Labor Department; publishing house director; executed 28 December 1937.

*Terhonen, Johan Martynovich (Martin)*     born 1903, Finland; emigrated from the USA in 1932; auto mechanic, Lososina transport center; executed 11 February 1938.

*Tolonen, Eino Venjaminovich (Benjamin)*     born 1888, Finland; emigrated from Detroit, Michigan, in 1931; mason; executed 28 April 1938.

*Tuomainen, Aksel Juhovich*     born 1895, Finland; emigrated from the USA in 1932; carpenter; executed 28 December 1937.

*Tuominen, Yrjo (Georg) Viktorovitsh*     born 1896, Finland; emigrated from the USA in 1932; director, railroad tie factory; executed 28 December 1937.

*Tuominen, Väinö Fedorovich (Heikki)*     born 1904, Finland; emigrated from the USA in 1931; driver; executed 10 February 1938.

*Turunen, Toivo Ottovich*     born 1912, Finland; emigrated from the USA in 1931; painter, city health department; Petrozavodsk; executed 20 January 1938.

*Unkuri (Bergman), Iohan Nikolaevich*     born 1891, Finland; emigrated from Cleveland, Ohio, in 1930; mechanic and carpenter; executed 3 April 1938.

*Uutela, Emil Matveevitsh (Matti)*     born 1890, Finland; emigrated from Clinton, Massachusetts, in 1932; blacksmith, Vilga machine station; executed 10 February 1938.

*Vaananen, Kaarlo Ivanovich (Juho)*     born 1905, Finland; emigrated from the USA in 1933; worker, Santala tractor station; executed 3 April 1938.

*Vahakari, Oskar Hannesovich*     born 1900, Finland; emigrated from the USA in 1931; logger, Vilga machine station; executed 28 December 1937.

*Wallen, August Martynovich (Martti)*     born 1878, Finland; emigrated from the USA in 1930; carpenter; executed 10 February 1938.

*Viger, Gabriel Isaakovich*     born 1885, Finland; emigrated from the USA in 1932; blacksmith, Vilga machine station; executed 10 February 1938.

*Viitanen, Yrjo Karlovitch*     born 1899, Finland; emigrated from the USA in 1932; logger, Santala tractor station; executed 6 March 1938.

*Vuori, Jaakko Viktorovich*     born 1912, Barry, Vermont; emigrated from the USA in 1932; tractor driver, Avneporog; executed 9 January 1938.

*Ylitalo, Jaakko Gustavovich (Kustaa)*     born 1898, Finland; emigrated from the USA in 1926 to "Sower" commune, Rostov oblast, from there to Karelia; stove mason, state farm N 2; executed 10 February 1938.

# NOTES

## Introduction

[1] Harvey Klehr, *Communist Cadre: The Social Background of the American Communist Party Elite* (Stanford, Calif.: Hoover Institution Press, 1978); Harvey Klehr, *The Heyday of American Communism: The Depression Decade* (New York: Basic Books, 1984); John Earl Haynes, *Dubious Alliance: The Making of Minnesota's DFL Party* (Minneapolis: University of Minnesota Press, 1984); John Earl Haynes, *Communism and Anti-Communism in the United States: An Annotated Guide to Historical Writings* (New York: Garland, 1987); Harvey Klehr, *Far Left of Center: The American Radical Left Today* (New Brunswick, N.J.: Transaction, 1988); Harvey Klehr and John Earl Haynes, *The American Communist Movement: Storming Heaven Itself* (New York: Twayne, 1992); Harvey Klehr, John Earl Haynes and Fridrikh Igorevich Firsov, *The Secret World of American Communism* (New Haven: Yale University Press, 1995); Harvey Klehr and Ronald Radosh, *The Amerasia Spy Case: Prelude to McCarthyism* (Chapel Hill: University of North Carolina Press, 1996); John Earl Haynes, *Red Scare or Red Menace? American Communism and Anticommunism in the Cold War Era* (Chicago: Ivan R. Dee, 1996); Harvey Klehr, John Earl Haynes and Kyrill M. Anderson, *The Soviet World of American Communism* (New Haven: Yale University Press, 1998); John Earl Haynes and Harvey Klehr, *Venona: Decoding Soviet Espionage in America* (New Haven: Yale University Press, 1999).

[2] Initially the archive was renamed the Russian Center for the Preservation of Documents of Recent History but later gained the title of Russian State Archive of Socio-Political History (RGASPI).

**249**

[3] Earl Latham, *The Communist Controversy in Washington: From the New Deal to McCarthy* (Cambridge, Mass.: Harvard University Press, 1966), 160. Latham himself dissented from this view and found her testimony credible.

[4] Fridrikh Igorevich Firsov, a Russian historian, coauthored *The Secret World of American Communism.*

[5] Kyrill M. Anderson, head of the RGASPI archive, coauthored this volume.

[6] George Will, "Cold Water on the Left's Myths," *Washington Post,* 20 April 1995; Arthur Schlesinger, "Party Circuits," *New Republic,* 29 May 1995: 36, 38–40; Murray Kempton, "Notes from Underground," *New York Review of Books,* 13 July 1995: 29–34.

## Chapter1: Revising History

[1] John Mendelsohn, ed., *The Wannsee Protocol and a 1944 Report on Auschwitz by the Office of Strategic Services,* vol. 11 of *The Holocaust: Selected Documents in Eighteen Volumes,* ed. John Mendelsohn and Donald S. Detwiler (New York: Garland, 1982), 19.

[2] Richard J. Evans, *Lying about Hitler: History, Holocaust, and the David Irving Trial* (New York: Basic Books, 2001).

[3] Werner Cohn, *Partners in Hate: Noam Chomsky and the Holocaust Deniers* (Cambridge, Mass.: Avukah Press, 1995).

[4] A sample of this literature can be found in Donald T. Critchlow and Agnieszka Critchlow, eds., *Enemies of the State: Personal Stories from the Gulag* (Chicago: Ivan R. Dee, 2002).

[5] To name but a few of their leading works: Adam Bruno Ulam, *The Bolsheviks: The Intellectual and Political History of the Triumph of Communism in Russia* (New York: Macmillan, 1965); Adam Bruno Ulam, *Stalin: The Man and His Era* (New York: Viking Press, 1973); Richard Pipes, *The Formation of the Soviet Union: Communism and Nationalism, 1917–1923* (Cambridge, Mass.: Harvard University Press, 1954); Richard Pipes, *The Russian Revolution* (New York: Knopf, 1990); Richard Pipes, *Russia under the Bolshevik Regime* (New York: Knopf, 1993); Martin E. Malia,

*The Soviet Tragedy: A History of Socialism in Russia, 1917–1991* (New York: Free Press, 1994).

[6] Edward E. Ericson, *Solzhenitsyn and the Modern World* (Washington, D.C.: Regnery Gateway, 1993), 5; Jerry F. Hough and Merle Fainsod, *How the Soviet Union Is Governed* (Cambridge, Mass.: Harvard University Press, 1979), 175–77; Sheila Fitzpatrick, *The Russian Revolution* (New York: Oxford University Press, 1982), 157; Robert Thurston, "On Desk-Bound Parochialism, Commonsense Perspectives, and Lousy Evidence: A Reply to Robert Conquest," *Slavic Studies* 45 (Summer 1986): 238–44; J. Arch Getty, *Origins of the Great Purges: The Soviet Communist Party Reconsidered, 1933–1938* (New York: Cambridge University Press, 1985), 8; Alfred J. Rieber and Robert Colby Nelson, *A Study of the USSR and Communism* (New York: Putnam, 1964), 90.

[7] Richard Pipes, *The Unknown Lenin: From the Secret Archive* (New Haven: Yale University Press, 1996); Dmitri Antonovich Volkogonov, *Lenin: A New Biography* (New York: Free Press, 1994); Dmitri Antonovich Volkogonov, *Stalin: Triumph and Tragedy* (New York: Grove Weidenfeld, 1991); Vladimir N. Brovkin, *Russia after Lenin: Politics, Culture and Society, 1921–1929* (London: Routledge, 1998); Anne Applebaum, *Gulag: A History* (New York: Doubleday, 2003); Jonathan Brent and Vladimir Pavlovich Naumov, *Stalin's Last Crime: The Plot against the Jewish Doctors, 1948–1953* (New York: HarperCollins, 2003); Joshua Rubenstein and Vladimir Pavlovich Naumov, *Stalin's Secret Pogrom: The Postwar Inquisition of the Jewish Anti-Fascist Committee* (New Haven: Yale University Press in association with the United States Holocaust Memorial Museum, 2001); Gennadi Kostyrchenko, *Out of the Red Shadow: Anti-Semitism in Stalin's Russia: From the Secret Archives of the Soviet Union* (Amherst, N.Y.: Prometheus Books, 1995); William J. Chase, *Enemies Within the Gates? The Comintern and the Stalinist Repression, 1934–1939* (New Haven: Yale University Press, 2001); F. Firsov, "Dimitrov, the Comintern and Stalinist Repression," in *Stalin's Terror: High Politics and Mass Repression in the Soviet Union,* ed. Barry

McLoughlin and Kevin McDermott (New York: Palgrave Macmillan, 2002); Alexander Dallin and Fridrikh Igorevich Firsov, *Dimitrov and Stalin, 1934–1943: Letters from the Soviet Archives* (New Haven: Yale University Press, 2000); Ronald Radosh, Mary R. Habeck and Grigory Nikolaevich Sevostianov, *Spain Betrayed: The Soviet Union in the Spanish Civil War* (New Haven: Yale University Press, 2001); Gerald Howson, *Arms for Spain: The Untold Story of the Spanish Civil* War (London: J. Murray, 1998). The most prominent of the European books is Stéphane Courtois and Rémi Kauffer, eds., *Le Livre noir du communisme: Crimes, terreur et répression* (Paris: R. Laffont, 1997), which appeared in English as Stéphane Courtois et al., *The Black Book of Communism: Crimes, Terror, Repression,* ed. and trans. Mark Kramer, ed. Jonathan Murphy (Cambridge, Mass.: Harvard University Press, 1999).

[8] For Yakovlev's summary of the tens of millions killed by Soviet communism, see A. N. IAkovlev [Alexander N. Yakovlev], *A Century of Violence in Soviet Russia,* trans. Anthony Austin (New Haven: Yale University Press, 2002).

[9] There are dozens of books on Katyn going back to the 1950s. Among the more comprehensive works are: J. K. Zawodny, *Death in the Forest: The Story of the Katyn Forest Massacre* ([Notre Dame, Ind.]: University of Notre Dame Press, 1962); Allen Paul, *Katyn: The Untold Story of Stalin's Polish Massacre* (New York: C. Scribner's Sons, 1991); Benjamin B. Fischer, "The Katyn Controversy: Stalin's Killing Field," *Studies in Intelligence,* Winter/Spring 1999, http://www.odci.gov/csi/studies/winter99–00/art6.html; U.S. House Select Committee on the Katyn Forest Massacre, *The Katyn Forest Massacre* (Washington, D.C.: U.S. Govt. Print. Off., 1952).

[10] Peter M. Irons, "The Test Is Poland: Polish Americans and the Origins of the Cold War," *Polish-American Studies* 30, no. 2 (August 1973): 20.

[11] Gabriel Kolko, *The Politics of War: The World and United States Foreign Policy, 1943–1945* (New York: Random House, 1968),

105–6. Kolko's views on Katyn are discussed in Jamie Glazov, "The Lies of Katyn," *Frontpage Magazine,* 8 August 2000, http://www.frontpagemag.com/.

[12] Nicholas Bethell, "Soviet Agent Reveals Terrible Truth of Polish Massacre," *Observer* (Great Britain), 6 October 1991, 1, 23. Russian accounts of the Katyn murders using Soviet-era archival sources include: N. S. Lebedeva, *Katyn prestuplenie protiv chelovechestva* (Moskva: Izdatel skaia gruppa "Progress" "Kultura," 1994); R. G. Pikhoia and Aleksander Gieysztor, eds., *Katyn plenniki neob iavlennoi voiny* (Moskva: Mezhdunarodnyi Fond "Demokratiia," 1997); Secretary of the Central Committee, All-Union Communist Party [CPSU] to Beria-NKVD, 5 March 1940, reproduced in *Revelations from the Russian Archives: Documents in English Translation,* eds. and trans. Diane Koenker and Ronald D. Bachman (Washington, D.C.: Library of Congress, 1997), 167–68; Dmitri Antonovich Volkogonov, *Autopsy for an Empire: The Seven Leaders Who Built the Soviet Regime,* ed. and trans. Harold Shukman (New York: Free Press, 1998), 220. The Katyn murders were also a part of a broader Stalinist terror against the Poles. Newly opened archival records show that in 1937, the CPSU Political Bureau, under Stalin's leadership, issued an order depicting ethnic Poles within the borders of the Soviet Union as "saboteurs" and "spies." By the end of 1938 the KGB had imprisoned more than 130,000 Poles and executed more than 110,000 of them. The Comintern also called the leadership of the Polish Communist Party to Moscow, where they were imprisoned and most executed, and the party itself was dissolved. During 1940 and 1941, in the portion of Poland annexed to the USSR, the KGB unleashed a reign of terror in which thousands were killed and tens of thousands were imprisoned. In order to reduce the ethnic Polish population in the annexed territory, Soviet security police deported more than a million Poles to remote areas of the USSR, with tens of thousands dying in transit or in exile from deprivation, disease and exposure. N. Petrov and A. Roginskii, "The 'Polish' Operation

of the NKVD, 1937–38," in *Stalin's Terror: High Politics and Mass Repression in the Soviet Union,* ed. Barry McLoughlin and Kevin McDermott (New York: Palgrave Macmillan, 2002); Jan Tomasz Gross, *Revolution from Abroad: The Soviet Conquest of Poland's Western Ukraine and Western Belorussia* (Princeton: Princeton University Press, 2002).

[13] J. Arch Getty and Oleg V. Naumov, *The Road to Terror: Stalin and the Self-Destruction of the Bolsheviks, 1932–1939* (New Haven: Yale University Press, 1999), xiii.

[14] J. Arch Getty, "The Future Did Not Work," *Atlantic Monthly,* March 2000, http://www.theatlantic.com/issues/2000/03/getty.htm. In view of what is known now, Conquest's earlier estimates may be high, although Alexander Yakovlev, who has had extensive access to the records, developed a total similar to that of Conquest. But even if Conquest's twenty million total is cut to ten or as low as five million, it is far closer in magnitude to the truth than the pre-1991 revisionists' estimates of thousands (Getty), or tens of thousands (Rieber), or low hundreds of thousands (Hough and Fitzpatrick). Martin Amis, *Koba the Dread: Laughter and the Twenty Million* (New York: Talk Miramax Books, 2002).

[15] Robert W. Thurston, *Life and Terror in Stalin's Russia, 1934–1941* (New Haven: Yale University Press, 1996), 227–28.

[16] Ibid., 227–28.

[17] Theodore Von Laue, "A Perspective on History: The Soviet System Reconsidered," *Historian* 61, no. 2 (Winter 1999): 387, 389.

[18] Ibid., 384–86.

[19] Ibid., 386–88.

[20] Barbara Foley, "Women and the Left in the 1930s," *American Literary History* 2, no. 1 (Spring 1990): 158, 167; Barbara Foley, *Radical Representations: Politics and Form in U.S. Proletarian Fiction, 1929–1941* (Durham, N.C.: Duke University Press, 1993), 8–9; Grover Furr, "Using History to Fight Anti-Communism: Anti-Stalinism Hurts Workers, Builds Fascism," *Cultural Logic* 1, no. 2 (Spring 1998), http://eserver.org/clogic/1–2/furr.html; Fredric Jameson, *Late Marxism: Adorno, or, the Persis-*

*tence of the Dialectic* (London and New York: Verso, 1990), 250. For a detailed discussion of Jameson's rationalization of mass murder by Stalin, Mao Tse-tung and Pol Pot, see John M. Ellis, "Fredric Jameson's Marxist Criticism," *Academic Questions* 7, no. 2 (Spring 1994): 30–43.

[21] John Earl Haynes, *Communism and Anti-Communism in the United States: An Annotated Guide to Historical Writings* (New York: Garland, 1987).

[22] For a detailed discussion of this historiography, see John Earl Haynes, "The Cold War Debate Continues: A Traditionalist View of Historical Writing on Domestic Communism and Anti-Communism," *Journal of Cold War Studies* 2, no. 1 (Winter 2000): 76–115; John Earl Haynes and Harvey Klehr, "The Historiography of American Communism: An Unsettled Field," *Labour History Review* (Great Britain) 68, no. 1 (April 2003).

[23] Theodore Draper, *The Roots of American Communism* (New York: Viking Press, 1957); Theodore Draper, *American Communism and Soviet Russia* (New York: Viking Press, 1960); Irving Howe and Lewis A. Coser, *The American Communist Party: A Critical History, 1919–1957* (Boston: Beacon Press, 1957).

[24] Thomas R Maddux, "Red Fascism, Brown Bolshevism: The American Image of Totalitarianism in the 1930s," *Historian* 40, no. 1 (November 1977); John L. Childs and George S. Counts, *America, Russia, and the Communist Party in the Postwar World*, pamphlet (New York: The John Day Company, 1943); Evron Kirkpatrick and Herbert McClosky, *Minnesota Daily*, 14 December 1944.

[25] Robert Griffith and Athan G. Theoharis, eds., *The Specter: Original Essays on the Cold War and the Origins of McCarthyism* (New York: New Viewpoints, 1974).

[26] David Caute, *The Great Fear: The Anti-Communist Purge under Truman and Eisenhower* (New York: Simon and Schuster, 1977), 21.

[27] Robert Griffith, *The Politics of Fear: Joseph R. McCarthy and the Senate* (Lexington: Published for the Organization of American Historians by University Press of Kentucky, 1970), 30–31.

[28] Leslie K. Adler and Thomas G. Paterson, "Red Fascism: The

Merger of Nazi Germany and Soviet Russia in the American Image of Totalitarianism, 1930's–1950's," *Journal of American History* 75, no. 4 (April 1970): 1049, 1061, 1063.

[29] Michael Denning, *The Cultural Front: The Laboring of American Culture in the Twentieth Century* (London and New York: Verso, 1997); Theodore Draper, "The Life of the Party," *New York Review of Books* 41 (13 January 1994): 47. Also see: Theodore Draper, "American Communism Revisited," *New York Review of Books* 32, no. 8 (9 May 1985); Theodore Draper, "The Popular Front Revisited," *New York Review of Books* 32, no. 9 (30 May 1985); Phyllis Jacobson, "The 'Americanization' of the Communist Party," *New Politics* 1, no. 1 (n.s.) (Summer 1986); Julius Jacobson, "The Soviet Union Is Dead: The 'Russian Question' Remains: Part I: The Communist Party—Myth and Reality," *New Politics* 5, no. 2 (n.s.) (Winter 1995), http://www.wpunj.edu/~newpol/issue18/jacobs18.htm.

[30] Maurice Isserman, "Three Generations: Historians View American Communism," *Labor History* 26, no. 4 (Fall 1985): 539–40; Maurice Isserman, *Which Side Were You On? The American Communist Party during the Second World War* (Middletown, Conn.: Wesleyan University Press, 1982).

[31] For a declaration and celebration that the "intellectual strength of the left" had come to dominate the academy, see Jon Wiener, *Professors, Politics, and Pop* (New York: Verso, 1991). For a critique of Wiener, see Ronald Radosh, "Jon Wiener's Pop Marxism," *New Criterion* 10, no. 7 (March 1992): 43–46.

[32] David Gelernter, "Hard Times for History," *Weekly Standard,* 16 September 1996: 35.

[33] Eugene D. Genovese, "The Question," *Dissent* 41, no. 3 (Summer 1994): 371–76.

[34] Communist Party of the USA, "The Communist Party Convention," *Political Affairs* 36 (April 1957): 3; William Z. Foster, "Draper's 'Roots of American Communism,'" *Political Affairs* 36 (May 1957): 37; Eugene Dennis, "Questions and Answers on the XXth Congress, CPSU," *Political Affairs* 35 (April 1956): 24. These and additional similar quotations can be found in

Aileen S. Kraditor, *"Jimmy Higgins": The Mental World of the American Rank-and-File Communist, 1930–1958* (New York: Greenwood Press, 1988), 84–85. Weiss is quoted in Joseph R. Starobin, *American Communism in Crisis, 1943–1957* (Cambridge: Harvard University Press, 1972), 308n.

[35] Eric Foner, "The Question: The Responses," *Dissent* 41, no. 3 (Summer 1994): 379–80; Eric Foner, "Restructuring Yesterday's News: The Russians Write a New History," *Harper's,* December 1990: 70–75, 78. Just as Foner did not want the blank pages of history filled in if they portrayed the USSR in a poor light, Rutgers University professor David Oshinsky denounced traditionalist historians as "too zealous in setting the record straight" in regard to American communism and espionage because their research threatened to complicate the academic consensus condemning anticommunism (David Oshinsky, "McCarthy, Still Unredeemable," *New York Times,* 7 November 1998, op-ed page). Eric Foner, "Lincoln's Lesson," *Nation,* 11 February 1991: 149, 164; Eric Foner, *The Story of American Freedom* (New York: W. W. Norton, 1998), 211; Theodore Draper, "Freedom and Its Discontents," *New York Review of Books* 46, no. 14 (23 September 1999): 59; John Patrick Diggins, "Fate and Freedom in History: The Two Worlds of Eric Foner," *National Interest* 69 (Fall 2002): 85.

[36] Herbert Aptheker, "The Truth about the Korean War," *Masses and Mainstream,* August 1950; Herbert Aptheker, *The Truth about Hungary* (New York: Mainstream Publishers, 1957); Herbert Aptheker, *The Fraud of "Soviet Anti-Semitism,"* pamphlet (Sydney: Current Book Distributors, 1963); Herbert Aptheker, *Czechoslovakia and Counter-Revolution: Why the Socialist Countries Intervened,* pamphlet (New York: New Outlook Publishers, 1969).

[37] Herbert Aptheker and Robin D. G. Kelley, "An Interview with Herbert Aptheker," *Journal of American History* 87, no. 1 (June 2000): 151–67.

[38] Ibid.; Robin D. G. Kelley, "Afterword," *Journal of American History* 87, no. 1 (June 2000): 168–71.

[39] Gerda Lerner, *Fireweed: A Political Autobiography* (Philadelphia: Temple University Press, 2002), 255, 370.

[40] Ibid., 278, 326.

[41] Norman Markowitz, "FDR and Socialism," *H-US1918–45,* 21 November 2001, archived at http://ww2.h-net.msu.edu/lists/.

[42] Paul Buhle, "Secret Subventions: Troubling Legacies," *OAH Newsletter* 28, no. 2 (May 2000): 27, http://www.oah.org/pubs/nl/2000may/buhle.html; Paul Buhle, "Spies Everywhere," *Radical History Review* no. 67 (Winter 1997): 187–98.

[43] Paul Buhle, "Truman's Heir," *Radical History Review* no. 60 (Fall 1994): 154; *Radical History Review* homepage: http://shnm.gmu.edu/Radical History Review/rht.htm; Paul Buhle, "Reflections of an Old New Leftist," *Radical History Review* no. 79 (Winter 2001): 81–84.

[44] Michael J. Heale, "Beyond the 'Age of McCarthy': Anticommunism and the Historians," in *The State of U.S. History,* ed. Melvyn Stokes (New York: Berg, 2002), 136, 140. Note Heale's use of quotation marks around "victory" as a device for expressing disapproval. One's perspective must be very radical if one finds it difficult to distinguish Kennedy's liberalism from the Nixonian conservatism of that era.

[45] Michael E. Brown, "Introduction: The History of the History of U.S. Communism," in *New Studies in the Politics and Culture of U.S. Communism,* ed. Michael E. Brown, Randy Martin, Frank Rosengarten and George Snedeker (New York: Monthly Review Press, 1993), 21, 28. Other authors in this volume include Rosalyn Baxandall, John Gerassi, Marvin Gettleman, Gerald Horne, Roger Keeran, Mark Naison, Stephen Leberstein, Ellen Schrecker, Annette Rubinstein, Alan Wald and Anders Stephanson. Wald later disassociated himself from what he termed Brown's "oddball opinions." Alan M. Wald, "Search for a Method: Recent Histories of American Communism," *Radical History Review* no. 61 (Winter 1995): 173n.

[46] Norman Markowitz, "The New Cold-War 'Scholarship,' " *Political Affairs* 62 (October 1983): 27–38; Gerald Horne, "Communists in Harlem during the Depression," *Political Affairs* 63 (September/October 1984): 36–38. Isserman differentiated

"new historians" of his sort from more extreme revisionists such as Markowitz and Horne whose views parallel the CPUSA's self-perception of its history.

[47] Lincoln Steffens, "Introduction," in *I Change Worlds: The Remaking of an American,* by Anna Louise Strong (Seattle: Seal Press, 1979), v.

[48] Paul Lyons, *Philadelphia Communists, 1936–1956* (Philadelphia: Temple University Press, 1982), 18, 238.

[49] Ellen Schrecker, *Many Are the Crimes: McCarthyism in America* (Boston: Little, Brown, 1998), xviii; Norman Markowitz, "FDR and Socialism," *H-US1918–45,* 14 November 2001, archived at http://ww2.h-net.msu.edu/lists/; Norman Markowitz, "What about 'Stalinism'?" *People's Daily World,* 11 April 1990.

[50] Alan Wald, "Communist Writers Fight Back in Cold War America," in *Styles of Cultural Activism: From Theory and Pedagogy to Women, Indians, and Communism,* ed. Philip Goldstein (Cranbury, N.J.: University of Delaware Press and Associated University Presses, 1994), 218; Lucas response to questions after delivery of Scott Lucas, "The U.S. Government and the Sponsorship of American Studies in Britain during the Cold War and Beyond," paper presented at Society for Historians of American Foreign Relations annual meeting (Washington, D.C., 2001); Joel Kovel, *Red Hunting in the Promised Land: Anticommunism and the Making of America* (New York: Basic Books, 1994), x.

[51] Gerald Horne, Letter to the Editor, *Journal of American History* 79, no. 2 (September 1992): 760; Gerald Horne, "The Bill Comes Due," News Release, Black Radical Congress (New York, 2001), http://www.blythe.org/nytransfer-subs/Labor/The_Bill_Comes_Due_-_Gerald_Horne; Rachel Neumann, "The Empire Strikes Back," *Village Voice,* 3 October 2001, http://www.villagevoice.com/issues/0140/neumann.php; Singer is a defender of Communist dual-union tactics. See, for example, Alan Singer, "Communists and Coal Miners: Organizing Mine Workers during the 1920s," *Science & Society* 55, no. 2 (Sum-

mer 1991). Eric Foner, "11 September," *London Review of Books* (Great Britain) 23, n. 19 (4 October 2001), http://www.lrb.co.uk/v23/n19/mult2319.htm.

[52] Rick Perlstein, "Left Falls Apart as Center Holds," *New York Observer,* 25 October 2001, 1.

[53] Schrecker, *Many Are the Crimes,* 46; David Evanier and Harvey Klehr, "Anticommunism and Mental Health," *American Spectator* 22, no. 2 (February 1989): 28–30. The Evanier-Klehr article reports on the 1988 "Anticommunism and the U.S.: History and Consequences" conference held at Harvard University by the Institute for Media Analysis, and concludes, "The conference (thirty-eight panels and plenaries) thoroughly covered the dire consequences of anticommunism; it deflowers us, poisons our bodily fluids, kills the poor, makes us fight wars against innocent people, demolishes time, spreads heterosexuality, destroys paid maternity leaves, fosters antilesbianism, eradicates abortion rights—well, it just poisons and ruins everything." Norman Markowitz, "Anti-Communism Old and 'New,'" *Political Affairs,* August/September 1999.

[54] Schrecker, *Many Are the Crimes,* 46, 375–76, 381, 390. Regarding the regrettable effects of anticommunism on U.S. State Department efficiency, Schrecker specifically cited the removal of Carl Marzani, a former OSS official, from his State Department job. What goes unmentioned is that Marzani had been a secret member of the CPUSA, was recruited as a Soviet agent by the KGB in 1939, and set up a publishing firm secretly subsidized by the KGB.

[55] Schrecker, *Many Are the Crimes,* 399–402, 415.

[56] Kovel, *Red Hunting,* xi–xii.

[57] Ibid., 101, 156.

[58] Ibid., x–xi, 74, 95, 233; Evanier and Klehr, "Anticommunism and Mental Health," 28, 30.

[59] T. Lerner [Tillie Olsen], "I Want You Women up North to Know," *Partisan* 1 (March 1934): 4; Moissaye J. Olgin, *Trotskyism: Counter-Revolution in Disguise* (New York: Workers Library Publishers, 1935), 148–49; Junius Irving Scales and Richard

Nickson, *Cause at Heart: A Former Communist Remembers* (Athens: University of Georgia Press, 1987), 93–94; Donald MacKenzie Lester, "Stalin—Genius of Socialist Construction," *Communist* 20 (March 1941): 257–58; Elizabeth Gurley Flynn, "He Loved the People," *Political Affairs*, April 1953: 43; Alexander Bittelman, "Stalin: On His Seventieth Birthday," *Political Affairs*, December 1949: 43. The above and other examples of the CPUSA's worshipful attitude toward Stalin and the USSR can be found in Aileen Kraditor's underappreciated book *"Jimmy Higgins."* (See n. 34 above.)

60 Venona 1635 KGB New York to Moscow, 21 November 1944; Ronald Radosh and Joyce Milton, *The Rosenberg File* (New Haven: Yale University Press, 1997), 29, 65.

61 Fraser M. Ottanelli, *The Communist Party of the United States: From the Depression to World War II* (New Brunswick, N.J.: Rutgers University Press, 1991), 4, 213.

62 *New York Times*, 24 August 1939: 9; *Daily Worker*, 23 August 1939: 1.

63 Browder report to CPUSA national committee, quoted in *Daily Worker*, 5 September 1939: 1.

64 Ottanelli, *The Communist Party*, 194.

## Chapter 2: The Archives Open

1 James Ryan, "Earl Browder and American Communism at High Tide: 1934–1945," Ph.D. diss. (Notre Dame, Indiana: University of Notre Dame, 1981); James G. Ryan, *Earl Browder: The Failure of American Communism* (Tuscaloosa, Ala.: University of Alabama Press, 1997), xi, 274.

2 Vernon L. Pedersen, "Riding the Wave: The Indiana Communist Party, 1929–1934," unpublished master's thesis (Terre Haute: Indiana State University, 1987); Vernon L. Pedersen, "Red, White and Blue: The Communist Party of Maryland, 1919–1949," Ph.D. diss. (Washington, D.C.: Georgetown University, 1993); Vernon L. Pedersen, *The Communist Party in Maryland, 1919–57* (Urbana and Chicago: University of Illinois Press, 2001), 3. Pedersen is a his-

torian and associate dean at Montana State University, Great Falls.

[3] Mark Solomon, "Red and Black: Negroes and Communism, 1929–1932," Ph.D. diss. (Harvard University, 1972), published as Mark I. Solomon, *Red and Black: Communism and Afro-Americans, 1929–1935* (New York: Garland, 1988). The quotation is in the latter's preface. Mark I. Solomon, *The Cry Was Unity: Communists and African Americans, 1917–36* (Jackson: University Press of Mississippi, 1998).

[4] Edward P. Johanningsmeier, *Forging American Communism: The Life of William Z. Foster* (Princeton, N.J.: Princeton University Press, 1994), 6–7, 284, 307.

[5] James R. Barrett, *William Z. Foster and the Tragedy of American Radicalism* (Urbana: University of Illinois Press, 1999), 4–5.

[6] Ellen Schrecker, "Post–Cold War Triumphalism and Historical Revisionism," paper presented at American Historical Association Annual Meeting (Boston, 2001); Scott Lucas, "Review of Venona: Decoding Soviet Espionage in America," *Journal of American History* 87, no. 3 (December 2000), http://www. historycooperative.org/journals/jah/87.3/br_108.html; Hugh Wilford, "The Communist International and the American Communist Party," in *International Communism and the Communist International: 1919–1943*, ed. Tim Rees and Andrew Thorpe (Manchester [U.K.] & New York: Manchester University Press distributed by St. Martin's Press, 1998), 229, 231; Robert Shaffer, "A Not-So-Secret Agenda," *Reviews in American History* 24, no. 3 (September 1996): 505.

[7] Among the prominent revisionist scholars giving papers were Maurice Isserman, Ellen Schrecker, Nelson Lichtenstein and Bruce Cummings. Isserman and Schrecker arraigned us and the diplomatic historian John Lewis Gaddis for triumphalism in Maurice Isserman and Ellen Schrecker, " 'Papers of a Dangerous Tendency': From Major Andre's Boot to the Venona Files," paper presented at Cold War Triumphalism conference (New York University International Center for Advanced Studies, 2002). The negative depiction of the war on terror was in

Corey Robin, "Toward a New Cold War? September 11, Civil Liberties, and Political Demonology," paper presented at Cold War Triumphalism conference.

[8] Ellen Schrecker, "Review of The Soviet World of American Communism," *Journal of American History* 85, no. 4 (March 1999): 1648.

[9] Ellen Schrecker and Maurice Isserman, "The Right's Cold War Revision: Current Espionage Fears Have Given New Life to Liberal Anticommunism," *Nation*, 24 July 2000: 22–24. In the same vein, Eric Alterman attempted to discredit Klehr and Radosh's *The Amerasia Spy Case* not by engaging its evidence but by accusingly noting that the Bradley Foundation had supported publication. Eric Alterman, "Replies," *Nation*, 30 September 1996: 26; Harvey Klehr and Ronald Radosh, *The Amerasia Spy Case: Prelude to McCarthyism* (Chapel Hill: University of North Carolina Press, 1996).

[10] For an even more strident and bizarre presentation of the notion that the American academy is besieged by a sinister right-wing conspiracy, see Dave Johnson, "Who's Behind the Attack on Liberal Professors?" (Commonwealth Institute, 2003), http://hnn.us/articles/1244.html; Victor Rabinowitz, *Unrepentant Leftist: A Lawyer's Memoir* (Urbana: University of Illinois Press, 1996), 164–65; Ellen Schrecker, *No Ivory Tower: McCarthyism and the Universities* (New York: Oxford University Press, 1986), viii.

[11] Frances Stonor Saunders, *The Cultural Cold War: The CIA and the World of Arts and Letters* (New York: New Press, 2000); Jeff Sharlet, "Tinker, Writer, Artist, Spy: Intellectuals during the Cold War," *Chronicle of Higher Education*, 31 March 2000: A19–A20; Arthur M. Eckstein, Paul Buhle and Dave Wagner, "Polonsky, Politics and the Hollywood Blacklist," *Filmhäftet* (Sweden) 30, no. 2 (March 2002): 26.

[12] In addition to reading Saunders, one would be wise to consult the more balanced accounts of Giles Scott-Smith, *The Politics of Apolitical Culture: The Congress for Cultural Freedom, the CIA and Post-War American Hegemony*, Routledge/PSA Political Studies

Series (New York: Routledge, 2002); Volker Rolf Berghahn, *America and the Intellectual Cold Wars in Europe: Shepard Stone between Philanthropy, Academy, and Diplomacy* (Princeton, N.J.: Princeton University Press, 2001); and Peter Coleman, *The Liberal Conspiracy: The Congress for Cultural Freedom and the Struggle for the Mind of Postwar Europe* (New York: Free Press, 1989). A revisionist who takes a somewhat more balanced view of the nature of CIA cultural funding than Saunders is Hugh Wilford, "Playing the CIA's Tune? The *New Leader* and the Cultural Cold War," *Diplomatic History* 27, no. 1 (Winter 2003): 15–34.

[13] Paul Buhle, "Secret Subventions: Troubling Legacies," *OAH Newsletter* 28, no. 2 (May 2000): 27, http://www.oah.org/pubs/nl/2000may/buhle.html; Sigmund Diamond, *Compromised Campus: The Collaboration of Universities with the Intelligence Community, 1945–1955* (New York: Oxford University Press, 1992), 133–34, 321 n23. Arnold Beichman, who was on the ACCF's executive committee at the time and was the ACCF's last chairman, confirmed that the ACCF's offer to assist the Communism in American Life series was declined. Arnold Beichman, "History Afflicted," *Washington Times*, 26 January 2003. We asked Paul Buhle to offer other evidence on this matter or withdraw his claim on the web journal *History News Network*, but he declined to do either. Harvey Klehr and John Earl Haynes, "A Challenge to Paul Buhle," *History News Network* [WWW], 14 January 2003, http://hnn.us/articles/1210.html.

[14] Victor Navasky, "My Hunt for Moscow Gold," *New York Times*, 21 October 2000, op-ed page.

[15] "Report, expended by the fund in 1973 . . . ," original from the Archive of the President of the Russian Federation, Heads of State file: Brezhnev, in Dmitri Volkogonov Papers, box 24, Manuscript Division, Library of Congress, Washington, D.C.; Michael Dobbs, "Panhandling the Kremlin: How Gus Hall Got Millions," *Washington Post*, 1 March 1992; Vladimir Bukovsky, "Secrets of the Central Committee," *Commentary*, October 1996: 33–41.

[16] David J. Garrow, *The FBI and Martin Luther King, Jr.: From "Solo"*

*to Memphis* (New York: W. W. Norton, 1981); John Barron, *Operation Solo: The FBI's Man in the Kremlin* (Washington, D.C.: Regnery, 1995).

[17] Edward P. Johanningsmeier, "Review of The Secret World of American Communism," *Labor History* 36, no. 4 (Fall 1995): 635; Schrecker, "Review of The Soviet World of American Communism," 1647.

[18] Paul Buhle, "Secret Work," in *Encyclopedia of the American Left,* ed. Mari Jo Buhle, Paul Buhle and Dan Georgakas, 2nd ed. (New York: Oxford University Press, 1998), 736.

[19] Paul Buhle and Dan Georgakas, "Communist Party, USA," in *Encyclopedia of the American Left,* 155; Paul Buhle, "Daily Worker," in *Encyclopedia of the American Left,* 2nd ed., 178; Buhle, "Secret Work," 737.

[20] Diane Koenker and Ronald D. Bachman, eds. and trans., *Revelations from the Russian Archives: Documents in English Translation* (Washington, D.C.: Library of Congress, 1997), 599–601.

[21] Michael Carley, Review of Klehr et al., Secret World of American Communism, in H-Russia, 6 July 1995, archived at <www2.h-net.msu.edu/lists/>. At the time of his review, Carley was affiliated with Carleton University (Canada).

[22] The same document was also transcribed in the Library of Congress's *Revelations from the Soviet Archives* with the same translation we used. Koenker and Bachman, *Revelations from the Russian Archives,* 596–98; Harvey Klehr and John Earl Haynes, "Haynes and Klehr Respond," in H-Russia, 10 July 1995; Michael Carley, "Re: Haynes and Klehr Respond," in H-Russia, 11 July 1995; Harvey Klehr and John Earl Haynes, "Review of Klehr and Haynes," in H-Russia, 13 July 1995; Michael Carley, "Re: Review of Klehr and Haynes," in H-Russia, 16 July 1995; all archived at www2.h-net.msu.edu/lists/.

[23] With similar carelessness, in the same essay Parrish wrote, "As Lovestone once quipped, pointing at Browder; 'There—there but for an accident of geography stands a corpse.' " It is a good line, known to many historians in the field, except that most

know that Max Shachtman, not Jay Lovestone, delivered it. It is from a 1950 debate between Shachtman and Browder in which the former recited a number of East European Communist leaders recently executed in Stalin's purges, pointed at Browder, and delivered this rhetorical knockout blow. Michael E. Parrish, a historian of American government and politics, should not be confused with Michael Parrish, a historian of the Soviet political police and intelligence services. Michael E. Parrish, "Review Essay: Soviet Espionage and the Cold War," *Diplomatic History* 25, no. 1 (Winter 2001): 108–9.

[24] Johanningsmeier, "Review of The Secret World," 635.

[25] Ibid.; Athan G. Theoharis, *Chasing Spies: How the FBI Failed in Counterintelligence but Promoted the Politics of McCarthyism in the Cold War Years* (Chicago: Ivan R. Dee, 2002), 237; David Caute, *The Great Fear: The Anti-Communist Purge under Truman and Eisenhower* (New York: Simon & Schuster, 1977), 54.

[26] Elizabeth Bentley, *Out of Bondage: The Story of Elizabeth Bentley* (New York: Devin-Adair, 1951).

[27] *Nation* editors, "The Shape of Things," *Nation*, 7 August 1948: 141; Herbert L. Packer, *Ex-Communist Witnesses: Four Studies in Fact Finding* (Stanford, Calif.: Stanford University Press, 1962), 222; Caute, *The Great Fear*, 56; Athan G. Theoharis and John Stuart Cox, *The Boss: J. Edgar Hoover and the Great American Inquisition* (New York: Bantam Books, 1990), 272, 297.

[28] James R. Barrett, "Review of The Secret World of American Communism," *Journal of American History* 82, no. 4 (March 1996): 1525–37; Kathryn S. Olmsted, *Red Spy Queen: A Biography of Elizabeth Bentley* (Chapel Hill: University of North Carolina Press, 2002). Olmsted also concluded that as the years passed, Bentley embellished, exaggerated, romanticized and even lied about details, but that the heart of her story was true. Lauren Kessler, *Clever Girl: Elizabeth Bentley's Life In and Out of Espionage* (New York: HarperCollins, 2003).

[29] Joseph Albright and Marcia Kunstel, *Bombshell: The Secret Story of America's Unknown Atomic Spy Conspiracy* (New York: Times

Books, 1997).

[30] Nick Cullather, "Review of Bombshell, A Century of Spies, and Secrets," *Journal of American History* 85, no. 3 (December 1998): 1146–48.

[31] Traditionalists are occasionally asked to review books, but that is a lesser task than authoring an essay.

[32] Lowell Dyson, "The Red Peasant International in America," *Journal of American History* 58, no. 4 (March 1972): 958–73. We would judge the following articles in *Journal of American History* to take a positive view of American communism or a negative view of domestic anticommunism: John A. Salmond, "Postscript to the New Deal: The Defeat of the Nomination of Aubrey W. Williams as Rural Electrification Administrator in 1945," 61, no. 2 (September 1974); Mary S. McAuliffe, "Liberals and the Communist Control Act of 1954," 63, no. 2 (September 1976); Athan Theoharis, "The Truman Administration and the Decline of Civil Liberties: The FBI's Success in Securing Authorization for a Preventive Detention Program," 64, no. 4 (September 1978); Robert Griffith, "Old Progressives and the Cold War," 66, no. 2 (September 1979); David Williams, "The Bureau of Investigation and Its Critics, 1919–1921: The Origins of Federal Political Surveillance," 68, no. 3 (December 1981); Kenneth O'Reilly, "A New Deal for the FBI: The Roosevelt Administration, Crime Control, and National Security," 69, no. 3 (December 1982); Gerald Zahavi, "Negotiated Loyalty: Welfare Capitalism and the Shoeworkers of Endicott Johnson, 1920–1940," 70, no. 3 (December 1983); Robert J. Norrell, "Caste in Steel: Jim Crow Careers in Birmingham, Alabama," 73, no. 3 (December 1986); JoAnne Brown, "'A Is for Atom, B Is for Bomb': Civil Defense in American Public Education, 1948–1963," 75, no. 1 (June 1988); Ellen Schrecker, "Archival Sources for the Study of McCarthyism," 75, no. 1 (June 1988); Robert Korstad and Nelson Lichtenstein, "Opportunities Found and Lost: Labor, Radicals, and the Early Civil Rights Movement," 75, no. 3 (December 1988); Jonathan M.

Wiener, "Radical Historians and the Crisis in American History, 1959–1980," 76, no. 2 (September 1989); Herbert Aptheker, "Welcoming Jonathan Wiener's Paper, with a Few Brief Dissents," 76, no. 2 (September 1989); Paul Buhle and Robin D. G. Kelley, "The Oral History of the Left in the United States: A Survey and Interpretation," 76, no. 2 (September 1989); Gerald Zahavi, "Passionate Commitments: Race, Sex, and Communism at Schenectady General Electric, 1932–1954," 83, no. 2 (September 1996); David W. Stowe, "The Politics of Café Society," 84, no. 4 (March 1998); Herbert Aptheker, "An Autobiographical Note," 87, no. 1 (June 2000); Herbert Aptheker and Robin D. G. Kelley, "An Interview with Herbert Aptheker by Robin Kelley," 87, no. 1 (June 2000); Robin D. G. Kelley, "Afterword," 87, no. 1 (June 2000); K. A. Cuordileone, "Politics in an Age of Anxiety: Cold War Political Culture and the Crisis in American Masculinity, 1949–1960," 87, no. 2 (2000), http://www. historycooperative.org/journals/jah/87.2/cuordileone.html; Robin D. G. Kelley, "But a Local Phase of a World Problem: Black History's Global Vision, 1883–1950," 86, no. 3 (December 1999), http://www.historycooperative.org/journals/jah/ 86.3/kelley.html.

[33] Alonzo L. Hamby, "The Vital Center, the Fair Deal, and the Quest for a Liberal Political Economy," 77, no. 3 (June 1972). Essays in the *American Historical Review* taking a revisionist stance include: Michael E. Parrish, "Cold War Justice: The Supreme Court and the Rosenbergs," 82, no. 4 (October 1977); Gerald Horne, "'Myth' and the Making of 'Malcolm X,'" 98, no. 2 (April 1993); David Joravsky, "Communism in Historical Perspective," 99, no. 3 (June 1994); James A. Miller, Susan D. Pennybacker and Eve Rosenhaft, "Mother Ada Wright and the International Campaign to Free the Scottsboro Boys," 106, no. 2 (April 2001); Eric Foner, "American Freedom in a Global Age," 106, no. 1 (February 2001).

[34] Ellen Schrecker, "Archival Sources for the Study of McCarthyism," *Journal of American History* 75, no. 1 (June 1988): 197; Ellen Schrecker, *Many Are the Crimes: McCarthyism in America*

(Boston: Little, Brown, 1998), x, xii, 75–76.

[35] Ethan Bronner, "Rethinking McCarthyism, If Not McCarthy," *New York Times,* 18 October 1998. The CPUSA was so apoplectic about the article's suggestion that Julius Rosenberg was guilty of espionage that its editorial writer falsely attributed authorship of the piece to "the head of an anti-Communist project at Yale." Bronner has no relationship to the Yale University Press. Editorial, "Reviving a Smelly Corpse," *People's Weekly World,* 24 October 1998: 12; Editorial, "Revisionist McCarthyism," *New York Times,* 23 October 1999.

[36] On our evaluation of Joseph McCarthy, see: Harvey Klehr and John Earl Haynes, *The American Communist Movement: Storming Heaven Itself* (New York: Twayne, 1992), 133–34; Harvey Klehr, John Earl Haynes and Fridrikh Igorevich Firsov, *The Secret World of American Communism* (New Haven: Yale University Press, 1995), 5–6, 15, 325; John Earl Haynes, *Red Scare or Red Menace? American Communism and Anticommunism in the Cold War Era* (Chicago: Ivan R. Dee, 1996), 161; Klehr and Radosh, *Amerasia Spy Case,* 219; John Earl Haynes and Harvey Klehr, "Soviet Espionage and Communist Subversion in the United States in the Early Cold War: What Do We Know?" paper presented at Eisenhower Center for American Studies "McCarthyism in America" conference (National Archives, Washington, D.C., 2000); John Earl Haynes, "Exchange with Arthur Herman and Venona Book Talk," paper presented at Herman and Haynes joint book talk, Borders Books, Washington, D.C., 2000, http://www.johnearlhaynes.org/page58.html.

[37] Schrecker, "Post–Cold War Triumphalism"; Schrecker and Isserman, "The Right's Cold War Revision," 23–24.

[38] Schrecker and Isserman, "The Right's Cold War Revision," 23–24.

[39] Schrecker, *Many Are the Crimes,* x.

[40] Schrecker and Isserman, "The Right's Cold War Revision," 23.

[41] The decisive importance of the struggle within liberalism is discussed in Klehr and Haynes, *The American Communist Movement: Storming Heaven Itself* and Haynes, *Red Scare or Red Menace?*

[42] Jacob Weisberg, "Cold War without End," *New York Times Sun-*

*day Magazine,* 28 November 1999: 116–23, 155–58.

[43] Ellen Schrecker and John Earl Haynes, "Schrecker on Haynes" (H-Diplo, 2000), archived at http://www2.h-net.msu.edu/lists/; Schrecker, "Post–Cold War Triumphalism"; Anna Kasten Nelson, "Illuminating the Twilight Struggle: New Interpretations of the Cold War," *Chronicle of Higher Education,* 25 June 1999: B5.

[44] Schrecker, "Post–Cold War Triumphalism."

## Chapter 3: See No Evil

[1] Scott Lucas, "Review of Venona: Decoding Soviet Espionage in America," *Journal of American History* 87, no. 3 (December 2000), http://www.historycooperative.org/journals/jah/87.3/br_108.html; Anna Kasten Nelson, "Illuminating the Twilight Struggle: New Interpretations of the Cold War," *Chronicle of Higher Education,* 25 June 1999: B5; Ellen Schrecker, *Many Are the Crimes: McCarthyism in America* (Boston: Little, Brown, 1998), 180.

[2] Nigel West and Oleg Tsarev, *The Crown Jewels: The British Secrets at the Heart of the KGB Archives* (New Haven: Yale University Press, 1999), 147–53, 159–68.

[3] Alexander Feklisov and Sergei Kostin, *The Man Behind the Rosenbergs,* trans. Catherine Dop (New York: Enigma Books, 2001), 69.

[4] John Earl Haynes and Harvey Klehr, *Venona: Decoding Soviet Espionage in America* (New Haven: Yale University Press, 1999), 41–42.

[5] Feklisov and Kostin, *The Man Behind the Rosenbergs,* 70.

[6] Venona 27 KGB New York to Moscow, 8 January 1945.

[7] The source, a journalist, had developed a genuine subsource in the U.S. State Department, for which the KGB paid him. He attempted to increase his income by inventing two fake subsources. After the KGB detected the fraud, it cut off the funding for the fake sources but, this being a business transaction, continued to pay for information from the genuine

subsource. Allen Weinstein and Alexander Vassiliev, *The Haunted Wood: Soviet Espionage in America—The Stalin Era* (New York: Random House, 1999), 35.

[8] Victor Navasky, "Tales from Decrypts," *Nation*, 28 October 1996: 5–6; William Kunstler, Letter to the Editor, *Nation*, 16 October 1995: 406; Brian Villa, remarks made during delivery of "The Chronology of VENONA," paper presented at Seventh Symposium on Cryptologic History (Fort Meade, Md., 1997); William A. Reuben, "The Latest Spy Hoax: 'Secret World's' False Secrets," *Rights*, 1995: 11–13.

[9] Bernice Schrank, "Reading the Rosenbergs after Venona," *Labour/Le Travail* 49 (Spring 2002): 195.

[10] With the bulk of its work done, the Venona project's staff declined rapidly after the 1950s, with only a few persons still assigned to the project by the time of its formal termination in 1980. Schrank, "Reading the Rosenbergs," 210.

[11] Venona 1749–1750 KGB New York to Moscow, 13 December 1944.

[12] Schrank, "Reading the Rosenbergs," 194–95.

[13] Aaron Katz, "On Feklisov and the Rosenbergs," *Jewish Currents*, June 1997: 36.

[14] William A. Reuben, *The Atom Spy Hoax* (New York: Action Books, 1955), unnumbered preface.

[15] This latter point is important because of the Soviet Union's strained industrial resources at the end of World War II. The United States invested a stupendous sum and devoted enormous amounts of industrial and technical resources to the atomic bomb program. Absent the huge cost saving provided by espionage, the Soviet Union would have been hard pressed to finance a similar program while maintaining, as it did, the world's most powerful land army and repairing the massive destruction it sustained in World War II. See David Holloway, *Stalin and the Bomb: The Soviet Union and Atomic Energy, 1939–1956* (New Haven: Yale University Press, 1994); Richard Rhodes, *The Making of the Atomic Bomb* (New York: Simon & Schuster, 1986); Richard Rhodes, *Dark Sun: The Making of the Hydrogen Bomb* (New

York: Simon & Schuster, 1995). Some of the Soviet documents on World War II atomic espionage are reproduced in appendixes 1–4 of Pavel Sudoplatov, Anatolii Pavlovich Sudoplatov, Jerrold L. Schecter and Leona Schecter, *Special Tasks: The Memoirs of an Unwanted Witness, a Soviet Spymaster* (Boston: Little, Brown, 1994), reproduced from *Voprosy istorii estestvoznaniia i tekhniki* [Questions about the History of Natural Science and Technology], Russian Academy of Science, no. 3 (1992): 107–34. Newly open archives have shown that Kim Il Sung, the Communist dictator of North Korea, asked Stalin's agreement for an invasion of South Korea in the spring of 1949 but Stalin refused. Stalin's assent was necessary because without massive Soviet military support (weaponry, munitions, vehicles, supplies and military technicians), North Korea was incapable of attacking the South. In early 1950, however, Stalin informed Kim that he was now willing to support an invasion. Later, in April, Stalin cited four reasons for his shift of view, one of which was that Soviet possession of the atomic bomb reduced the likelihood of American intervention, something Stalin wished to avoid. Evgenii P. Bajanov, "Assessing the Politics of the Korean War, 1949–1951," *Cold War International History Project Bulletin,* no. 6–7 (Winter 1995): 87; Kathryn Weathersby discussion of an April 1950 Stalin document, meeting of the Chesapeake regional chapter of The Historical Society, 4 November 2000.

[16] Reuben, *The Atom Spy Hoax,* 56, 78. The Gouzenko investigation led to the conviction of eight Canadians, including Fred Rose, a Communist member of the Canadian Parliament; Sam Carr, national organizing secretary of the Communist Party of Canada; and Dr. Allan Nunn May, a scientist taking part in the Canadian contribution to the American-British atomic bomb project.

[17] Reuben, *The Atom Spy Hoax,* 170, 228, 231; Herbert Romerstein and Eric Breindel, *The Venona Secrets: Exposing Soviet Espionage and America's Traitors* (Washington, D.C.: Regnery, 2000), 225. Coplon's convictions were overturned on technicalities when appeals courts ruled that the evidence against her could not

be used because the FBI had lacked probable cause to seize it. There are fourteen deciphered Venona messages discussing Coplon's recruitment and work as a Soviet spy.

18 Norman Markowitz, "Rosenberg, Ethel, and Julius Rosenberg," in *American National Biography,* vol. 18 (New York: Oxford University Press, 1999), 879–81, http://www.anb.org/articles/index. html. In 2002 Markowitz announced that he had been a member of the CPUSA for twenty-four years. History News Network Staff, "Are You Now or Have You Ever Been a Member of the Communist Party?" *History News Network* [WWW Journal] (2002), http://hnn.us/articles/288.html; Norman Markowitz, "The Witch-Hunter's Truth," in *Our Right to Know, Special Issue— The Rosenberg Controversy Thirty Years Later* (Fund for Open Information and Accountability, 1983), 11.

19 Markowitz, "Rosenberg, Ethel, and Julius Rosenberg."

20 Ibid.

21 William Reuben, "The Hiss Case," in *Encyclopedia of the American Left,* ed. Mari Jo Buhle, Paul Buhle and Dan Georgakas, 2nd ed. (New York: Oxford University Press, 1998), 315–18.

22 Mari Jo Buhle, Paul Buhle and Dan Georgakas, eds., *Encyclopedia of the American Left,* 1st ed. (New York: Garland, 1990); Mari Jo Buhle, Paul Buhle and Dan Georgakas, eds., *Encyclopedia of the American Left,* 2nd ed. (New York: Oxford University Press, 1998), vii.

23 Attention: Inspector M. E. Gurnea, 17 May 1945, FBI file 100-267360, serial 221, Box 117, folder 4 and Washington FBI memo, 26 May 1945, FBI file 100-267360, serial 237, box 117, folder 6, Philip Jaffe Papers, Emory University.

24 Ibid.

25 The Truman administration, fearing political embarrassment from the case, hushed it up with a quick plea bargain on lesser charges. Harvey Klehr and Ronald Radosh, *The Amerasia Spy Case: Prelude to McCarthyism* (Chapel Hill: University of North Carolina Press, 1996).

26 Frederick Vanderbilt Field, *From Right to Left: An Autobiography*

(Westport, Conn.: L. Hill, 1983).

[27] Paul Buhle, "Secret Work," in *Encyclopedia of the American Left,* 2nd ed., 735–37.

[28] Harvey Klehr, John Earl Haynes and Fridrikh Igorevich Firsov, *The Secret World of American Communism* (New Haven: Yale University Press, 1995), 324.

[29] Labor Zionists and the Jewish Joint Distribution Committee coordinated the vast majority of the fundraising and arms shipments that went to Israel in 1947–48, not, as Buhle seems to imply, Communists. The Soviet bloc supplied some arms to the nascent Israeli state through Czechoslovakia, and the Irish Republican Army, motivated by anti-British animus, also supplied some weaponry. It is possible that one or another individual American Communist was involved in one of these operations. Even if that were the case, it would be a minor affair, not the "largest incident" of Buhle's imagination. And, in any case, he provides no evidence of any such event. We contacted Professor Buhle directly and asked for the documentary basis for these claims. He responded that it was based on oral history interviews but he could remember the name of only one of the interviewees and was not sure if that was the correct one. We obtained a copy of the interview from the Tamiment Library at New York University. It contained no support for the *Encyclopedia's* assertion. Additional inquiries to Professor Buhle requesting the documentary basis for his published claims in the *Encyclopedia* produced no specific sources. Yehuda Bauer, telephone interview with Harvey Klehr, 13 June 2001; Simon Spiegelman, telephone interview with Harvey Klehr, 10 July 2001; Arthur Liebman, *Jews and the Left* (New York: Wiley, 1979). American Communists would have trumpeted this sacrifice in the late 1940s, but there is no evidence they ever did. *Jewish Currents,* a magazine published by ex-Communists, whose writers and editors have run innumerable articles about Israel and communism, has never mentioned the "prominent role" played by American Communists fighting and dying in the Israeli War of Independence.

[30] Michael Karni, "Finnish Americans," in *Encyclopedia of the Amer-*

*ican Left,* 2nd ed., 227.

[31] Michael G. Karni, "Yhteishyva—Or, For the Common Good: Finnish Radicalism in the Western Great Lakes Region, 1900–1940," Ph.D. diss. (Minneapolis: University of Minnesota, 1975).

[32] Tom [McEwen] to Dear Friends, 11 August 1938, Russian State Archive of Social and Political History (RGASPI), Archive of the Secretariat of the Executive Committee of the Communist International, *fond* 495, *opis* 18, *delo* 1290. Tom McEwen, a Canadian Communist, served on the staff of the Comintern's Anglo-American Secretariat.

[33] Mayme Sevander, *Of Soviet Bondage* (Duluth, Minn.: OSCAT, 1996), 51.

[34] James T. Patterson, "The Enemy Within," *Atlantic Monthly,* October 1998: 111.

[35] Adam Hochschild, "Never Coming Home: An Exclusive Look at the KGB's Secret Files on Americans in Stalin's Prisons," *Mother Jones,* October 1992: 50–56. Hochschild included additional details about the persecution of American Communists in the USSR in Adam Hochschild, *The Unquiet Ghost: Russians Remember Stalin* (New York: Viking, 1994).

[36] Alan Cullison, "The Lost Victims," *Associated Press Wire Service,* 9 November 1997. Reprinted in part in Alan Cullison and Associated Press, "How Stalin Repaid the Support of Americans," *Washington Times,* 9 November 1997; and Alan Cullison, "Stalin's Lost American Victims," *Moscow Times* (Moscow, Russia), 12 November 1997: 1.

[37] Until that day comes, the most comprehensive work on the tragedy of the Finnish Americans who emigrated to Karelia has been done not by academics but by an amateur historian, Mayme Sevander (née Corgan). As a young teenager, the American-born daughter of Oscar Corgan came to Karelia in the early 1930s with her father, mother and two siblings. After he was arrested, the rest of the family was reduced to dire straits but survived. Sevander eventually became a teacher in Petrozavodsk, the chief city of Karelia. In the late 1980s she finally had

the opportunity to visit America and reestablish contact with relatives, and later she returned permanently to the United States. Appalled that professional historians had given so little attention to the subject, she gathered documentary evidence in the United States and Russia and interviewed other survivors and family members of those murdered. Sevander wrote three short books: *They Took My Father* (1992), *Red Exodus* (1993) and *Of Soviet Bondage* (1996). While she may have been an untrained historian, Sevander filled her books with rich detail and documentation unavailable elsewhere. None of her books has been reviewed in a major journal of history and, with the single exception of one review in the *Michigan Historical Review,* we have been unable to locate any scholarly journal that has reviewed any of these three books. (There are hundreds of major and minor scholarly and semischolarly journals, some with highly specialized audiences, and we cannot say we have checked all of them. However, we do see a great many journals and have made a variety of internet searches.) Mayme Sevander and Laurie Hertzel, *They Took My Father: A Story of Idealism and Betrayal* (Duluth, Minn.: Pfeifer-Hamilton Publishers, 1992); Mayme Sevander, *Red Exodus: Finnish-American Emigration to Russia* (Duluth, Minn.: OSCAT, distributed by the Duluth International Peace Center, 1993); Sevander, *Of Soviet Bondage.*

[38] Sam Sills, "Abraham Lincoln Brigade," in *Encyclopedia of the American Left,* 2nd ed., 2–4.

[39] Schrecker, *Many Are the Crimes,* 105; Fraser M. Ottanelli, *The Communist Party of the United States: From the Depression to World War II* (New Brunswick, N.J.: Rutgers University Press, 1991), 176; Robin Kelley, "African Americans and the Communist Party, USA" (Africana.com Inc., 2002); Robin D. G. Kelley, "Preface," in *The Lincoln Brigade: A Picture History,* by William Loren Katz and Marc Crawford (New York: Apex Press, 2001); Robbie Lieberman, *The Strangest Dream: Communism, Anticommunism and the U.S. Peace Movement, 1945–1963* (New York: Syracuse University Press, 2000), 18; Michael P. Rogin, "When the CIA Was the NEA," *Nation,* 12 June 2000, archived at

http://www.thenation.com; Bernard Knox, "'Premature Anti-Fascist,'" paper presented at Bill Susman Lecture Series (King Juan Carlos I of Spain Center—New York University, 1998), http://www.alba-valb.org/lectures/1998_knox_bernard.html.

[40] John Gerassi, *The Premature Antifascists: North American Volunteers in the Spanish Civil War, 1936–39: An Oral History* (New York: Praeger, 1986), 165–66, 172.

[41] One of the few was a passing 1944 reference that the FBI used the term "prematurely anti-Fascist," by a left-wing journalist who provided no details, no examples and no specific instances. Matthew Josephson and Russell Mahoney, "The Testimony of a Sinner," *New Yorker* 20 (22 April 1944): 26. We thank the historian George Nash for bringing this usage to our attention.

[42] Peter N. Carroll, *The Odyssey of the Abraham Lincoln Brigade: Americans in the Spanish Civil War* (Stanford, Calif.: Stanford University Press, 1994), 259.

[43] Mary Burkee to John E. Haynes, e-mail of 10 November 1999.

[44] Peter Carroll to John Haynes, 28 May 2000. Peter Carroll, "Premature Anti-Fascist," ALBA [WWW Discussion List], 25 May 2000, archived at http://forums.nyu.edu.

[45] "John Haynes raises a matter of ..." in "Research in Progress and Research Queries" section, *Newsletter of the Historians of American Communism* 17, no. 4 (December 1998): 3. Inquiries were raised on the H-Pol (http://www2.h-net.msu.edu/lists/), H-Diplo (http://www2.h-net.msu.edu/lists/), and ALBA (http://forums.nyu.edu) internet historical discussion lists in May 2000. Marvin Gettleman to John Haynes, e-mail of 26 January 1999; Marvin Gettleman, "Premature Anti-Fascist Designation," in ALBA forum, http://www.alba-valb.org/albadiag.htm, 1 January 2002.

[46] Carroll, "Premature Anti-Fascist."

[47] Carroll, *The Odyssey of the Abraham Lincoln Brigade*, 244–46.

[48] The document, Fitin to Dimitrov, 13 May 1942, is translated and transcribed in its entirety in Klehr, Haynes and Firsov, *The Secret World of American Communism*, 260–63.

[49] Klehr, Haynes and Firsov, *The Secret World of American Commu-*

*nism*, 271–73.

[50] Milt Felsen, *The Anti-Warrior: A Memoir* (Iowa City: University of Iowa Press, 1989), 151–52; Maurice Isserman, *Which Side Were You On? The American Communist Party during the Second World War* (Middletown, Conn.: Wesleyan University Press, 1982), 183; Robert A. Rosenstone, *Crusade of the Left: The Lincoln Battalion in the Spanish Civil War* (New York: Pegasus, 1969), 350.

[51] Testimony of Milton Wolff, transcript of the proceedings held before the Subversive Activities Control Board in the matter of *Herbert Brownell, Attorney General, v. Veterans of the Abraham Lincoln Brigade*, 1954, pp. 3695, 4119, 4123, 4272, 4275, 4323–28.

[52] The former is transcribed and the latter is cited in Harvey Klehr, John Earl Haynes and Kyrill M. Anderson, *The Soviet World of American Communism* (New Haven: Yale University Press, 1998), 85, 254–56.

[53] Roy MacLaren, *Canadians behind Enemy Lines, 1939–1945* (Vancouver: University of British Columbia Press, 1981), 133–35; David Stafford, *Camp X* (Toronto: Lester & Orpen Dennys, 1986), 171–73.

[54] MacLaren, *Canadians behind Enemy Lines*, 133–35; Stafford, *Camp X*, 171–73.

[55] Keynote speech of Milton Wolff to May 1941 VALB convention, reprinted as Petitioners' Exhibit 98, proceedings held before the Subversive Activities Control Board in the matter of *Herbert Brownell, Attorney General, v. Veterans of the Abraham Lincoln Brigade*, 1954.

[56] John Gates, "A Soviet-German Military Pact?" February 1940, reproduced in *A Documentary History of the Communist Party of the United States*, ed. Bernard K. Johnpoll (Westport, Conn.: Greenwood Press, 1994), vol. 6, 295–98.

[57] Paul Buhle and Dan Georgakas, "Communist Party, USA," in *Encyclopedia of the American Left*, 2nd ed., 146–56.

[58] "First Speech Delivered in the Presidium of the E.C.C.I. on the American Question, May 14, 1929," in Iosif Stalin, *Stalin's Speeches on the American Communist Party, Delivered in the Ameri-*

*can Commission of the Presidium of the Executive Committee of the Communist International, May 6, 1929, and in the Presidium of the Executive Committee of the Communist International on the American Question, May 14th, 1929...*, pamphlet ([New York]: Central Committee, Communist Party, U.S.A., 1931).

59 Buhle is not the only revisionist who sought to distance Peters from the CPUSA. Athan Theoharis erroneously refers to "Soviet agent Joszef Peters." Athan G. Theoharis, *Chasing Spies: How the FBI Failed in Counterintelligence but Promoted the Politics of McCarthyism in the Cold War Years* (Chicago: Ivan R. Dee, 2002), 57. Similarly confused, Professor Alfred Rieber refers to Peters as "a man of ... alleged importance to the Comintern." Alfred J. Rieber, "Review of The Secret World of American Communism," *Slavic Review* 54, no. 2 (Summer 1995): 430.

60 Paul Buhle, "Spies Everywhere," *Radical History Review*, no. 67 (Winter 1997): 190, 192.

61 Maurice Isserman, "Three Generations: Historians View American Communism," *Labor History* 26, no. 4 (Fall 1985): 544–45.

62 Tony Judt, "Rehearsal for Evil," *New Republic,* 10 September 2001: 35. The two-party theory is also critiqued in Julius Jacobson, "The Soviet Union Is Dead: The 'Russian Question' Remains: Part I: The Communist Party—Myth and Reality," *New Politics* 5, no. 2 (n.s.) (Winter 1995), http://www.wpunj.edu/~newpol/issue18/jacobs18.htm.

## Chapter 4: Lies about Spies

1 Whittaker Chambers, *Witness* (New York: Random House, 1952); Allen Weinstein, *Perjury: The Hiss-Chambers Case* (New York: Knopf, 1978); Sam Tanenhaus, *Whittaker Chambers: A Biography* (New York: Random House, 1997).

2 Victor Navasky, "The Case Not Proved against Alger Hiss," *Nation,* 8 April 1978; Victor Navasky, "New Republic, New Mistakes," *Nation,* 6 May 1978; Victor Navasky, "The Hiss-Weinstein File," *Nation,* 17 June 1978; Victor Navasky, "Weinstein, Hiss, and the Transformation of Historical Ambiguity into Cold War

Verity," in *Beyond the Hiss Case: The FBI, Congress, and the Cold War,* ed. Athan G. Theoharis (Philadelphia: Temple University Press, 1982); Victor Navasky, "Nixon and Hiss," *Nation,* 4–11 January 1993; Victor Navasky, "Allen Weinstein's Docudrama," *Nation,* 3 November 1997; Victor Navasky, "Alger, Ales, Tony, and Time," *Tikkun* 14, no. 5 (October 1999).

³ Donald Kirk, "Checking Up on Peter's Smile," *Nation,* 6 May 1978: 525–26.

⁴ Navasky, "The Case Not Proved," 400.

⁵ Elinor Langer, "The Secret Drawer," *Nation,* 30 May 1994: 756; Elinor Langer, *Josephine Herbst* (Boston: Little, Brown, 1984).

⁶ John J. Abt, *Advocate and Activist: Memoirs of an American Communist Lawyer,* assisted by Michael Myerson (Urbana: University of Illinois Press, 1993), 39–42, 45–46, 178–79; Langer, "The Secret Drawer," 756; Langer, *Josephine Herbst;* Hope Hale Davis, *Great Day Coming: A Memoir of the 1930s* (South Royalton, Vt.: Steerforth Press, 1994); Hope Hale Davis, "Looking Back at My Years in the Party," *New Leader,* 11 February 1980.

⁷ Harvey Klehr, John Earl Haynes and Fridrikh Igorevich Firsov, *The Secret World of American Communism* (New Haven: Yale University Press, 1995), 73–96, 105–10.

⁸ Maurice Isserman, "Notes from Underground," *Nation,* 12 June 1995: 853; William A. Reuben, "The Latest Spy Hoax: 'Secret World's' False Secrets," *Rights,* 1995: 12.

⁹ The "Peters, John" personal biographical file, which Reuben insists does not exist, can be found in *fond* 495, *opis* 261, *delo* 5584 at the RGASPI archive. Reuben is one of the featured authorities on the Hiss defense website http://www.homepages.nyu.edu/~th15/home.html. For an example of his citation by younger revisionists, see Bruce Craig, " 'Treasonable Doubt': The Harry Dexter White Case," Ph.D. diss. (Washington, D.C.: American University, 1999), 482.

¹⁰ Quoted in Maria Schmidt, "A Few New Aspects to the Story of the American Alger Hiss and the Hungarian Laszlo Rajk's Affair," unpublished essay [translated from Hungarian]

(Budapest, Hungary, 2001).

[11] Karel Kaplan, *Report on the Murder of the General Secretary* (Columbus: Ohio State University Press, 1990), xiii, 19–25.

[12] Quoted from Czech National Archives, Ministry of National Security File #4523, 30 March 1955, in Herbert Romerstein and Eric Breindel, *The Venona Secrets: Exposing Soviet Espionage and America's Traitors* (Washington, D.C.: Regnery, 2000), 133.

[13] Noel Field statement of 23 September 1954 and Noel Field handwritten statement in German, 23 June 1954, Noel Field material, Historical Institute Archive (former Ministry of Interior Archive), Budapest, Hungary, quoted in Schmidt, "A Few New Aspects."

[14] Noel Field statement, 23 September 1954, quoted in Schmidt, "A Few New Aspects." Ethan Klingsberg, a Hiss defender, claimed that Field's account to the Hungarian security police should not be believed because it was coerced. That charge, however, made no sense. Why would Communist security police coerce Field into falsely implicating Hiss as a Soviet spy? The Communist position was that Hiss was not a spy. And as for Field attempting to ingratiate himself to the Hungarian Communist police by falsely claiming he had worked for Soviet intelligence, Schmidt noted, "Field was faced by the Hungarian State Security Authority that worked under Soviet instruction. Thus he could not easily claim that he or the others had worked for Soviet intelligence if it was not true. After all the Russians and the Hungarians could verify his claims." Ethan Klingsberg, "Case Closed Alger Hiss?" *Nation*, 8 November 1993: 528–32; Schmidt, "A Few New Aspects." See also Maria Schmidt, "The Hiss Dossier: A Historian's Report," *New Republic*, 8 November 1993: 17–18, 20.

[15] Gompertz [Massing] report, April 1936; and NKVD personnel file on Laurence Duggan, Archive of the Russian Intelligence Service (Moscow), Case 36857, Book 1, pp. 21, 23, 81; both quoted in Allen Weinstein, *Perjury: The Hiss-Chambers Case* (New York: Random House, 1997), 182–84.

[16] Victor Navasky, "Cold War Ghosts," *Nation*, 16 July 2001,

http://www.thenation.com/doc.mhtml?i=20010716&s=navasky.

[17] Charlotte A. Crabtree and Gary B. Nash, *National Standards for United States History: Exploring the American Experience* (Los Angeles: National Center for History in the Schools, 1994), 215.

[18] James T. Patterson, *Grand Expectations: The United States, 1945–1974* (New York: Oxford University Press, 1996), 195; Ellen Schrecker, *Many Are the Crimes: McCarthyism in America* (Boston: Little, Brown, 1998), 173–75; Ellen Schrecker and John Earl Haynes, "Schrecker on Haynes" (H-Diplo, 2000), archived at http://www2.h-net.msu.edu/lists/.

[19] John Lowenthal, "Venona and Alger Hiss," *Intelligence and National Security* 15, no. 3 (Autumn 2000): 98–130.

[20] Lowenthal, "Venona and Alger Hiss," 101. The material included a handwritten summary of a 1938 cable from the U.S. embassy in Paris to the State Department dealing with the Sino-Japanese war (a conflict of intense interest to the Soviets at the time), Chinese purchases of French aircraft, and reports of possible Japanese moves against the USSR's maritime provinces in the East, a State Department cable on British naval maneuvers and new combat ships, notes on a cable on the Japanese order of battle and troop movements, and Hiss's handwritten summary (nearly a complete transcript) of an American diplomatic cable from Moscow on the Robinson/Reubens case. The latter dealt with American diplomats stumbling over evidence of Soviet espionage in the United States, another matter of great interest to Hiss if he was a Soviet spy but of no relevance whatsoever to his official duties at the U.S. State Department in an office dealing with American foreign economic policy.

[21] Allen Weinstein demonstrated the asinine nature of the claim that the Woodstock at the trial was a fake in "'Forgery by Typewriter': The Pursuit of Conspiracy, 1948–1997," in Weinstein, *Perjury* (1997), 515–32.

[22] Venona 1822 KGB Washington to KGB Moscow, 30 March 1945. Our discussion of the flaws in Lowenthal's analysis of the Ales message benefited greatly from Eduard Mark's rigorously researched "Who Was Venona's Ales? Cryptanalysis and the

Hiss Case," forthcoming in *Intelligence and National Security.* We greatly appreciate his generosity in sharing his research with us prior to publication of his article.

[23] Eduard Mark in "Who Was Venona's Ales?" suggests that the KGB's Akhmerov approached Hiss, a GRU source, as a result of an urgent order from Moscow, contained in a March 3 cable, demanding information on American diplomatic plans for the San Francisco United Nations conference and tasking Akhmerov with the job. Hiss was the U.S. State Department's point man for the U.N. conference. Akhmerov, who had been aware since the mid-1930s that Hiss was a GRU source, used the KGB's predominance in intelligence matters to approach the GRU's asset. Venona 195 KGB Moscow to New York, 3 March 1945.

[24] Weinstein, *Perjury* (1997), 154.

[25] Tanenhaus, *Whittaker Chambers,* 519; Weinstein, *Perjury* (1997), 321–22.

[26] We thank Eduard Mark for his information on the activities of the Stettinius party in Moscow.

[27] Bentley deposition (FBI file 65-14603). The reliability of Bentley's testimony regarding the chief persons in this passage, Victor Perlo, Harold Glasser and Charles Kramer, is well documented. See chapters 4 and 5 of John Earl Haynes and Harvey Klehr, *Venona: Decoding Soviet Espionage in America* (New Haven: Yale University Press, 1999). Also see Hayden B. Peake, "Afterword," in *Out of Bondage: The Story of Elizabeth Bentley,* by Elizabeth Bentley (New York: Ivy Books, 1988); and Hayden B. Peake, "OSS and the Venona Decrypts," *Intelligence and National Security* 12, no. 3 (July 1997).

[28] Venona 769 and 771 KGB New York to Moscow, 30 May 1944. Haynes and Klehr, *Venona,* 125–28. The mutual corroboration of the real identities behind code names between the Venona messages and Weinstein and Vassiliev's KGB documents is discussed in Haynes and Klehr, *Venona,* 40; and John Earl Haynes and Harvey Klehr, "Venona and the Russian Archives: What Has Already Been Found," paper presented at Seventh Sym-

posium on Cryptologic History (Fort Meade, Md., 1997).

[29] KGB file 43072, vol. 1, 88–89, quoted in Allen Weinstein and Alexander Vassiliev, *The Haunted Wood: Soviet Espionage in America—The Stalin Era* (New York: Random House, 1999), 268–69. We have substituted our own convention for how to show cover names, keeping the original text with cover name and adding the real name in brackets. Weinstein and Vassiliev prefer simply to use the latter.

[30] Scott Lucas, "Review of Venona: Decoding Soviet Espionage in America," *Journal of American History* 87, no. 3 (December 2000), http://www.historycooperative.org/journals/jah/87.3/br_108.html.

[31] Lowenthal, "Venona and Alger Hiss," 108.

[32] Ibid., 108–9.

[33] Ibid.

[34] The fourteen were: John Abt, Solomon Adler, Frank Coe, Robert Coe, Lauchlin Currie, Laurence Duggan, Noel Field, Isaac Volkov [Folkoff], Alger Hiss, Charles Kramer, Vincent Reno, Philip Rosenblit, Julian Wadleigh and Harry White. Including Priscilla Hiss would make this fifteen. The ten were: Abt, Adler, Frank Coe, Currie, Duggan, Field, Folkoff/Volkov, Hiss, Kramer and White. Of the latter, only Field did not appear in Venona.

[35] Joseph P. Lash, *Dealers and Dreamers: A New Look at the New Deal* (New York: Doubleday, 1988), 442. Years later, however, Berle told journalist Arnold Beichman that he had discussed the matter with the president, who had dismissed it as paranoid fantasy. Arnold Beichman to John Earl Haynes, personal communication, September 1999. Athan Theoharis claims, "Berle never briefed the president about Chambers' allegations chiefly because the assistant secretary did not understand that Chambers' 'underground' group reference suggested a Soviet espionage operation." Athan G. Theoharis, *Chasing Spies: How the FBI Failed in Counterintelligence but Promoted the Politics of McCarthyism in the Cold War Years* (Chicago: Ivan R. Dee, 2002), 36. This theory is sheer nonsense. Berle's notes, typed person-

ally, were labeled by him "Underground *Espionage* Agent" (emphasis added). For a chronology of the contact between Berle, Chambers and the FBI, see Ladd to Hoover, 29 December 1948, reproduced in Robert Louis Benson and Michael Warner, *Venona: Soviet Espionage and the American Response, 1939–1957* (Washington, D.C.: National Security Agency; Central Intelligence Agency, 1996), 121–28.

[36] Lowenthal, "Venona and Alger Hiss," 110.

[37] Ibid.

[38] Vladimir Pozniakov, "A NKVD/NKGB Report to Stalin: A Glimpse into Soviet Intelligence in the United States in the 1940's," *Cold War International History Project Bulletin*, no. 10 (March 1998), http://cwihp.si.edu/publications.htm. Pozniakov wrote that the documents listed Gregory Silvermaster as "George Silvermaster," possibly a confusion with George Silverman, a leading member of Silvermaster's network.

[39] We thank the diplomatic historian Eduard Mark for providing documentation of Vishinski's whereabouts in this period. Professor Athan Theoharis, like Lowenthal, suggests the Ales message could be read to say that Ales was not in Moscow but only the "Soviet personage," Vishinski, who later spoke with Ales. But this argument runs into the same insolvable problem of Vishinski not being in the U.S. to speak with Ales from the time of the Yalta conference to the time of the Ales message. Theoharis also argues that Ales cannot be Hiss because the message "describes Ales as having worked with the *GRU* 'continuously since 1935.' ... Hiss was employed in the Justice Department's Solicitor General office in 1935, however, and did not transfer to the *State Department* until 1936." This is a non sequitur. The message states that Ales had worked for the GRU continuously since 1935, not that Ales had worked for the State Department continuously since 1935. Theoharis also halfheartedly suggests, "the suspected Ales more logically would be either John Carter Vincent, who headed the Far Eastern desk at State, or Assistant Secretary of the Treasury Harry Dexter White." But he makes no attempt to explain how either would fit the particu-

lars about Ales contained in the Venona message. Theoharis advances his suggestion about Vincent and White on the basis of an Ales document located by Weinstein and Vassiliev, who write that the document is about Hiss. Theoharis, without evidence or a reasonable argument, suggests that the document is actually about the *Amerasia* case and that Vincent and White are more logical suspects. Theoharis, *Chasing Spies*, 30–31.

[40] The others were: John Costello and Oleg Tsarev, *Deadly Illusions* (New York: Crown Publishers, 1993); Nigel West and Oleg Tsarev, *The Crown Jewels: The British Secrets at the Heart of the KGB Archives* (London: HarperCollins, 1998); David E. Murphy, Sergei A. Kondrashev and George Bailey, *Battleground Berlin: CIA vs. KGB in the Cold War* (New Haven: Yale University Press, 1997).

[41] Volkogonov to Lowenthal, 14 October 1992, reprinted in "In Re: Alger Hiss," *Cold War International History Project Bulletin*, no. 2 (Fall 1992): 33; Lowenthal, "Venona and Alger Hiss," 115; Jeffrey A. Frank, "Stalin Biographer Offers Latest Twist in Hiss Case," *Washington Post*, 31 October 1992; William E. Pemberton, "Hiss, Alger," in *Encyclopedia of U.S. Foreign Relations*, vol. 2, ed. Bruce W. Jentleson and Thomas G. Paterson (New York: Oxford University Press, 1997), 297–98.

[42] Lowenthal, "Venona and Alger Hiss," 129.

[43] On November 11, 1992, Volkogonov told the researcher Herbert Romerstein that the GRU archives on foreign intelligence were closed and he had not searched them for material on Hiss. Romerstein and Breindel, *The Venona Secrets: Exposing Soviet Espionage and America's Traitors*, 140; *Neazavisimaya Gazeta* (Moscow), 24 November 1992, p. 4; Serge Schmemann, "Russian General Retreats on Hiss," *New York Times*, 17 December 1992.

[44] U.S. Senate Internal Security Subcommittee, *Interlocking Subversion in Government Departments* (Washington, D.C.: U.S. Govt. Print. Off., 1953), Part 6, 329–30.

[45] In the first edition of *Venona* we incorrectly had the 1942 visit lasting several months, an error noted by Roger Sandilands.

The mistake was corrected in the 2000 edition. John Earl Haynes and Harvey Klehr, *Venona: Decoding Soviet Espionage in America* (New Haven: Yale University Press [Nota Bene], 2000), 146. Chambers had identified three of Bentley's sources (Adler, Coe and Currie according to Berle's notes) or four (adding White according to Levine's notes) in his 1939 interview with Berle.

[46] A fellow economist, John Kenneth Galbraith, who knew Silvermaster in New Deal days, told the historian Bruce Craig that Silvermaster "was incessantly vocal about his political beliefs." Quoted in Craig, " 'Treasonable Doubt,' " 113.

[47] File card of Patterson contacts in regard Silvermaster, Box 203, Robert P. Patterson Papers, Library of Congress; General Bissell to General Strong, 3 June 1942; Silvermaster reply to Bissell memo, 9 June 1942; Robert P. Patterson to Milo Perkins of BEW, 3 July 1942, all reprinted in "Interlocking Subversion in Government Departments," August 30, 1955, 84th Cong., 1st sess., part 30, 2562–67; Lauchlin Currie testimony, 13 August 1948, U.S. Congress, House of Representatives, Committee on Un-American Activities, 80th Cong., 2d sess., 851–77.

[48] The 1943 date was misstated as 1944 in our 1999 edition and corrected to 1943 in the 2000 edition of Haynes and Harvey Klehr, *Venona* (2000), 47.

[49] Robert Louis Benson and Cecil Philips, *History of Venona*, unpublished classified manuscript (Fort Meade, Md.: National Security Agency, 1995), 37–38 (declassified).

[50] Roger J. Sandilands, *The Life and Political Economy of Lauchlin Currie: New Dealer, Presidential Adviser, and Development Economist* (Durham, N.C.: Duke University Press, 1990), vii–ix.

[51] Ibid., 144.

[52] Levine was author of one of the earliest English-language accounts of the Russian Revolution of 1917, one of the earliest full-length biographies of Joseph Stalin in English, and the earliest biography of Ramond Mecader, Leon Trotsky's assassin. Isaac Don Levine, *The Russian Revolution* (New York: Harper & Brothers, 1917); Isaac Don Levine, *Stalin* (New York: Cosmopolitan Book Corporation, 1931); Isaac Don Levine, *The*

*Mind of an Assassin* (New York: Farrar, Straus & Cudahy, 1959).

[53] The special weight that Soviet leaders gave to intelligence information is discussed in V. M. Zubok and Konstantin Pleshakov, *Inside the Kremlin's Cold War: From Stalin to Khrushchev* (Cambridge, Mass.: Harvard University Press, 1996), 14, 104, 107, 145–46.

[54] By this time Bentley had been removed from contact with the Silvermaster network for six months. Consequently, Currie's delivery of documents may have occurred after her time.

[55] Venona 253 KGB Moscow to New York, 20 March 1945.

[56] Roger J. Sandilands, "Guilt by Association? Lauchlin Currie's Alleged Involvement with Washington Economists in Soviet Espionage," *History of Political Economy* 32, no. 3 (2000): 478.

[57] Elizabeth Bentley, "Elizabeth Bentley FBI Deposition of 30 November 1945," FBI file 65-14503 (1945).

[58] Sandilands, "Guilt by Association?" 480–81.

[59] Ibid., 491.

[60] Ibid.

[61] Ibid., 483, 485.

[62] Ibid., 501–2.

[63] Ibid., 494–95.

[64] Ibid., 495, 513.

[65] Ibid., 498.

[66] KGB file 70545, vol. 1, 405–6, quoted in Weinstein and Vassiliev, *The Haunted Wood,* 106.

[67] Sandilands, "Guilt by Association?" 503.

[68] Lucas, "Review of Venona"; Lowenthal, "Venona and Alger Hiss," 113–15.

[69] Weinstein, *Perjury* (1997), 212.

[70] In *Venona* we included Victor Perlo in this list. James Boughton corrects us on this, noting that Perlo was hired after White left the Treasury, albeit with the assistance of other members of the Silvermaster network inside Treasury. He also objects to the inclusion of William Taylor, stating, "no evidence supports that accusation. Taylor was cleared of all charges in 1956." There is very good evidence about Taylor: the new archival evi-

dence that has appeared since the 1950s supports Elizabeth Bentley's testimony and her credibility. Consequently, we include him in the list. James M. Boughton, "The Case against Harry Dexter White: Still Not Proven," *History of Political Economy* 33, no. 2 (Summer 2001): 238.

71 Transcripts of Glasser's promotions and job rating forms signed by Coe, Ullmann and White are in U.S. Senate Internal Security Subcommittee, *Interlocking Subversion*, Part 2, 81–82, 98–99: Hottel to Hoover, 14 January 1947, FBI Silvermaster file, serial 2028.

72 File card of Patterson contacts in regard Silvermaster, Box 203, Robert P. Patterson Papers, Library of Congress; General Bissell to General Strong, 3 June 1942; Silvermaster reply to Bissell memo, 9 June 1942; Robert P. Patterson to Milo Perkins of BEW, 3 July 1942, all reprinted in U.S. Senate Internal Security Subcommittee, *Interlocking Subversion*, Part 30, 2562–67.

73 Paul Appleby to L. C. Martin and J. Weldon Jones, 23 March 1944, reprinted in U.S. Senate Internal Security Subcommittee, *Interlocking Subversion*, Part 30, xii. White also facilitated the employment of a Communist spy, Chi Ch'ao-ting, in the Nationalist Chinese government. Chi was educated at Tsinghua College in Peking and then attended the University of Chicago and Columbia University. He secretly joined the American Communist Party in 1926 and was part of its Chinese bureau until 1941. Chiang Kai-shek's government depended heavily on American aid and with the support of the U.S. government arranged through White, Chi became an official of the Chinese Nationalist government's finance ministry in 1941. When Chiang Kai-shek and his Nationalist government retreated to Taiwan in 1949, Chi stayed on the mainland, announced his status as a veteran Chinese Communist Party operative, and became a senior official of Mao Tse-tung's regime. Harvey Klehr and Ronald Radosh, *The Amerasia Spy Case: Prelude to McCarthyism* (Chapel Hill: University of North Carolina Press, 1996), 21–22, 37, 159, 171–72, 197.

74 James M. Boughton, *The Case against Harry Dexter White: Still*

*Not Proven,* publication no. WP/00/149, IMF Working Paper (Washington, D.C.: International Monetary Fund, 2000); Boughton, "The Case against Harry Dexter White" (2001).

[75] Boughton, "The Case against Harry Dexter White," 222. At the Hiss trial, Meyer Shapiro, who actually purchased the rugs for Chambers in New York, produced the receipts, for $876.71, and there were additional shipping costs. Chambers remembered Bykov as giving him "a thousand dollars, or close to a thousand dollars, to buy the four rugs." Chambers, *Witness,* 415.

[76] Boughton, "The Case against Harry Dexter White," 222; Chambers, *Witness,* 414–15. Der Advokat (the Lawyer) was Bykov's cover name for Hiss.

[77] Boughton, "The Case against Harry Dexter White," 222, 227.

[78] Ibid., 223.

[79] Ibid., 225. The Schecters' KGB documents appeared after Boughton's essay in *History of Political Economy.* Jerrold L. Schecter and Leona Schecter, *Sacred Secrets: How Soviet Intelligence Operations Changed American History* (Washington, D.C.: Brassey's, 2002).

[80] Boughton, "The Case against Harry Dexter White," 232–33.

[81] Venona 195 KGB Moscow to New York, 3 March 1945.

[82] Venona 235–236 KGB San Francisco to Moscow, 5 May 1945. Boughton, "The Case against Harry Dexter White," 236.

[83] Boughton, "The Case against Harry Dexter White," 234–35.

[84] Alexander Feklisov and Sergei Kostin, *The Man Behind the Rosenbergs,* trans. Catherine Dop (New York: Enigma Books, 2001), 70–71.

[85] Venona 1119–1121 KGB New York to Moscow, 4–5 August 1944. White's proposal that he brief his KGB contacts during auto rides parallels Chambers' report that White also preferred this method of meeting in the mid-1930s. Boughton, "The Case against Harry Dexter White," 236.

### Chapter 5: From Denial to Justification

[1] Maurice Isserman, "Guess What—They Really Were Spies,"

*Forward,* 29 January 1999: 11.

[2] Maurice Isserman, "They Led Two Lives," *New York Times Book Review,* 9 May 1999: 35.

[3] Maurice Isserman, "Disloyalty as a Principle: Why Communists Spied," *Foreign Service Journal* 77, no. 10 (October 2000): 30, 34.

[4] We also note that Isserman corrected us on the matter of one document in *The Secret World.* We reproduced a report written by Rudy Baker, head of the CPUSA's underground arm, describing the work during 1942 of a covert network that included a covert radio operator with the code name Louis, who had been working in South America and operated for a time in Gilla, the code name for an unknown location. We thought Louis was Morris Cohen, an American Communist who was in the party's underground and became a career KGB spy. We made the link because a memoir by a retired KGB officer who discussed Morris Cohen's work stated that Cohen had the cover name Louis in 1942 and we knew that Cohen had been trained in covert radio work. Isserman thought the identification unlikely for several reasons. Subsequently, with the assistance of our colleague Fridrikh Firsov, we found documents in the archive of the Communist International establishing that Louis could not have been Cohen and most likely was Victorio Codovilla, an Argentine Communist on Comintern assignment. We corrected the misidentification of Cohen as Louis in *Venona: Decoding Soviet Espionage in America.*

[5] Navasky, "Cold War Ghosts."

[6] J. Peters, *The Communist Party: A Manual on Organization* ([New York]: Workers Library Publishers, 1935), 104–5.

[7] Athan G. Theoharis, Chasing Spies: *How the FBI Failed in Counterintelligence but Promoted the Politics of McCarthyism in the Cold War Years* (Chicago: Ivan R. Dee, 2002), 237–38; Bernice Schrank, "Reading the Rosenbergs after Venona," *Labour/Le Travail* 49 (Spring 2002): 200.

[8] Unless, of course, Theoharis and Navasky believe that the defendants of the Moscow trials of the mid-1930s and the victims of

the Great Terror really were agents of American imperialism or that the victims of Stalin's late 1940s and early 1950s purges really were agents of American and Zionist conspiracies recruited by American intelligence before and during World War II.

[9] Schrank, "Reading the Rosenbergs," 205.

[10] Theoharis, *Chasing Spies*, 16, 236; Athan G. Theoharis, *Seeds of Repression: Harry S. Truman and the Origins of McCarthyism* (Chicago: Quadrangle Books, 1971); Athan G. Theoharis, *Spying on Americans: Political Surveillance from Hoover to the Huston Plan* (Philadelphia: Temple University Press, 1978); Athan G. Theoharis and John Stuart Cox, *The Boss: J. Edgar Hoover and the Great American Inquisition* (Philadelphia: Temple University Press, 1988). The FBI was, after all, a security agency charged with monitoring potential security threats from persons inside the United States and the Germans were citizens of a nation with whom the United States was at war. Most, to be sure, were anti-Nazi refugees. But one of the oldest techniques of espionage is to send agents into a foreign country pretending to be refugees fleeing oppression and hostility in their native land. The only practical way to deal with this threat is for security agencies to monitor exiles for signs of someone playing a double game.

[11] Theoharis, *Chasing Spies*, 16–17.

[12] Nikita Sergeevich Khrushchev, *Khrushchev Remembers: The Glasnost Tapes*, trans. and ed. Vyacheslav V. Luchkov and Jerrold L. Schecter (Boston: Little, Brown, 1990); Walter Schneir, "Time Bomb," *Nation*, 3 December 1990: 688; Pavel Sudoplatov, Anatolii Pavlovich Sudoplatov, Jerrold L. Schecter and Leona Schecter, *Special Tasks: The Memoirs of an Unwanted Witness, a Soviet Spymaster* (Boston: Little, Brown, 1994), 177, 191, 213–17; Walter Schneir, "Sudo-History," *Nation*, 6 June 1994: 804, 806–8.

[13] Alexander Feklisov and Sergei Kostin, *The Man Behind the Rosenbergs*, trans. Catherine Dop (New York: Enigma Books, 2001), 160.

[14] Venona 1053 KGB New York to Moscow, 26 July 1944.

[15] Walter Schneir and Miriam Schneir, "Cables Coming in from the Cold," *Nation,* 5 July 1999: 26; Walter Schneir and Miriam Schneir, "Cryptic Answers," *Nation,* 14 August 1995: 152.

[16] Venona 1600 KGB New York to Moscow, 14 November 1944.

[17] Schneir and Schneir, "Cables Coming in from the Cold," 30; Walter Schneir and Miriam Schneir, "Rosenbergs Redux," *Nation,* 16 October 1995: 445.

[18] Eric Foner, "History, Politics and 'The Rosenberg File,'" *Guardian,* 26 October 1983: 1, 19; Eric Foner, "Foreword," in *We Are Your Sons: The Legacy of Ethel and Julius Rosenberg,* by Robert Meeropol and Michael Meeropol (Urbana: University of Illinois Press, 1986); Eric Foner, Letter to the Editor, *New Republic,* 11 September 1995: 6–7.

[19] Gerda Lerner, *Fireweed: A Political Autobiography* (Philadelphia: Temple University Press, 2002), 332–33.

[20] Venona 1340 KGB New York to Moscow, 21 September 1944.

[21] Venona 1657 KGB New York to Moscow, 27 November 1944.

[22] Some of these were convicted of perjury rather than espionage, but this is a distinction without substance. The underlying offense was espionage, but the government found the perjury statute an easier vehicle for prosecution.

[23] Schrank, "Reading the Rosenbergs," 193. One could also add William Weisband, imprisoned for failing to answer a Grand Jury summons, and Ilya Wolston, convicted of contempt of court, both charges being more easily proved substitutes for an espionage indictment.

[24] Schrank, "Reading the Rosenbergs," 206, 208–9. Oddly, after her denunciation of playing "connect the dots " by reading the Venona messages in light of other evidence, Schrank closes her essay with a call for reading the messages in light of other evidence. We cannot see how these contradictory passages can be reconciled.

[25] Schrank, "Reading the Rosenbergs," 208.

[26] Ellen Schrecker, *Many Are the Crimes: McCarthyism in America* (Boston: Little, Brown, 1998), 166.

27 Ibid., 178–79.

28 Ibid., 166, 178–79, 188.

29 Ibid., 172.

30 Bruce Craig, "'Treasonable Doubt': The Harry Dexter White Case," Ph.D. diss. (Washington, D.C.: American University, 1999), 579–80.

31 Michael E. Parrish, "Review Essay: Soviet Espionage and the Cold War," *Diplomatic History* 25, no. 1 (Winter 2001): 116.

32 Nor do the people who once lived within it share Parrish's nostalgia for the Soviet "sphere of influence in Eastern Europe." Only one nation, Belarus, has expressed any desire to surrender its national independence and return to a revived USSR. And Belarus is a dictatorship whose leader rules with terror and force. As for the rest, the notion that the world was a better place when the people of Poland, Hungary, the Czech Republic, Slovakia, Estonia, Lithuania, Latvia, Rumania, Bulgaria and eastern Germany lived under Communist tyranny and Soviet hegemony is not a proposition that most inhabitants of those countries would find compelling. Even the reformed Communist parties in those nations pledge never to return to that brutal reality. This type of nostalgia for the Cold War can only be based on a loathing for American power and a belief that powerful, nuclear-armed, antidemocratic rivals are a good tonic for what ails the United States. For an examination of the flagrant distortions found in Professor Parrish's attacks on historical works that cause discomfort to radical historians, see Harvey Klehr and Ronald Radosh, Letter to the Editor, *Reviews in American History* 25, no. 3 (1997): 526–30.

33 Joan Hall, "Family of Spies: Interview with Joan Hall," in *Secrets, Lies, and Atomic Spies* (NOVA, 2002), http://www.pbs.org/wgbh/nova/venona/fami_joanhall.html; Ruth Hall, "Family of Spies: Interview with Ruth Hall," in *Secrets, Lies, and Atomic Spies* (NOVA, 2002), http://www.pbs.org/wgbh/nova/venona/fami_ruthhall.html. Ruth Hall's rhetoric is muddled. Her father did not "come forward," but the reverse, dropping back into the shadow world of espionage. And only in the feverish world

of far-leftist anti-American bigotry can tank-busting solid shot made of uranium U-238 (minimal radioactivity, less than a microwave oven, not the U-235 used in atomic bombs) used in U.S. tank cannons be described as "nuclear weapons," or can American intervention in Kosovo to save Albanian Muslims from ethnic cleaning or rescuing Kuwait from Saddam Hussein be perceived as obvious evidence of America's evil.

[34] Kathleen Hulser, curator, and Sam Roberts, consultant, *The Rosenbergs Reconsidered: The Death Penalty in the Cold War Era*, exhibit captions (New York City: New York Historical Society, 2001), http://www.nyhistory.org/index.html.

[35] Joel Kovel, *Red Hunting in the Promised Land: Anticommunism and the Making of America* (New York: Basic Books, 1994), dedication page, x.

[36] David Blank, "Corliss Lamont and Civil Liberties," private paper sent to the Trustees of Columbia University, 1999; Edward S. Shapiro, "Corliss Lamont and Civil Liberties," *Modern Age* 42, no. 2 (April 2000): 158–75.

[37] Harvey Klehr and John Earl Haynes, "Communists and the CIO: From the Soviet Archives," *Labor History* 35, no. 3 (Summer 1994); Harry Bridges Center for Labor Studies and James Gregory, "Communism in Washington State—History and Memory Project" (Harry Bridges Center for Labor Studies of the University of Washington, 2002), http://faculty.washington.edu/gregoryj/cpproject/.

[38] Craig, "'Treasonable Doubt,'" 7.

[39] Ibid., 569, 571–74.

[40] Ibid., 558.

[41] Schrank, "Reading the Rosenbergs," 199; Robert Meeropol and Michael Meeropol, "Family of Spies: Interview with Robert and Michael Meeropol," in *Secrets, Lies, and Atomic Spies* (NOVA, 2002), http://www.pbs.org/wgbh/nova/venona/fami_meeropol.html; Navasky, "Cold War Ghosts"; Hall, "Family of Spies: Joan Hall."

[42] Craig, "'Treasonable Doubt,'" 574; Athan Theoharis, "Review of Venona: Decoding Soviet Espionage in America," *American Historical Review* 106, no. 1 (February 2001), http://historycoop.

com/journals/ahr/106.1/br_90.html. We cannot rule out that Professor Theoharis is playing word games with his statement. If the "majority" of the reported information did not compromise U.S. security interests, does he mean a *minority* did compromise security interests? Theoharis, *Chasing Spies,* 17.

[43] Christopher M. Andrew and Vasili Mitrokhin, *The Sword and the Shield: The Mitrokhin Archive and the Secret History of the KGB* (New York: Basic Books, 1999), 111, 118, 129.

[44] On the value of Soviet technical intelligence, see Vladimir Pozniakov, "A NKVD/NKGB Report to Stalin: A Glimpse into Soviet Intelligence in the United States in the 1940's," *Cold War International History Project Bulletin,* no. 10 (March 1998), http://cwihp.si.edu/publications.htm.

[45] Craig, " 'Treasonable Doubt,' " 581, 585–86.

[46] Ibid., 263–64, 306.

[47] Ibid., 261, 408–9.

[48] Ibid., 588.

[49] Ibid., 589–90.

[50] Allen Weinstein and Alexander Vassiliev, *The Haunted Wood: Soviet Espionage in America—The Stalin Era* (New York: Random House, 1999), 300. Note that many revisionists reject the authenticity of Weinstein and Vassiliev documents demonstrating the guilt of Hiss, White, Rosenberg and Currie but this document wins revisionist approval because it can be used to advance their agenda.

[51] Ellen Schrecker, "The Spies Who Loved Us?" *Nation,* 24 May 1999: 28–31.

[52] While Schrecker presents Soviet espionage in the U.S. as having been shattered by Gouzenko and Bentley, other revisionists look at the same situation and argue that American counterespionage efforts failed. This is the expressed theme of Athan Theoharis's *Chasing Spies: How the FBI Failed in Counterintelligence but Promoted the Politics of McCarthyism in the Cold War Years.* He also remarks that "the tangible results of the Venona project are remarkably thin," a claim as well of Bernice Schrank's "Reading the Rosenbergs after Venona" (p. 192).

Both cite the small number of espionage convictions as proof. This view ignores the counterespionage dilemma the FBI faced between gathering evidence that could be used in criminal trial (risking the continued loss of secrets while legally admissible evidence is gathered) or choosing to identify and quickly neutralize a security breach (ending the loss of secrets but often precluding criminal prosecution because the evidence was gathered in a manner that ruled out its use in a criminal trial). The FBI chose the latter course, like almost every counterespionage agency. Criminal prosecution is almost always a secondary objective in counterespionage operations.

53 In addition to what is in Weinstein and Vassiliev's *The Haunted Wood,* Andrew and Mitrokhin in *The Sword and the Shield* also show that KGB operations in the U.S. were seriously degraded by the Gouzenko and, particularly, the Bentley defections. Joseph Albright and Marcia Kunstel, *Bombshell: The Secret Story of America's Unknown Atomic Spy Conspiracy* (New York: Times Books, 1997), 182–85, 189–200; Andrew and Mitrokhin, *The Sword and the Shield,* 147–48.

54 His exposure in 1950 came as a consequence of Venona and the FBI investigation of the Rosenberg network.

55 Ellen Schrecker, *Many Are the Crimes: McCarthyism in America,* 2nd ed. (Princeton, N.J.: Princeton University Press, 1999), ix–x.

56 Andrew and Mitrokhin, *The Sword and the Shield,* 148.

57 Ibid., 279–82.

## Conclusion

1 Ellen Schrecker, *Many Are the Crimes: McCarthyism in America,* 1st ed. (Boston: Little, Brown, 1998), 369, 374.

2 Robert Korstad and Nelson Lichtenstein, "Opportunities Found and Lost: Labor, Radicals, and the Early Civil Rights Movement," *Journal of American History* 75, no. 3 (December 1988): 800, 811.

3 George Lipsitz, *Class and Culture in Cold War America: A Rainbow at Midnight* (New York: Praeger, 1981).

4 Rachel Neumann, "The Empire Strikes Back," *Village Voice,* 3
October 2001, http://www.villagevoice.com/issues/0140/neu-
mann.php; Alan Wald, "Communist Writers Fight Back in Cold
War America," in *Styles of Cultural Activism: From Theory and Pedagogy to Women, Indians, and Communism,* ed. Philip Goldstein
(Cranbury, N.J.: University of Delaware Press & Associated University Presses, 1994).

5 By this we mean the publication of essays and articles. On occa-
sion, traditionalists are allowed to review books.

6 Martin Malia, "Judging Nazism and Communism," *National
Interest* 69 (Fall 2002): 74.

7 Ibid.

## Appendix

1 This list is based on Mayme Sevander's research in archives in
Petrozavodsk, Russia, and we thank her for generously sharing
her research. We also wish to acknowledge our gratitude to
Jukka Pietilainen and Carl Ross for their assistance in translat-
ing a similar list from the Finnish language journal *Carelia* (issues
2–9, 1998) published in Petrozavodsk. The names in KGB
archives are in Russian and follow Russian naming conventions
which include patronymics. The latter, however, were not customary among North American Finns. To preserve the authenticity of KGB documents the Russian patronymics have been
preserved, while the Finnish/English spelling is given in paren-
theses. Russian patronymics have double markers: OVA/EVA,
indicating the possessive case; and ICH—masculine, NA—fem-
inine. Thus, Ivanovich—son of Ivan; Ivanovna—daughter of
Ivan. In addition to KGB and other archival records, Sevander
made use of Yuri Dmitriev, *Mesto Rasstrela Sandarmokh* [San-
darmokh Is Where They Were Executed] (Petrozavodsk [Rus-
sia], 1999); Eila Lahti-Argutina, *Olimme Joukko Vieras Vaan* [We
Were Just a Bunch of Strangers] (Turku [Finland]: Siirtolaisuusinstituutti, 2001); Mayme Sevander, *Vaeltajat* [Wanderers]

(Turku [Finland]: Siirtolaisuusinstituutti, 2000).

[2] Nelson had been active in the left wing of the American Socialist Party in 1919 and was one of the members of the founding generation of American communism.

# Index